LifeTraining

by
Dr. Joe White

Tyndale House Publishers, Wheaton, Illinois

LIFETRAINING

Library of Congress Cataloging-in-Publication Data
White, Joe, 1948-
          p. cm.
     Includes bibliographical references.
     ISBN 1-56179-726-X
     1. Teenagers—Prayer books and devotions—English. 2. Family—Prayer books and devo-
tions—English. 3. Christian life—Prayer books and devotions—English. I. Title.
BV4531.2.W477   1998
242'. 63—dc21

                                                                                        97-47626
                                                                                             CIP

A Focus on the Family book published by Tyndale House Publishers, Wheaton, Illinois.

Unless otherwise noted, Scripture taken from the *New American Standard Bible*®, Copyright © 1960, 1962, 1963, 1971, 1972, 1973, 1975, 1977 and 1995 by The Lockman Foundation. Used by permission.

Scripture quotations marked NIV are from the HOLY BIBLE, NEW INTERNATIONAL VERSION ®. Copyright © 1973, 1978, 1984 by the International Bible Society. Used by permission of Zondervan Publishing House. All rights reserved.

Editor: Betsy L. Holt
Cover Design: Candi Park D'Agnese
Cover Photo: John Terence Turner/FPG International LLC.
Interior Design: Big Cat Studios

Printed in the United States of America
99 00 01 02 03 04/10 9 8 7 6 5 4 3 2

To Jamie —
Because you led Courtney, Brady, and Cooper to Jesus
with your precious childhood faith...
and because, in my heart, you'll always be
"Daddy's little girl"

With special thanks to my mom
and my great friends Will Cunningham, Elizabeth Jones,
and the Kanakuk summer staffs for their many contributions to this book
and, most importantly, to my life

Contents

Introduction

There's No Place Like Home

Although it happened more than 20 years ago, it seems like just yesterday that my precious wife brought Jamie, our first little girl, home from the hospital. I called her "Peanut" because she was so small and had her mom's big, brown eyes. She was everything I'd ever wanted in a child.

Before I had time to catch my breath, 18 years went streaking by, and Peanut was 5'6" tall and off to college some 450 long miles away from our Ozark mountain home. She's still my little girl, but our day-to-day closeness was never the same after she packed her bags for that long trip to Texas and higher education.

Now, a few years after I sent Jamie off to college, I'm tearfully, happily preparing to walk my Peanut down the chapel aisle as she gets married to the man of her dreams. I know Jamie will bring everything but regret to the altar of holy matrimony.

Why? She carries a lifetime of faith in Jesus Christ with her.

I gave Jamie (and the rest of my kids) clothes, vacations, hugs, and love, but no gift ever came close to the time I spent with her and her siblings studying God's Word. Those devotional times—memorizing Bible verses and reading Scripture—were by far the most significant, cherished, irreplaceable activities we did as a family.

I never commanded Jamie to have a daily quiet time, but she spent time with God almost every day throughout her high school years.

I never ordered her to treat her mom and I with grace, but she respected and honored us with love.

I never forced her to witness to her friends, but she would often come home smiling when one of her friends took a step closer to God because of the time they'd spent together.

I never told Jamie to have a peer Bible study group, but every Tuesday morning she was the first one up and out of the house to join her friends for "God time."

Her homecoming-queen nominations didn't come from some outward beauty bought with expensive makeup or fancy clothes. Jamie never sought to be on the cover of *Seventeen* magazine. Her friends told me those votes were cast out of respect for her Christian character.

Am I bragging about my kid or getting prideful? Nope. My family has had its share of failures, problems, and trials. We're far from perfect. I'm bragging about God's Word and the way it shapes lives when it's presented consistently, creatively, and enthusiastically in the home.

I'm not a noted theologian or a seminary professor, but when Jamie was five, Courtney was two, Brady was one, and Cooper was just an idea, I set a goal to help my kids grow spiritually. Every night, I'd lie or kneel by each child and discuss the day's adventures. Then we'd memorize a Bible verse together and finish with prayer. At breakfast or supper, my wife, Debbie-Jo, and I had a family Bible devotional with whomever was within shouting distance.

Honestly, it takes tough personal discipline to ensure that we'll have family time day after day. Our lives are hectic (just as your life probably is, too). Visitors are constantly in our home, but I excuse myself from *whatever* is going on to get the "daddy" job done first.

I've realized that the time I spend with my kids in God's Word is of eternal importance.

The Critical Years

Folks, this book is written for families with kids in the "critical years," ages 11-18.

These are the years when the hormones peak.

These are the years when Hollywood begins marketing sexually graphic movies and TV shows toward young people.

These are the years when politically-correct public schools continually tell teenagers that God is irrelevant and science has all the answers.

These are the years in which peer groups pressure kids so much that even the strongest young Christians can be pushed to the breaking point.

Unfortunately, this is also the time when many families stop having Bible times together. Folks, these aren't the years to taper off. You should be turning up the heat if your child is an adolescent or teenager. There's no better time to teach your son or daughter about God than during the critical years. And you'll be rewarded for doing it. You can have fantastic discussions with your child, and you'll rejoice as you watch your teenager make good decisions and learn to develop a godly lifestyle.

Family devotional time is not an option. God commands moms and dads to teach their children about Him. Read Deuteronomy 6:6-7:

> *These words, which I am commanding you today, shall be on your heart.*
> *You shall teach them diligently to your sons and shall talk of them*
> *when you sit in your house and when you walk by the way*
> *and when you lie down and when you rise up.*

The Bible doesn't say, "Teach your kids about God's Word." It says, "*Teach them God's Word*" and then help them apply it to their daily lives. God didn't issue this command to Sunday school teachers and educators. He gave it to ordinary parents like you and me.

Does it pay off? Does it work? You'll know when your son or daughter hits junior high. You'll get a second report card after his or her freshman year in college. You'll get a third when you see how your grandkids are raised. As a counselor of teenagers, I've heard hundreds of horror stories detailing drug addictions, alcohol-related accidents, date rape, unwanted pregnancies, abortions, eating disorders, and more from kids whose parents didn't consistently spend quality time with them. On the flip side, as the Kanakuk-Kanakomo Kamp director, I've also seen thousands of kids with strong character and an even stronger faith, raised by parents who've guided their spiritual paths.

The Family Devotional Time

> *Open my eyes, [Lord,] that I may behold wonderful things from Your law.*
> ↪ Psalm 119:18

The devotionals in this book are designed to help your kids earn "straight A's" on their life report cards. Each devotion brings God's Word to life—and the results are *guaranteed*.

Says who? Not me! God guarantees these family devotional times. I simply cling to His promise. Read it with me in Psalm 1:

> *How blessed is the man [child, mom, dad]*
> *who does not walk in the counsel of the wicked,*
> *nor stand in the path of sinners, nor sit in the seat of scoffers!*
> *But his delight is in the law of the Lord,*
> *and in His law he meditates day and night.*
> *He will be like a tree firmly planted by streams of water,*

which yields its fruit in its season, and its leaf does not wither;
and in whatever he does, he prospers (verses 1-3).

Start today. Then when your child leaves home, you will be sure you've given him or her the gift that never gets outdated, the gift that will join your family together—forever.

Every family will do the devotions differently, but here are some suggestions that helped our family get the most out of God's Word:

1. Ask someone to open in prayer.
2. Read the Scripture passage.
3. Ask someone what he or she hears God saying in the passage.
4. Read the devotional amplification.
5. Discuss each question.
6. If needed, make each other accountable in following through with the devotional's challenge.
7. Close with prayer.
8. More hints:
    a) Alternate which family members lead the reading and discussion each day.
    b) Strive for equal discussion time for each family member.
    c) Participate in green-light thinking! Find the good in each person's response. In our family, criticisms or put-downs some times cost the critic a quarter, which he or she must put into the family charity fund.

Bedside Memory

Your word I have treasured in my heart, that I may not sin against You.

⌁ *Psalm* 119:11

This book is written by an ordinary dad with four ordinary children and an ordinary wife, with invaluable input from my mom, my friends Will Cunningham and Elizabeth Jones, and a group of kid-loving counselors at Kanakuk-Kanakomo, our Christian sports camp in the Ozark mountains. Together, we picked Bible memory verses for you and your kids to learn that will give them (and you) a firm foundation to stand on as they grow up. These verses will also strengthen your teenager's spiritual state when he or she goes to college. Statistics show that 7 out of 10 Christian kids walk away from their Christian faith and get washed away into moral decay by the harsh anti-Christian collegiate atmosphere.

Do all you can not to let your teenager become one of those statistics.

What we put into our minds can stick with us—long term. In second grade, I memorized a little poem, four lines long. It was about a mushroom and an oak tree. I'll never forget it. In fourth grade, I spent about an hour memorizing a few verses from the Sermon on the Mount in Matthew 5. Those amazing words still come to mind 40 years later! Regretfully, in high school, my brother was given a decadent recording by a music group that rivals some of the street rap of today. I'm ashamed to say that even though I only listened to it a few times, I still remember those raunchy lyrics.

Proverbs rightly tells us, "For as he thinks within himself, so he is" (23:7). If we think God's thoughts, we'll do God's will. If our mind is captured by trash, we'll do things that bring us grief and regret.

The practice of memorizing Scripture together, adopted when my kids were young, has welded our family like epoxy cement. Each night, from the time they were three years old, I'd lay beside them for a few minutes and we'd memorize a Bible verse together. It was simple, fun, and accompanied by hugs and good end-of-the-day conversation. As the years went by, the verses became chapters, the chapters became books, and now (although none of us are scholars or seminary graduates) we have hearts that are chock-full of the best book ever written—the Bible. That book has bonded our family and helped us overcome many problems that, as in every home I've ever known, creep up in our household.

And don't worry—your kids *aren't* too old for this.

My older son, Brady, is 6'3" tall and dunks a basketball as easily as he used to dunk his younger brother in the swimming pool. My second son, Cooper, is an aggressive outside linebacker on his high school football team. He'd rather flatten an opposing running back than eat breakfast. I still tuck 'em in at night and lie on their pillows as we read Scripture and memorize Bible verses together.

As my kids reached about age 10, I told them they would get the car keys when they were old enough to drive *and* they had memorized two books of the Bible. (No, Philemon, Titus, and Jude weren't allowed!) Cooper, my youngest, and I finished the book of James together last summer, one week before the big driver's license test. (Yes, we had to cram a little at the end!)

If my family can do it, there's no reason yours can't, too. At the end of this book, you'll find 100 Bible verses that every teenager should know. They'll give your kids the inside strength to resist the outside pressure they face in this challenging world. I suggest that you take two verses a week for 50 weeks. (Everyone should get a two-week vacation each year, don't you think?)

There's no one correct formula for memorizing Scripture with your child, but I've found a few ways to make it more effective. Here are my suggestions for developing meaningful memorization times with your teenager:

1. Set a goal and stick with it!
   For example:
   a) "We will enjoy Scripture memory together every night, six nights a week."
   b) Or, "We will memorize two new verses (and review previous verses) twice a week."
2. It works *far* better if you memorize together. Set a goal to be there with your child every night (or however often you decide to memorize Scripture).
3. When you spend time with your teenager, start by visiting casually about the day. Ask him or her, for example:
   a) "How was your day today?"
   b) "What was the highlight of your day?"
   c) "Did anything sad happen to you today?"
   d) "What did you learn at school today?"
   e) "Tell me about your friends. What did they do today?"
4. After chatting, begin the memory time.
5. Finally, end in prayer.

Remember—however you do it best is fantastic. Have fun! I pray that this experience brings you even half the joy, fulfillment, and peace it has given my kids and me.

Matthew

It's fitting that the gospel account according to Matthew, one of Jesus' 12 hand-picked disciples, leads the 27 books of New Testament writings. Matthew knew Jesus as "King of the Jews"—the Messiah, the fulfillment of all Old Testament prophecies about "the One who is to come." Matthew also records more of Jesus' majestic teachings than any other book in the Bible. The reading and understanding of this book will enable your family to truly understand the Savior's heart, mind, and intentions for sound biblical living.

THE NIGHT THAT WAS

"But when he had considered this, behold, an angel of the Lord appeared to him in a dream, saying, 'Joseph, son of David, do not be afraid to take Mary as your wife; for the Child who has been conceived in her is of the Holy Spirit. She will bear a Son; and you shall call His name Jesus, for He will save His people from their sins.' Now all this took place to fulfill what was spoken by the Lord through the prophet; 'Behold, the virgin shall be with child and shall bear a Son, and they shall call His name Immanuel,' which translated means, 'God with us.'"

↜ Matthew 1:20-23

There will never be another night like it.

Two young people, singled out by the Lord, were picked to become parents of the Messiah. God chose Mary for her purity and dedication to Him. Purity mattered to God then, and purity matters to God today. God chose Joseph because he was a righteous man. Righteous living mattered to God then, and righteous living matters to God today.

Jesus' parents were righteous, and His conception was pure. The Bible tells us He was conceived by the Holy Spirit. Many people such as the late Joseph Smith, the founder of Mormonism, believe that's just a story—there's no way Mary was a virgin.[1] But that couldn't be further from the truth. God is powerful. If God can turn a pitiful caterpillar into an inexplicably graceful butterfly, if He can create the universe with a word, then He can easily conceive a life inside a mother's womb.

Jesus *was* conceived within a virgin.

Baby Jesus, growing in Mary's womb, would transform "the law" into "grace" as He gave His followers forgiveness from sin and the hope of eternity. This baby would allow our biggest failures to lead to God's biggest acts of mercy. This baby demonstrated, once and for all time, that God's heart overflows with love toward His people.

Discussion Starters:

1. Is that night significant to you? Why or why not?
2. Why does God value righteousness and purity?
3. How does God turn our sinfulness into righteousness?

Lifeline:

God's love was expressed to its fullest extent when He sent His Son to earth to die for our sins. Discuss how you, as a family, can show God's love to one another.

GIFTS TO THE MANGER CHILD

"After hearing the king, they went their way; and the star, which they had seen in the east, went on before them until it came and stood over the place where the Child was. When they saw the star, they rejoiced exceedingly with great joy. After coming into the house they saw the Child with Mary His mother; and they fell to the ground and worshiped Him. Then, opening their treasures, they presented to Him gifts of gold, frankincense, and myrrh."

⌒ Matthew 2:9-11

We aren't much different from the wise men of Jesus' time. Like them, we have gifts to offer our Savior.

The apostle Paul wrote of some. In Romans 12:1-2, he urged us to give our bodies to Jesus as a holy sacrifice. Paul also said that we shouldn't let the world mold our minds, but instead we need to allow Christ to make us more and more like Him every day.

Keeping our bodies and minds pure are gifts that please Jesus.

In Matthew 25:31-40, Jesus also spoke of gifts. He promised that when we give our time or money to the poor, the lonely, the hurt, or the downtrodden, we are actually giving gifts to Him. When you befriend an unpopular student from your high school, for example, give money each month to a starving child, or even comfort your brothers or sisters when they're hurting, your love will reveal Christ in you.

Your love for people is a gift to Christ.

Gift-giving is easy. Your trip to the manger begins each day when you decide to say no to premarital sex or refuse to look at a trashy magazine. Your purity is a gift. You also give to Jesus when you wake up and consider the needy people around you. A decision, a smile and a kind word, part of your savings, or a missionary trip are a few gifts you can offer your Savior. You may not have precious objects such as the wise men offered, but you do have an eternal gift to offer the Messiah—yourself.

Discussion Starters:

1. How can you keep your mind pure for Jesus? Your body?

2. What did Jesus mean when He said, "When you give it to the least of these, you give it to me" (see Matthew 25:40)?

3. What is the greatest gift God has given you?

Lifeline:

Discuss what manger gifts you (individually or as a family) can give to Christ.

PERSPECTIVE

"Then when Herod saw that he had been tricked by the magi, he became very enraged, and sent and slew all the male children who were in Bethlehem and all its vicinity, from two years old and under, according to the time which he had determined from the magi. Then what had been spoken through Jeremiah the prophet was fulfilled: 'A voice was heard in Ramah, weeping and great mourning, Rachel weeping for her children; and she refused to be comforted, because they were no more.'"

↜ Matthew 2:16-18

In northwest Arkansas, a beautiful wilderness cave with millions of pristine crystal formations lies beneath the Ozark Mountains. My boys and I love to visit and explore that cave. The utter darkness of it is foreboding and cold, but when we turn on our bright cave lights, the underground treasure chest comes alive.

Darkness and light cannot coexist. The rays of light beaming into the cave's darkness immediately eliminate its blackness.

That's how it was with the light of Christ. His life chased away the darkness of sin and corruption among His followers in Israel. But King Herod, with his black heart, couldn't stand the thought of Jesus, the pure ray of light, coming into the world. Herod tried to destroy the baby Messiah and ended up murdering countless innocent babies. But Jesus' light prevailed— and it always will.

How can you shine your light for Christ? When you carry your Bible to school, when you refuse to join the party scene, when you avoid ungodly movies, and when your actions match your words of faith, you are a witness for Christ. As they did with Jesus, the people who live in darkness will try to put out your light. They'll laugh at you, gossip about you, and belittle you.

When it happens, continue to love those people as Christ did. As a witness for Jesus, you'll be rewarded with eternal light—heaven, where there will be no more darkness.

Discussion Starters:

1. How have you represented Christ in your school? At work?
2. Have you ever been put down or ridiculed for representing Jesus? If so, how?
3. Which biblical people were mistreated because of their faith? How did they respond to their "persecutors"?

Lifeline:

Discuss how your family can bring Christ's light to your neighborhood.

OBEDIENCE

"Then Jesus arrived from Galilee at the Jordan coming to John, to be baptized by him. But John tried to prevent Him, saying, 'I have need to be baptized by You, and do You come to me?' But Jesus answering said to him, 'Permit it at this time; for in this way it is fitting for us to fulfill all righteousness.' Then he permitted Him."

⌐ Matthew 3:13-15

I was pretty sure my happy-go-lucky son Cooper would have a tough time keeping his foot off the accelerator of his "slightly used" Ford Explorer during his beginning months as a new driver. Sure enough, to his horror, one of his first views in the rearview mirror was the flashing red lights of a police car.

Cooper called me immediately.

"Hey, Dad, uh, guess what I just got?" His voice sounded sheepish.

"Hmmm. (I was almost scared to ask.) Tell me." I chuckled nervously.

"Uh, well, I sorta got a speeding ticket. I'll give you back my license as soon as I get home. I'm sorry, Dad," Cooper said, sighing.

We had prearranged a deal that his first ticket would cost him his license for a month. His second would cost him six months, etc. As crazy and fun and outgoing as he is, I appreciated his obedience that day. I knew it would kill him to give up his driving privileges, but his cooperation meant so much to me. It makes our relationship honest, open, and fun.

Jesus was a *perfect* Son. He was perfectly obedient.

"Why in the world," you might ask about today's Scripture passage, "is Jesus, the perfect man, getting baptized?"

Because, as a Jewish boy, Jesus had been asked by God to "fulfill all righteousness" (verse 15). Similarly, Jesus observed the Passover even though He was the Passover Lamb. He was obedient to Mary and Joseph even though He created them. He gave Himself up for sacrifice on a Roman cross even though He had never sinned.

No wonder His Dad said proudly at Jesus' baptism, "This is My beloved Son, in whom I am well-pleased" (Matthew 3:17).

Discussion Starters:

1. Why is obedience sometimes seen as a harsh or distasteful word?

2. Why is it hard to be obedient to authority figures (like Mom and Dad)?

Lifeline:

How can your family create an environment where obedience is more palatable?

"IT'S TEMPTING, BUT I'LL PASS"

"Again, the devil took Him to a very high mountain and showed Him all the kingdoms of the world and their glory; and he said to Him, 'All these things I will give You, if You fall down and worship me.' Then Jesus said to him, 'Go, Satan! For it is written, "You shall worship the Lord your God, and serve Him only."'"

⌐ Matthew 4:8-10

Justin, a high school sophomore in Memphis, is nervous about the party at Jennifer's house. He's deciding if he should smoke a joint with his friends before the party. Satan whispers, "It would be a lot better to feel relaxed from the marijuana than to act tense and uncool without it."

Sarah is working the grocery store checkout line when a customer accidentally gives her an extra $20. Satan reminds Sarah, "You're in charge of the money. No one will know if you pocket it."

Eric, an eighth grader in San Diego, notices a *Playboy* magazine on the counter at a surf shop. Satan knows that Eric's curiosity for girls has been getting the best of him lately. Satan nudges Eric, "Go ahead. Catch a few glimpses while nobody is looking."

Janelle, a 16-year-old beauty from Boston, is chatting with her friends at lunchtime. They want her to date Todd, the cute basketball player. Janelle has always wanted to go out with someone like him but isn't sure it's the best idea. Satan tells her, "So what if Todd has a bad reputation with girls? All your friends say you'd look great as a couple."

Temptation. Deception. Satan's the master of them both. He always tries to give us the things we think we want now—without giving us a clue of the consequences we'll face later.

Jesus knew that, so He dealt with Satan in the only surefire way he can be immediately defeated. Jesus didn't argue; He didn't rationalize; He didn't play around. Jesus simply put the arrow of Scripture right through Satan's heart—and that knocked the devil right off his feet.

Discussion Starters:

1. How are you being tempted this week?

2. What Scripture verse can you memorize to help you the next time you're tempted?

3. Why does Satan flee when we toss Scripture at him?

Lifeline:

Family devotions build an arsenal of scriptural weapons that your family can use to overcome temptation.

FISHERS OF MEN

"Now as Jesus was walking by the Sea of Galilee, He saw two brothers, Simon who was called Peter, and Andrew his brother, casting a net into the sea; for they were fishermen. And He said to them, 'Follow Me, and I will make you fishers of men.'"

⟿ Matthew 4:18-19

My gran'ma was 100 years old when the curtain between life on earth and eternal life with Jesus was raised and her new heavenly theater became her home. I always called her "Pardner" because she let me know in clear terms that she wasn't old enough to be my gran'ma.

Pardner taught me to fish when I was a young lad. We caught more fish together in my growing-up days than I could even begin to count. During the last few years of Pardner's life she was confined to a wheelchair, but her big, caring smile and the twinkle of love in her pretty brown eyes never dimmed. Just before her 100th birthday, I took her fishing, and she caught a beautiful rainbow trout in the Ozark mountain lake in front of my house.

Her 100th birthday party was the greatest, as I'm sure you can imagine. As I walked in the door to wish her happy birthday, her eyes caught mine, and she never looked away until I knelt by her side.

"Joe Boy," she said sincerely, "take me fishing."

"Aw, Pardner, I can't take you fishing today," I responded lovingly. "This is your 100th birthday, and everybody is here to see you."

Her eyes narrowed in gran'ma-style sternness as she said, "Joe Boy, if you love me, you'll take me fishing."

When Jesus spoke to Peter and Andrew in today's passage, He invited them to go fishing, too. But His call was to a different kind of fishing— "fishing" for the souls of men and women, boys and girls.

Discussion Starters:

1. What do you think the disciples thought of Jesus' invitation as they stood on the shore of the Sea of Galilee?

2. Their trade was fishing. Yours might be basketball, school, cheerleading, band, work, home, or family. How would Jesus tell you to witness for Him in your trade?

3. When Jesus wants to take you "fishing for men," what does He want you to do?

Lifeline:

Have each family member make a list of people for whom he or she can "fish." Then follow up on Jesus' command, and keep one another accountable for doing it.

RADICAL FORGIVENESS

"'But I say to you that everyone who is angry with his brother shall be guilty before the court; and whoever says to his brother, "You good-for-nothing," shall be guilty before the supreme court; and whoever says, "You fool," shall be guilty enough to go into the fiery hell. Therefore if you are presenting your offering at the altar, and there remember that your brother has something against you, leave your offering there before the altar and go; first be reconciled to your brother, and then come and present your offering.'"

↩ Matthew 5:22-24

Jesus demands radical forgiveness. But forgiveness is not easy.

Mr. Jefferson knows that full well. His son Alonzo was murdered by a teenaged gang member during a drive-by shooting. Mr. Jefferson was devastated, but then he decided to adopt the boy and bring him into his home. The teenager who took Alonzo's life is now treated with all the honor Mr. Jefferson gave his own deceased son. That's radical forgiveness.

My close friend "Ad" Coors also knows forgiveness. His father was murdered in cold blood. It took a lot of courage for Ad to visit the prison and release his bitterness toward the man who robbed him of many wonderful years with his father. Ad forgave the man, which was a monumental accomplishment. But Ad went even further and actually apologized to the man for holding that bitterness against him. That's radical forgiveness.

Many of us may not have experienced such severe wrongdoings, but regardless of circumstances, it's always difficult to forgive. We like to hold on to our hurt and let others know how much they have wronged us. It takes humility and devotion to God for us to release our bitterness.

Jesus knew that. That's why He talked so much about the need to forgive. When we know God, it's much easier to do, because we remember that we've been forgiven, too. And when we know God, we remember that all things "work together for good to those who love God, to those who are called according to His purpose" (Romans 8:28).

Is there someone you need to forgive today?

Discussion Starters:

1. Why did Jesus command us to forgive others (especially family members) before we come to God in worship, prayer, or offering?
2. Do you need to seek reconciliation with someone? If so, with whom? How will reconciliation be reached?

Lifeline:

How well do you forgive each other in your family? How can you do it better?

INTEGRITY

"'But I say to you, make no oath at all, either by heaven, for it is the throne of God, or by the earth, for it is the footstool of His feet, or by Jerusalem, for it is the city of the great King. Nor shall you make an oath by your head, for you cannot make one hair white or black. But let your statement be, "Yes, yes" or "No, no"; anything beyond these is of evil.'"

⟿ Matthew 5:34-37

My oldest brother, Bob, at 6'3" tall and with 210 pounds of solid muscle, is a man's man to the core of his heart. He's a successful dentist, avid bird dog trainer, and skilled outdoorsman. He's one of my heroes.

Thirty years ago, Bob married the first girl he ever loved. He said yes to the preacher on that wedding day and gave his word that he'd give Mary Evelyn his life, *no matter what*. Two summers ago, Mary Evelyn's kidneys quit. Her blood was poisoning her (according to the charts) almost to the point of death. She needed a donor kidney immediately to stay alive. No kidney that matched her biological chemistry was available. Immediately, Bob volunteered his. He was tested for compatibility and, amazingly enough, his matched perfectly.

Soon after, the doctors opened up Bob from his belly button to his backbone, took three ribs and the kidney, placed the kidney into his bride's abdomen, and hooked up the tubes and vessels. The next day, Mary Evelyn was alive and well. Now she feels like a million bucks. Bob feels pain every day, but he just smiles and shrugs it off as a small expression of love for his "wife of a lifetime."

When Jesus said, "Let your yes be a yes," he meant, Keep your word. Unfortunately, it's easy to see that our culture doesn't often hold to its promises. Politicians say "I promise" and then forget those promises, magazines feature celebrities who've gotten yet another divorce, and so-called best friends will quickly forget their commitment to friendship if someone more exciting comes along. It makes you wonder if anyone values commitment anymore.

But Brother Bob showed me that followers of Jesus keep their word.

Discussion Starters:

1. When is it hardest for you to keep a commitment? Why?
2. Why is a person's *yes* the most important word in his or her life?
3. How can you become a more reliable person?

Lifeline:

Make honesty the only policy in your home!

HUMILITY

"'Beware of practicing your righteousness before men to be noticed by them; otherwise you have no reward with your Father who is in heaven.... But when you give to the poor, do not let your left hand know what your right hand is doing, so that your giving will be in secret; and your Father who sees what is done in secret will reward you.'"

↩ Matthew 6:1,3-4

How many times have you heard prideful remarks like these?

> "I give 15 percent of my paycheck to the Lord's work."
> "I'm fasting and praying today."
> "I support that ministry, too."
> "I go to church every Sunday."
> "I would never do a thing like that."

Those words remind me of the way an NFL receiver looks when he catches a great pass and goes strutting into the end zone like a peacock courting his girlfriend. A while back, when the NCAA began to enforce stiffer penalties for such ego flaunting, Notre Dame coach Lou Holtz glibly said to his players, "When you get into the end zone, act like you've been there before."

Humility. Discreetness. Secret giving. Silent offering. These are the kinds of qualities that get God's attention and please Him deeply. Jesus makes it clear that when you do something special, God wants all the glory. If you take the glory, there's none left for Him. (He'll get His chance to return the glory to you when you meet Him at heaven's gate.) Heaven will be the final awards ceremony! That's where the rewards, honors, and glory will really matter.

Next time you get a chance to take the credit for something God has honored you with, have some fun and discreetly let Him or someone else get the glory. Be careful, it may become habit-forming!

Discussion Starters:

1. Why is it hard to give the glory to God?
2. What did Jesus mean by saying that hypocrites already "have their reward in full" (verse 2)?
3. Why is humility such an attractive quality?
4. Who is the most humble person you know? Why?

Lifeline:

Discuss ways in which your family can encourage humility at home.

TREASURES

" 'Do not store up for yourselves treasures on earth, where moth and rust destroy, and where thieves break in and steal. But store up for yourselves treasures in heaven, where neither moth nor rust destroys, and where thieves do not break in or steal; for where your treasure is, there your heart will be also.' "

↪ Matthew 6:19-21

Sunday was the greatest day for me! I got to do what I absolutely *treasure* the most. First, I had the whole day off to play. I cooked homemade blueberry cinnamon muffins for my 17-year-old boy, Brady, and chocolate-chocolate chip muffins for my 14-year-old son, Cooper. (Yes, I ate one of each.) After a fantastic breakfast devotional together, we went to our little country church and sang those super old hymns I used to sing with my daddy when I was a pip-squeak. After church, my boys and I played catch with the football and hit golf balls. Then I was lucky to get phone calls from Jamie and Courtney, my two girls who are in college. And if that wasn't enough, I was fortunate enough to hold my precious wife's hand as we prayed together before bed.

I treasure those times with my God, my wife, and my kids. You can burn down my house, steal my car, and take everything I own (except my dog), but leave my treasures and life will still be a "10" for me.

God says it's dangerous to treasure the wrong things. Last night, a dear family friend told me a sad story. My friend said that his 18-year-old daughter, Shauna, is dating a troubled guy. Shauna treasures her popularity and wants to be loved, so she's begun compromising her beliefs for her boyfriend. He's pressuring her into drinking and partying. Now she's confused, depressed, and feels as if her whole world is falling apart.

It's easy to treasure popularity, expensive toys, power and position, houses, careers, sex, and cars. But Jesus tells us to treasure eternal things.

And most of all, God says, "Treasure Me."

Discussion Starters:

1. What things do you treasure? Is your heart in the right place?

2. Why is it so hard to treasure what really matters more than the stuff that clutters our lives?

3. What do you really want to treasure more today? How can you do that?

Lifeline:

Talk through how your family can better treasure the things that matter most.

MONKEY SEE, MONKEY DO

" 'The eye is the lamp of the body; so then if your eye is clear, your whole body will be full of light. But if your eye is bad, your whole body will be full of darkness. If then the light that is in you is darkness, how great is the darkness! No one can serve two masters; for either he will hate the one and love the other, or he will be devoted to one and despise the other. You cannot serve God and wealth.... But seek first His kingdom and His righteousness, and all these things will be added to you.' "

↩ Matthew 6:22-24,33

What you see is what you get.

It's true. Your eyes are windows into your mind and heart. What you see, what you choose to put into your mind each day, will have a profound impact on you. Are you too materialistic for your own good? Are you being selective enough in choosing magazines and TV programs? What kinds of movies do you watch? It's hard to keep your eyes on Jesus and not on money or the world. It's difficult to stay sexually pure and drug- and alcohol-free. But it's even harder when you let the culture constantly parade money, sex, and alcohol in front of your eyes.

Temptation is everywhere. A reviewer for *Rolling Stone* magazine remarked that after only a few hours of watching MTV, he had seen more than 100 women scantily clad and portrayed like the seductive models who grace the cover of *Cosmopolitan* magazine.[2] The soaps and sitcoms aren't much better. *USA Today* reported that a survey of more than 500,000 fourth graders said "TV prompts them the most" to try drugs and alcohol.[3] It isn't any wonder when you consider that the average TV viewer will see 100,000 beer commercials by age 18[4] and 14,000 sexual references *per year*.[5]

The apostle Paul, knowing where true peace and happiness lie, urged us to "set your mind on the things above, not on the things that are on earth" (Colossians 3:2). Place your eyes on God, and all good and righteous things will be given to you.

Discussion Starters:

1. Why does Jesus talk so much about the eyes?

2. Are you trying to serve two masters? Explain.

3. How can your family create a healthy media environment?

Lifeline:

Have each person set goals to help him or her develop eyes for God.

LOG EYE

"'Do not judge so that you will not be judged.... Why do you look at the speck that is in your brother's eye, but do not notice the log that is in your own eye? ...You hypocrite, first take the log out of your own eye, and then you will see clearly to take the speck out of your brother's eye.'"

⇝ Matthew 7:1,3,5

Old "Log Eye," according to Paul Aldrich, a Christian recording artist and comedian, is a funny ol' critter. He roams in every home, every school hallway, every church, every business, every human mind. He's a weird-looking dude because he has a magnifying glass in front of one eye, a big, bowed-up log in the other eye, and a sharp, pointy finger always showing somebody else's faults. The first word out of his mouth is always "You."

I fight with Log Eye in my own mind every day. The big chump! He makes me so critical of my wife and kids that I want to take the log out and hit him with it! One time when one of my boys was young, I was "rantin' and ravin'" about something he had done (a hillbilly term for being overly critical and vocal) when my sweet wife, Debbie-Jo, stopped me dead in my tracks.

"Honey," she said to me, "your son sees himself in your eyes." Oooo, that hurt. But she was right. I was so bent on criticizing my son, I forgot the damage I could cause to him. Log Eye was ruling my life that day!

God instructs parents to teach godly principles and to correct bad behavior, but He never intended our *focus* to be critical or judgmental. Our first priority is to love God and then love others (see Matthew 22:37-40).

With that in mind, for *all* members of the family, the motto I like is:

"Catch each other in the act of doing something *good* and tell 'em about it."

Discussion Starters:

1. Why is it so dangerous to be judgmental?
2. What is a blind spot? Why are logs so hard to see?
3. Why is it sometimes easier to be critical rather than loving?
4. How can your family kick ol' Log Eye out of the family circle?

Lifeline:

Have each family member say something affirming to two others.

LEGITIMACY

"'Not everyone who says to Me, "Lord, Lord," will enter the kingdom of heaven, but he who does the will of My Father who is in heaven will enter. Many will say to Me on that day, "Lord, Lord, did we not prophesy in Your name, and in Your name cast out demons, and in Your name perform many miracles?" And then I will declare to them, "I never knew you; depart from Me, you who practice lawlessness."'"

⇜ Matthew 7:21-23

Imagine what we'd all look like if we were completely transparent and could see the inside of other people's hearts. What if others could see the inside of *your* heart?

Your motives. Your intentions. Your true self. Your agenda.

No baloney, no excuses, no hoopla, just truth. What would people see in you?

Unlike our fellow men and women, the Lord looks *only* at our hearts (see 1 Samuel 16:7). Many Christians are dedicated and sincere in their faith. But many of them run around churches and Christian homes calling themselves "Christians" when they've never completely given their hearts to Him. In this passage, Jesus was talking to those half-hearted souls. Are you one of them?

The chronicler expresses God's focus this way: "For the eyes of the Lord move to and fro throughout the earth that He may strongly support those whose heart is completely His" (2 Chronicles 16:9).

I believe that once we're truly His, we're always truly His. But if we have lawless, rebellious, or dishonest hearts, we have to wonder if we ever were His in the first place.

The apostle Paul urged us to search our hearts. He said, "Test yourselves to see if you are in the faith; examine yourselves!" (2 Corinthians 13:5). Do you consider anything in your life to be more important than God? Are you only a "Sunday Christian"? If so, ask God for forgiveness, and give Him your whole heart. Then you'll have a faith that is, as people say, "the real thing."

Discussion Starters:

1. What does it mean to do the will of the Lord?
2. What do you think Jesus meant when He said, "I never knew you"?
3. Are you giving God your whole heart? Explain.

Lifeline:

Discuss specific ways to help one another put God first in your hearts.

THAT SPECIAL TOUCH

"When Jesus came down from the mountain, large crowds followed Him. And a leper came to Him and bowed down before Him, and said, 'Lord, if You are willing, You can make me clean.' Jesus stretched out His hand and touched him, saying, 'I am willing; be cleansed.' And immediately his leprosy was cleansed."

⤸ Matthew 8:1-3

Cathy hardly ever went out. In fact, the boys in our high school didn't even notice her. As a little girl, Cathy had battled a rare illness that left her neck and mouth grossly distorted. Even though Cathy was as sweet as any girl in my school, no boy would ask her for a date because of her strangely disfigured features...that is, until her senior prom.

David was the president of our student council and was about as nice a guy as I've ever met. He not only asked Cathy to the prom, but he also took her there and treated her like a queen. Cathy looked stunningly beautiful in her baby blue dress trimmed with white lace.

That prom night was significant for another reason as well. Alfonse, a quiet but sincere country boy, was also at the prom, and he noticed Cathy's previously hidden beauty. Alfonse took a special interest in Cathy after that dance, and they developed a wonderful relationship. Eventually, Alfonse asked for her hand in marriage.

Imagine the good we could do if we all reached out with hands of love and compassion! David, the boy who asked Cathy to the prom, demonstrated Christ's loving touch when he looked beyond Cathy's appearance, beyond what other kids might think of him, and asked her to the dance. Christ was able to work through David, beautifully fulfilling Cathy's need for love and attention.

The miracle that happened with David, Cathy, and Alfonse always reminds me of the story of Jesus and the leper. Jesus, with unfathomable compassion, reached out His hand in love. He risked disease and rejection from society and touched the disfigured leper right in front of everyone. While others backed away and turned their heads in disgust, Jesus reached His hand straight into the heart of the man's greatest need.

Discussion Starters:

1. What would be a modern equivalent to Jesus' touching a leper with compassion?
2. Are you in need of Jesus' loving touch? Explain.
3. Do you know someone who needs your hand of compassion? If so, who? How can you help him or her?

Lifeline:

Discuss how your family can both receive and give Jesus' healing love.

SUFFICIENT FAITH

"When He got into the boat, His disciples followed Him. And behold, there arose a great storm on the sea, so that the boat was being covered with the waves; but Jesus Himself was asleep. And they came to Him and woke Him, saying, 'Save us, Lord; we are perishing!' He said to them, 'Why are you afraid, you men of little faith?' Then He got up and rebuked the winds and the sea, and it became perfectly calm."

↪ Matthew 8:23-26

My friend Shannon is an actress in Hollywood. She is talented, beautiful, capable, sought after...and poor. She has read dozens of scripts from wooing directors and producers, but to this date in her young career, she has not accepted one. Every script has suggestive romance. Every script has crude language. And every time, she says the same thing—"No thanks. I'll wait for a script my conscience can live with."

My dear friend Shannon has faith that God will meet her needs.

God *will* meet your needs. But so often we struggle to believe it.

Even the disciples struggled with their faith. All day long in the boat, before the big storm, the disciples had heard Jesus deliver the greatest sermon on faith ever preached. But when the clouds came in and the rain poured down, they floundered. Had they really listened to their teacher?

"Save us, Lord; we are perishing!" they cried (verse 25).

We read the Bible and wonder, *How could the disciples forget Jesus' words so soon?* But how do *you* deal with life's storms?

You haven't had a date in months. You could lower your standards.

Your weight lifting program for football training has gone flat. Several guys have a higher bench-press max. You could take steroids.

Algebra is becoming impossible. The tests are killers. That girl sitting next to you always gets it right. Just one look at her paper would help.

There will always be storms, but your God is bigger than the storms in your life. Is your faith big enough?

Discussion Starters:

1. What is testing your faith today?

2. Where is Jesus in your boat?

3. Why is it so hard to believe that Jesus can silence and calm our storms?

4. How can you find peace and serenity in the midst of your storm right now?

Lifeline:

Next time your family encounters a storm, remember, "And...God will supply all your needs according to His riches in glory in Christ Jesus" (Philippians 4:19).

TRUE FRIENDS

"And they brought to Him a paralytic lying on a bed. Seeing their faith, Jesus said to the paralytic, 'Take courage, son; your sins are forgiven.'"

⇔ Matthew 9:2

Have you ever thought about the paralytic's friends?

His friends knew him. They knew he needed help, and they knew he needed the Savior. They went out of their way, went to work, and took their friend to the only place he could get the help he desperately needed. They were true friends.

I'm sure you've learned that not everyone is a true friend, though. Some so-called friends help friends sneak out of the house at night. Other "friends" buy beer and drugs so friends can party. Some "friends" take friends to suggestive movies. And many supposed "friends" push their girlfriends or boyfriends to have sex. These wanna-be friends are dangerous. I know— almost all the mistakes my teenage friends make are due to their "friends" who have led them in the wrong direction.

That's not the case with Andy, Justin, Chris, Brady, Skippy, Jared, and Isaac, though. These high school juniors are star athletes, so drinking and partying aren't even options for them. They know that drugs and alcohol are completely uncool, and they remind each other of that at their weekly Bible study. They encourage each other to keep off drugs, to be sexually pure, and to be moral leaders in their school.

Want to be a true friend? Build others up. Encourage your friends to do the right thing. And let your friendship reveal Christ's unconditional love.

That's what real friendship is all about.

Discussion Starters:

1. What's the difference between a "friend" and a true friend?

2. Who are your true friends? Why do you consider them to be true friends?

3. To *have* a true friend, you need to *be* a true friend. Describe the kind of friend you'd like to be.

4. In what ways is Jesus a friend to you?

Lifeline:

How can your family be true friends to one another? How can you encourage one another to develop true friendships?

JUST A TOUCH

"And a woman who had been suffering from a hemorrhage for twelve years, came up behind Him and touched the fringe of His cloak; for she was saying to herself, 'If I only touch His garment, I will get well.' But Jesus turning and seeing her said, 'Daughter, take courage; your faith has made you well.' At once the woman was made well."

⤷ Matthew 9:20-22

Jesus loves it when His children reach out to Him in faith.

Just look at how He responded to the thief on the cross (see Luke 23). This criminal hung next to Jesus, dying. In the final breath of his futile life, the thief looked to the Savior nailed on the cross beside him and squeaked out a tiny plea for mercy. Immediately, Jesus promised him life in heaven.

Peter, one of Jesus' reckless disciples, also called out to Him in faith. Peter and the other disciples had watched Jesus walk on the Sea of Galilee. Eager to follow in his Master's footsteps (literally), Peter impulsively stepped out of the boat to walk on the sea. But his fear caught up with him, and he began to sink. Peter cried desperately, "Lord, save me!" (Matthew 14:30). In a heartbeat, Jesus' hand was there, and Peter's life was spared.

The hemorrhaging woman had great faith in Jesus' power as well. After 12 years of continuous bleeding, the woman realized she needed a touch from Jesus. She approached Him in a crowd and, amidst the pushing and shoving, reached out in faith and touched not Him but His garment! Jesus responded to her hopefulness and courage, and her faith was rewarded.

What about you? Is your situation hopeless? Are you sinking in despair? Does your heart bleed? Do you have faith that Jesus can help you?

Your coach hasn't noticed you in weeks. Your close friend has cancer. You cringe every time you look in the mirror. Spanish class is killing you. Your girlfriend just called it quits. Everyone makes fun of you. Your bleeding just won't stop, and you need a Savior.

Christ is your ultimate problem solver, and He's ready to rescue you. All it takes is a tiny prayer and a speck of faith because He's only an arm's reach away. He'll be there. Count on it.

Discussion Starters:

1. What is faith? Why is faith so important to God?

2. Can you relate to any of the biblical people in today's devotional? If so, how?

3. How can you touch His garment when your heart's bleeding?

Lifeline:

Discuss a situation in which your family must reach out to Jesus in faith.

SODOM AND GOMORRAH
DALLAS AND SAN FRANCISCO

"'And whatever city or village you enter, inquire who is worthy in it, and stay at his house until you leave that city.... Whoever does not receive you, nor heed your words, as you go out of that house or that city, shake the dust off your feet. Truly I say to you, it will be more tolerable for the land of Sodom and Gomorrah in the day of judgment than for that city.'"

↩ Matthew 10:11,14-15

It's a sunny Thursday afternoon. School has just ended, and Cindy and Rebecca are racing out the door to the parking lot. They hop into Rebecca's four-wheel-drive jeep, and Cindy pops in the newest CD. Jamming down the road, singing, they drive to the mall, where Cindy sees this sweater she "has to have." She doesn't have any cash, but—not to worry—she can always charge it to Mom and Dad's platinum card. Cindy's got to have a new outfit for her date on Friday with Brian. It's a *necessity*.

Maybe you can't afford the lifestyle Cindy and Rebecca enjoy, but chances are you know someone who can. We live in a rich country where Americans have it all! Our poorest people would be among the rich in other lands. The things we take for granted, like indoor plumbing and electricity, are luxuries in other countries.

As spoiled as we are, we still want more. That's why we trade in our cars, rack up debts on credit cards, move to bigger houses, "hit the mall," and upgrade to more expensive stereos. Yet, with all our God-given blessings, our music, TV shows, books, and movies continue to blaspheme God.

God has sent a steady stream of His disciples to us for 400 years. We have churches on almost every corner and Bibles all over the house. But God is quickly being taken out of our schools, courtrooms, and businesses. If God leveled Sodom and Gomorrah in a flash, what will become of America if we don't repent and heed God's Word? America's blessings will mean nothing if the hearts of its people are still sinful.

Discussion Starters:

1. Would the disciples have to "shake the dust off their feet" if they came to your house today? Why or why not?
2. How can your family remain humble and live lives that are pleasing to God?

Lifeline:

Building a godly home is the best way to begin rebuilding America (or any nation).

UNASHAMED

"'Do not fear those who kill the body but are unable to kill the soul; but rather fear Him who is able to destroy both soul and body in hell.... Therefore everyone who confesses Me before men, I will also confess him before My Father who is in heaven.'"

↪ Matthew 10:28,32

The secret had slipped out. It was the mid-1970s, during the days of fierce Russian Communism and the ruthless suppression of Christianity. A group of more than 100 Christians was singing hymns and worshiping God in an "underground" church when the service was abruptly interrupted by KGB soldiers equipped with automatic guns.

The congregation immediately became deathly silent as the guards demanded that all true followers of Jesus Christ stand up. Those not willing to confess Christ were free to leave. With fear and trepidation, a few dozen devout believers stood on their feet, knowing the next sound they'd probably hear would be gunshots snuffing out their final breath. The rest desperately fled from the building.

When the scuffling ended and the room was silent, one of the KGB gunmen spoke up. "All right," he said, "we've also converted to Christianity, and we just wanted to know who the true Christians were. Now let's have a real worship service together." The worship that night was powerful.

No, we don't live in the old USSR, and the United States isn't communist, but this "one nation under God" can be awfully cruel to Christians sometimes. Speaking up or saying no in high school often brings on heavy persecution. The evolutionists will sneer, the popular crowd will gossip, the partyers will laugh, and sometimes your friends will leave you. Standing up for Jesus is not easy.

But He defended you. He subjected Himself to ridicule, persecution, and even death—all for you, because He loves you. Is your love for Him strong enough to stand?

Discussion Starters:

1. If you lived in a communist country and were convicted of being a Christian, what evidence would the witnesses bring up to convict you?

2. If you were one of the Russian worshipers that day, would you have stood or fled the scene?

3. Have you ever been persecuted for your faith? If so, how did you persevere through it? Was your faith strengthened? Why or why not?

Lifeline:

Pray together that God will enable your family to stand up for Jesus.

IS HE GOD, OR WHAT?

"Now when John, while imprisoned, heard of the works of Christ, he sent word by his disciples and said to Him, 'Are You the Expected One, or shall we look for someone else?' Jesus answered and said to them, 'Go and report to John what you hear and see.'"

⟿ Matthew 11:2-4

"I and the Father are one" (John 10:30).
"I am the good shepherd" (John 10:11).
"I am the true vine" (John 15:1).
"I am the door" (John 10:9).
"I am the way" (John 14:6).

Make no mistake about it—whatever the world thinks about Jesus, He is convinced that He's God in the flesh. You can call Him crazy; you can call Him delirious; you can call Him grossly misinformed; but don't label Him as a good man, another prophet, a great moral teacher, or any other title of mere human significance, because either He is God or He is the most misleading person who ever lived.

But Jesus does not lie. He is God incarnate.

John the Baptist, another man with a definite mission from God, had given his life to proclaiming the coming of Christ. Sitting in his prison cell, he wanted to make sure he was sold out for the right person. In so many words, Jesus told John's disciples to tell him the same thing He'd tell you the next time you ask. "I do things that only God can do. I'm the fulfillment of all Messianic prophecy. I have power that no mere man could ever have. Yes, John, when you see Me, you've seen the Father."

If Jesus was anything less than God, His sacrifice on the cross could never have paid for your sins. At the same time, He had to become a man and identify with your sinfulness so that He could literally die for those sins. As God, He had the holiness and authority; as man, He had the empathy and the humanity.

John was convinced. Are you?

Discussion Starters:

1. Why did God have to become a man?
2. What did He mean when He said, "I and the Father are one"?

Lifeline:

As a family, come up with a brief answer you could give to others who claim that Jesus was just a great moral teacher.

THE LIGHT BURDEN

"'Come to Me, all who are weary and heavy-laden, and I will give you rest. Take My yoke upon you and learn from Me, for I am gentle and humble in heart, and you will find rest for your souls. For My yoke is easy and My burden is light.'"

↜ Matthew 11:28-30

The night before my college football team played the University of Oklahoma in a major New Year's Eve bowl bash, we went to a professional ice hockey game to ease our nerves and forget the tension of the upcoming duel on the field. The hockey game was brutal. The hitting, checking, and fighting made our game of football seem more like Nintendo. We moaned, groaned, and empathized with the physical punishment each player dealt to his opponent. We left the arena, relieved to be putting on our football gear the next day and playing such a comparatively tame sport!

My buddy Shane plays goalie for his high school hockey team. It's no small task. The goalie takes the heat with every play. The frozen puck slams into his face mask at speeds up to 100 mph, and every opponent longs to shove him away from the goal so his teammates can score into the net. But Shane plays the game fearlessly because in hockey, the goalie is protected by his teammates at all costs. In one critical game, a crazed opponent bashed into Shane with both fists. Immediately, Shane's teammates leaped on the intruder with protective vengeance. The goalie's burden of protecting the goal is light. He has no fear of the opposing players because at all times, his teammates are ready, willing, and able to defend him.

As a Christian, you are the goalie. The pressure of life is intense. You may be weary and burdened by the demands around you. The opponents—peer pressure, guilt, perfectionism, failure, and lust—are constantly before you, desiring to eliminate you from the game. But thanks to our caring, self-sacrificing, protective Savior, Jesus Christ, the game is fun! We know that Jesus will respond immediately to our prayers. He'll overpower the enemy as we look to Him in faith and let Him intercede for our daily needs.

Discussion Starters:

1. What burden have you been carrying this week?

2. How can you give it to Jesus?

3. How has Jesus taken up your burdens in the past?

Lifeline:

Pray with the family member who's burdened today, and help him or her give the load to Christ.

THE LORD OF THE SABBATH

"At that time Jesus went through the grainfields on the Sabbath, and His disciples became hungry and began to pick the heads of grain and eat. But when the Pharisees saw this, they said to Him, 'Look, Your disciples do what is not lawful to do on a Sabbath.' ...[And Jesus said,] 'Have you not read in the Law, that on the Sabbath the priests in the temple break the Sabbath and are innocent? But I say to you that something greater than the temple is here.... For the Son of Man is Lord of the Sabbath.'"

⮠ Matthew 12:1-2,5-6,8

Until the time Jesus came, the word *law* was a stumbling block for everyone who lived according to it. It meant keeping tons of nitpicky rules, and many people who lived by it were judgmental and hypocritical.

Jesus changed all that. He said that it's not just sinful to murder, but it's also sinful to hate a guy enough to want to kill him.

It's not only sinful to fornicate, commit adultery, and practice homosexuality, but it's also sinful to entertain sexual thoughts about anyone except your spouse.

It's not just sinful to talk in a derogatory manner behind your parents' or children's backs, but it's also sinful to harbor unresolved bitterness in your heart.

The letter of the law didn't matter so much to Jesus. He cared about the spirit of the law: Your motives. Your thoughts. What's in your heart.

In Scripture, Jesus is referred to as "the Christ" (John 11:27), "the Word" (John 1:1), the co-creator of the universe (Colossians 1), and the "Lord of the Sabbath" (Matthew 12:8). As you love Him and worship Him in all things, you are keeping the law. The name of the game on the Sabbath (as well as the other six days of the week) is not to keep from breaking a sweat, but to think of Him, worship Him, live for Him, and love Him.

On Sundays, we're supposed to focus on God and remember His command to rest one day a week. But whatever we do, our *hearts* matter most to God. If we're truly devoted to Him, we'll try to stay pure, represent Christ, be reconciled with our families, and honor Him in all we do.

Discussion Starters:

1. The Jewish leaders had gotten off track in their view of the law. How do we often lose track of the meaning of God's words?

2. We fulfill God's law when we simply, sincerely love Jesus. How does knowing that bring you freedom?

Lifeline:

How can your family honor Christ better this next Sabbath?

IT'S ALL OR NOTHING

"And knowing their thoughts Jesus said to them, 'Any kingdom divided against itself is laid waste; and any city or house divided against itself will not stand.... He who is not with Me is against Me; and he who does not gather with Me scatters.'"

↪ Matthew 12:25,30

Sonya follows Christ and tries to spend time praying and reading the Bible each day. She wants her life to reflect her love for God and other people. Ted, on the other hand, is defiant and rebellious. He cusses up a storm and uses Christ's name in vain—all the time. Crystal and Tony are in a completely different group. They're not living for God, but they're not out to get Him, either. They party a little and go to church a little, too. They believe in God, but they don't want to be associated with Him.

Folks, Jesus didn't mince words when He said, "He who is not with Me is against Me" (verse 30). Jesus' half brother James put it this way: "Whoever wishes to be a friend of the world makes himself an enemy of God" (James 4:4). For decades, I've heard stories of kids and adults who cop out on God by saying, "I'm not doing anything that bad. I'm just not ready to commit my life to Christ." In case after case, it was only a matter of time before each person was reeling in emotional pain because her "friendship with the world" had led her into some disaster.

No one *wants* to be a drug addict, but one little joint doesn't look all that bad. No one *wants* to be a hopeless alcoholic, but one little beer looks pretty harmless. No one *wants* to be a porn addict, but that *Cosmopolitan* magazine doesn't look that dangerous. One joint, one beer, or one flip through a questionable magazine can start you on a path toward a bunch of bad habits, though.

Jesus knew what He was talking about when He warned, in effect, "Either you love me with your whole heart or you don't love me at all." Our Lord is demanding. He wants all of you. Have you made that total commitment?

Discussion Starters:

1. Why does Satan like to see us walk down the middle of the road, morally speaking?
2. Are you facing any compromising circumstances this week? Explain.
3. How can you love Jesus with your whole heart? What things do you need to change so you can do that?

Lifeline:

Discuss and reflect on Revelation 3:15-16. What significance does this have for your family?

HIS FAMILY MATTERS

"And stretching out His hand toward His disciples, He said, 'Behold My mother and My brothers! For whoever does the will of My Father who is in heaven, he is My brother and sister and mother.'"

⌒ Matthew 12:49-50

I'll never forget the sting of rejection I felt that day as a shy and insecure seven-year-old. It was after one of Elvis Presley's small concerts during his early performance days, before he hit the big time. Presley had given me his autograph earlier, but I'd lost it somewhere in the crowd. He must have remembered my nervous and embarrassed face the second time around because he said, annoyed, "Hey, kid, didn't I already do this once tonight?" After I fumbled a torn piece of paper and a pencil into his hands, he reluctantly scribbled "Elvis Presley" a second time. I ducked my head in complete embarrassment and scurried off to find my bike and pedal home.

Some people collect Elvis albums like diamonds and even call him "the King of Rock and Roll." To each his own, I guess, but I'd rather invest my money and soul in the real King—Jesus Christ. Christ gave me a longer-lasting autograph than Elvis did. Christ's words are written "on the tablet of my heart" because He died for me, and through His Spirit, He lives in me (see 2 Corinthians 3).

But even better, Jesus actually calls me family! As I choose to follow Him, He chooses me to be His son. First John 3:1 says, "See how great a love the Father has bestowed on us, that we should be called children of God; and such we are." I'm part of His family because He loves me so much. As His child, I even share in His heavenly inheritance. Now, that's love! Some people would do anything for my old Elvis autograph, but I'd trade in the rock 'n' roll king's paper for the almighty King's eternal riches and love any day.

He has invited you to be His child, too. Have you joined His family?

Discussion Starters:

1. What does it mean to be invited into God's family?

2. Why does He call His obedient followers "family"?

3. What do you see when you picture your heavenly Father?

4. How do you feel knowing you are part of God's divine family?

Lifeline:

Since you are members of God's family, how should you act toward each other?

HEARTFELT GROWTH

"And He spoke...to them in parables, saying, 'Behold, the sower went out to sow; and as he sowed, some seeds fell beside the road, and the birds came and ate them up. Others fell on the rocky places, where they did not have much soil; and immediately they sprang up, because they had no depth of soil. But when the sun had risen, they were scorched; and because they had no root, they withered away. Others fell among the thorns, and the thorns came up and choked them out. And others fell on the good soil and yielded a crop, some a hundredfold, some sixty, and some thirty.'"

↩ Matthew 13:3-8

I had just spent an exciting week snowboarding in the Rockies with my five best friends—my wife and four kids. As we sat in the Denver International Airport, waiting for our flight home, a petite seven-year-old girl and her daddy caught my eye. The girl's long, brown ponytail bobbed up and down each time she caught the small, red, bouncy ball her daddy tossed her way. For several minutes, I watched them giggle together as they played catch. With each bounce of the ball, he sowed another seed of love in her heart. With each assuring word and positive glance, her tiny heart expanded as she smiled back at her daddy.

After they left, I thought, *What will happen to her when she's 16, 17, and 18?* I looked over at my own daughters, ages 18 and 21, and wondered, *Will she and her dad still be friends? What decisions will she make? What kind of friends will she run with? Will she make her parents proud?* As a father, I could see that the little girl's daddy had sown seeds of love and planted them with high expectations that someday a fulfilled, happy, productive woman would grow from those innocent days of childhood.

I hoped that love would take root. That was my desire for the little girl, and that is Jesus' desire for us. He hopes that the thorns—temptations—of work and school won't choke the growth in our hearts. He has faith that bad attitudes, bitterness, and jealousy won't harden our hearts. Jesus has sown seeds from the fruit of His Spirit—love, joy, peace, patience, kindness, goodness, faithfulness, gentleness, and self-control—into the hearts of His children. If we spend time with the Sower, Jesus, His seeds *will* take root.

Discussion Starters:

1. How have God's seeds grown in your heart this year? Be specific.

2. Have any thorns crept into your life? If so, how can you uproot them?

Lifeline:

Family time with God creates deep and fertile soil.

40

WEEDS AND FLOWERS

"Jesus presented another parable to them, saying, 'The kingdom of heaven may be compared to a man who sowed good seed in his field. But while his men were sleeping, his enemy came and sowed tares among the wheat, and went away. But when the wheat sprouted and bore grain, then the tares became evident also.... [So the landowner said], "Allow both to grow together until the harvest; and in the time of the harvest I will say to the reapers, 'First gather up the tares and bind them in bundles to burn them up; but gather the wheat into my barn.'"'"

↪ Matthew 13:24-25,30

As a kid, I dreaded certain Saturdays. My brothers and I would trudge out to the yard to begin our least favorite chore—weeding. Weeding out the Bermuda grass from the flower gardens that surrounded our Texas home was no small task. Bermuda grass is tough as all get-out, and its long, gnarly roots grab the soil. We would pull and complain, dig and grumble for hours on Saturday mornings in the spring and fall. The flowers that grew after we weeded were beautiful, and I loved cutting a handful of them for my mom, but I couldn't get rid of those weeds fast enough. Weeds are such a big pain that they can make beautiful flowerbeds a chore!

Weeds and tares are like rotten habits, bad TV shows, sick music, and bitter thoughts. Once they plant themselves in your heart, it's hard to pull them out. I'm ashamed to tell you I can *still* remember the lyrics from some of the foul songs that I listened to in junior high. Those weeds are brutal, and they're often deeply buried in your heart. The worst part of all is that they choke out your wheat.

What's your wheat? Reading and memorizing Scripture, spending time with family and uplifting friends, praying, volunteering your time, doing family devotionals...all those things can be the wheat—the good—in your life. And when you weed out the tares from the wheat, the result is rich and enduring! My mom had me memorize some of the Sermon on the Mount when I was nine, and do you know what? I still remember those verses!

When Christ comes, the tares go into the fire, and the wheat becomes a bouquet of flowers that is presented to God.

If He came today, what would *your* "crop" look like?

Discussion Starters:

1. Describe the wheat in your life today.

2. What tares or weeds have lodged themselves in your mind?

3. What kind of bouquet do you want to present to God?

Lifeline:

How can your family encourage spiritual weeding?

THE BEST OF THE BEST AND THE WORST OF THE WORST

" 'The kingdom of heaven is like a treasure hidden in the field, which a man found and hid again; and from joy over it he goes and sells all that he has and buys that field.... Again, the kingdom of heaven is like a dragnet cast into the sea, and gathering fish of every kind; and when it was filled, they drew it up on the beach; and they sat down and gathered the good fish into containers, but the bad they threw away. So it will be at the end of the age; the angels will come forth and take out the wicked from among the righteous, and will throw them into the furnace of fire; in that place there will be weeping and gnashing of teeth.' "

↪ Matthew 13:44,47-50

My son Brady stood past the half-court line, ready to make the three-point, tie-breaking shot. This was Brady's sophomore year, and he'd been sitting on the varsity bench most of the season. But Brady was ready. He had practiced the shot millions of times. Brady fired the ball through the air, and the ball swished through the net just as the buzzer sounded. The crowd went wild! Brady felt as if he were perched on the front row of heaven as the mob embraced him. It was the thrill of victory! The best of the best!

During his bitterly disappointing junior year, he missed the same last-second shot five times in game after game. Each time, Brady's miss cost his team the game. He felt personally responsible for each defeat and spent most of the season perched on the bench of despair. It was the agony of defeat! The worst of the worst!

What do you think is the best thing the world has to offer? What's worth your sacrifice and patience? A BMW convertible? An Ivy League scholarship? Making it to the NFL? Being voted homecoming queen?

On the flip side, what's your worst nightmare? A broken heart? Public humiliation? A tragic car wreck? Flunking out of school?

Nothing on earth, no matter how seemingly wonderful, will compare to the treasure of heaven. And the worst nightmare on earth will pale in comparison to a second spent in hell. Jesus always shot it straight. He told us what to expect based on how we respond to His offer of salvation.

Discussion Starters:

1. Why did Jesus compare heaven to a treasure?
2. Why did Jesus say that in hell there will be "weeping and gnashing of teeth" (verse 50)?

Lifeline:

Discuss what you picture heaven to be like and why. (We'll learn more about it when we look at the book of Revelation.)

A PROMISE IS A PROMISE

"But when Herod's birthday came, the daughter of Herodias danced before them and pleased Herod, so much that he promised with an oath to give her whatever she asked. Having been prompted by her mother, she said, 'Give me here on a platter the head of John the Baptist.' Although he was grieved, the king commanded it to be given because of his oaths, and because of his dinner guests. He sent and had John beheaded in the prison."

⌐ Matthew 14:6-10

Have you ever had a friend who always called you at the last minute to cancel plans? A friend who stood you up? A friend who backed out on an offer to help? A friend who said one thing and then did another?

Not many people weigh their words these days.

In the movie *Hook*, Robin Williams played a Wall Street businessman who was also a preoccupied father. He was so busy working that he left no time for family. During a trip with his son, Williams said to the boy, "When we get back, I'll go to all the rest of your ball games. I promise. My word is my bond."

His son had already seen too many broken promises and replied with disgust, "Yeah—junk bonds."

Like the busy businessman, King Herod also spoke thoughtlessly. Swayed by the moment and his guests, Herod rashly promised to give Herodias's daughter whatever she asked. Later, the king "was grieved" to realize that keeping his promise would mean beheading John the Baptist (verse 9-10). He probably would've given anything to take back his promise.

What about you? How dependable are your promises? Do you always think before you give your word? Do you count the cost before you sign your name to an agreement? Are you someone who follows through?

Your word is the key that will open the door to every important relationship you'll ever have. If you're trusted, you will be able to talk openly with people, and they will listen. If you break your word, everything you say will be suspect and insignificant to others. By simply watching what you say and then standing by those words, you will become a trustworthy, dependable, credible friend.

Discussion Starters:

1. How often do you think before you sign your name or give your promise?
2. In what areas do you need to work on your level of honesty?

Lifeline:

Remember to forgive one another for making mistakes in this sensitive area.

THE STORM OF REJECTION

"And in the fourth watch of the night He came to them, walking on the sea.... But immediately Jesus spoke to them, saying, 'Take courage, it is I; do not be afraid.' Peter said to Him, 'Lord, if it is You, command me to come to You on the water.' And He said, 'Come!' And Peter got out of the boat, and walked on the water and came toward Jesus. But seeing the wind, he became frightened, and beginning to sink, he cried out, 'Lord, save me!' Immediately Jesus stretched out His hand and took hold of him, and said to him, 'You of little faith, why did you doubt?'"

↪ Matthew 14:25,27-31

It's been decades, but I can still remember the pain of rejection I felt as a fifth grader. I was playing out in front of our house, and my "buddies" were inside my neighbor's house, watching a football game on TV. The door was locked, so I knocked to be let in.

"There's no one home," one of the giggly voices inside called out.

I näively responded, "What do you mean? I can see you in there."

The voice turned cutting and cruel. "Go away. Can't you take a hint?"

Rejection. It cuts like a knife. During junior high and high school, it's probably the worst kind of pain. I can almost laugh today when I think about my first girlfriend, Jenny, back in seventh grade, but it wasn't funny then! We "went out" (whatever that meant) for a few months. One day, Jenny told her best friend to tell me that she liked my best friend better than me. Getting dumped by Jenny cut me to the quick.

I'm sure the disciple Peter could relate to my need for love. He denied Jesus three times, undoubtably to gain others' approval. He tried to walk on the water, perhaps to gain Jesus' and the disciples' acceptance.

Like Peter, I often feel I'm "outside the boat," trying to build friendships and dreams. The wind and waves of rejection and difficulty seem overpowering. My faith weakens, and I get discouraged. Then I remember Peter's plight, look to my Savior, and pray Peter's prayer:

"Lord, help. I'm sinking. I'm lonely, hurting. Please take my hand."

The same hand that reached out to Peter will pull you to safety when the waves of life threaten to drown you. Jesus will always be there, lifting you up with His amazing forgiveness and love. And He won't let go.

Discussion Starters:

1. How can you relate to Peter today? When did you last pray his prayer?
2. How does Jesus calm your waves and bring you peace?

Lifeline:

Resolve to lift one another up in prayer through difficult times.

A MATTER OF THE HEART

"'You hypocrites, rightly did Isaiah prophesy of you: "This people honors Me with their lips, but their heart is far away from Me. But in vain do they worship Me, teaching as doctrines the precepts of men."'"

↩ Matthew 15:7-9

Steve was a little arrogant. The night before his 16th birthday (and the day before he was to take his driving test), he called Tanya up for a date. "Hey, how'd you like to go to the school dance with me on Friday? I'll pick you up in my brand-new, fully-loaded, high-rise truck," he said. Tanya agreed, and Steve hung up smugly, anticipating the 100 percent he'd receive on his test and the look of admiration on Tanya's face when he came to get her.

Steve's birthday came, and his mother drove him to the DMV. Steve got behind the wheel, nodded to the instructor, and pulled forward. Or, he tried to. The poor guy put the car in reverse instead of first gear and backed into the car behind him. Steve'd had so much confidence in his new truck that he hadn't practiced driving enough. His red-faced instructor promptly drew a big, fat "F" across Steve's test, forcing Steve to ride home with his mother and, worse, to ask Tanya if *she* could drive them to the dance.

As Steve learned, who's in the driver's seat is more important than the type of car you drive. The driver makes the judgment calls, acts and reacts, and directs the vehicle. Likewise, your heart is the driver of your life. It is the volitional center where life makes up its mind. Your heart tells you to say yes when things are right and no when situations are wrong. That's why Jesus wants to occupy your heart. He can direct you when other people and things lead you in a dozen different directions. When Jesus is in your heart, in your driver's seat, you'll always travel on the right road.

Discussion Starters:

1. How will having a Christ-centered heart help you pass life's tests?
2. What was Dale Carnegie urging when he said, "Flattery is from the teeth out. Sincerity is from the heart out"?[6]
3. Why do you think the heart is so significant?
4. Who is the most sincere, Christ-centered person you know? Why?

Lifeline:

The media focus all their attention on people's outsides. How can your family emphasize the importance of the heart?

MULTIPLICATION

"And Jesus called His disciples to Him, and said, 'I feel compassion for the people, because they have remained with Me now three days and have nothing to eat; and I do not want to send them away hungry, for they might faint on the way.' ...And Jesus said to them, 'How many loaves do you have?' And they said, 'Seven, and a few small fish.' ...And He took the seven loaves and the fish; and giving thanks, He broke them and started giving them to the disciples, and the disciples gave them to the people. And they all ate and were satisfied, and they picked up what was left over of the broken pieces, seven large baskets full. And those who ate were four thousand men, besides women and children."

↩ Matthew 15:32,34,36-38

Two times two is four. Four times four is sixteen. Sixteen times sixteen is... I always loved multiplication tables as a kid. I remember setting up a chalkboard with multiplication tables written on it, trying to prepare for tests. What I really liked about multiplication, though, was that the numbers increased so much faster than they did with addition.

That's one of the things I love about Jesus, too. Jesus is a multiplier.

Give Him a talent and He makes a career.

Give Him a date and He builds a friendship.

Give Him a need and He fills it completely.

Give Him a family and He creates a home.

Jesus sees to people's needs. After preaching to the multitudes, He knew they were hungry. The food was scarce, but Jesus, the multiplier, filled their empty stomachs and empty hearts—and had leftovers!

Sadly, not everyone allows Jesus to bring her fulfillment. Yesterday I learned that a young friend of mine, "Angie," died from a drug overdose. She was a popular cheerleader and class officer. She seemed to have everything—except happiness. To numb her pain, Angie turned to alcohol. She started drinking in junior high, and by high school she was an alcoholic. Soon Angie turned to drugs. I wish she had turned to Jesus.

Jesus can fill you with true happiness and peace. If you look to Him, He will multiply love and joy in your life—no matter how hopeless the conditions appear, no matter how great the need may be.

Discussion Starters:

1. What do you hunger for today? How can Jesus fill that need?

2. What was Angie's first mistake? How can you learn from her?

Lifeline:

Discuss why and how Jesus is the great multiplier, the great fulfiller, in your family.

IT'S ALL ABOUT FAITH

"But He replied to them, 'When it is evening, you say, "It will be fair weather, for the sky is red." And in the morning, "There will be a storm today, for the sky is red and threatening." Do you know how to discern the appearance of the sky, but cannot discern the signs of the times? An evil and adulterous generation seeks after a sign; and a sign will not be given it, except the sign of Jonah.' And He left them and went away."

↬ Matthew 16:2-4

Do you believe the sun will come up tomorrow morning? Do you believe your bed won't collapse tonight when you climb into it? Do you believe you'll find enough to eat tomorrow? Do you believe your car will start the next time you turn the key? Do you believe your house will be there when you return from a family trip?

Do you believe that God loves you? Are you convinced He knows and guides your future?

Belief. Faith. The writer of Hebrews described it like this: "Now faith is the assurance of things hoped for, the conviction of things not seen" (11:1). Everyone has faith. Lots of it. Each day, we place our faith in people, places, and things we believe in—even though we never know what the future holds.

So why is it so hard to place our faith in Christ? Even though we haven't seen Him face to face, Jesus has proved—through His unconditional love for us—that He can be trusted. If you need to have God constantly prove His abilities, your trust is shallow and your love for Him is weak. Next time you pray, instead of commanding God, "Lord, show me that You're here," say to Him, "Lord, I'm so thankful You're always with me."

Faith means "**F**ather, **A**ll **I**n **T**hy **H**ands." Jesus loves it when we give our belief and trust to Him—and we *should*, whether or not we see one of His mighty deeds.

Discussion Starters:

1. How have you put your faith in God the Father and Son?

2. Why does God value our faith so highly?

3. Could God show us great signs and wonders each day if He wanted to? Why doesn't He?

4. Why is it often so hard to trust God?

Lifeline:

Remind each other of the little ways in which God shows Himself in your home.

I CALL IT AS I SEE IT

"He said to them, 'But who do you say that I am?' Simon Peter answered, 'You are the Christ, the Son of the living God.' And Jesus said to him, 'Blessed are you, Simon Barjona, because flesh and blood did not reveal this to you, but My Father who is in heaven.'"

↜ Matthew 16:15-17

"I think so." "Uh, I'm not sure, but..." "Well, I sorta guess that you're the..." "I'm thinkin' I might be able to..." "One of these days I'm gonna do that, but..." "Well, maybe...."

In the hills, we call it "hum-hawing" around. My urban friends call it "copping out."

The University of Texas versus Texas A&M baseball game was hot, and the rivalry was intense. The count on the batter was three balls and two strikes, a full count. The pitcher wound up and greased a fastball across the inside corner of the plate. The ball stung the catcher's mitt with fire. The umpire gazed intently at the plate and said absolutely nothing. The catcher jumped up and screamed, "What is it, ump? Is it a ball or a strike?"

The seasoned old umpire glared right into the catcher's eyes and quietly responded, "It ain't nothin' 'til I call it, boy."

Peter also called it as he saw it. He said, in effect, "Yes, You're the Messiah, plain and simple. You're the One the Old Testament prophets spoke of for 1,500 years. You're the Anointed One. You're God in the flesh."

As I counsel teens in trouble, college folks in stress, and adults in despair, I see people afraid to call it as they see it. They're scared to say:

"It's a lie, and I'm not going to say it."

"It's pornography, and I won't look at it."

"He's God, so I won't say words that are derogatory to His name."

"It's alcohol, and my body's a temple of the Holy Spirit, so I won't drink it."

"It may be rated PG, but it doesn't glorify Christ, so count me out."

Real men and women call a spade a spade. They say, "No, thanks, that's not for me." Peter was such a man.

Do you have that kind of honesty and courage?

Discussion Starters:

1. Who do you say that Jesus is? What does that answer mean to you?

2. Why do you respect people who shoot straight?

3. When are you tempted to "cop out"?

Lifeline:

Home should be the safe place to be honest, especially over tough issues.

IN WHOSE OPINION?

"Six days later Jesus took with Him Peter and James and John his brother, and led them upon a high mountain by themselves. And He was transfigured before them; and His face shone like the sun, and His garments became as white as light.... And behold, a voice out of the cloud said, 'This is My beloved Son, with whom I am well-pleased; listen to Him!'"

↪ Matthew 17:1-2,5

Next Christmas or Easter, go check out the grocery store magazine stand. Chances are, it'll have masses of magazines doing their traditional feature about the mysteries of Jesus of Nazareth. Usually the content is watered down and liberal, written by people who don't know Jesus at all. They mention that Jesus is a literary figure who's been the main focus of humankind for centuries. But you and I know that Jesus is much more than that. I wonder why they don't quote those who knew Him best.

Why don't they quote from God Himself, who said, "This is My beloved Son, with whom I am well-pleased" (verse 5)? Or they could talk of Peter, who proclaimed, "You are the Christ, the Son of the living God" (Matthew 16:16). Even those who crucified Him posted a sign above His head which read, "This Is Jesus the King of the Jews" (Matthew 27:37).

How well do you know Him? Who is He in your life? Your Friend? Father? Almighty Lord? Guide? Comforter? How important is He to you? If you don't know Christ, your faith is only religion—a bunch of beliefs and rules. But when He's close to your heart, your faith becomes something much deeper. It becomes a *relationship* with a holy and loving God.

Next time you want to read more about Jesus, pick up the Bible. It's packed with people who knew Him intimately. They all attested to the fact that He was God in the flesh, the second Person of the triune Godhead, the Living Word, Immanuel, God with us.

Who do *you* say that He is?

Discussion Starters:

1. What was the significance of the transfiguration?
2. Why does our culture tend to belittle the deity of Jesus?
3. How can you best discern the truth about Jesus?
4. How would you respond if a friend vehemently denied that Jesus is Lord?

Lifeline:

Discuss how well you (individually) know Christ. How can your family members help each other to know Him better?

FAITH THAT MOVES THINGS

"And He said to them, 'Because of the littleness of your faith; for truly I say to you, if you have faith the size of a mustard seed, you will say to this mountain, "Move from here to there," and it will move; and nothing will be impossible to you.'"

↩ Matthew 17:20

Christina has a faith that could move mountains. She also has an illness that could easily put her in valleys of despair. Most of the time, she's sick in bed with a fever, the flu, insomnia, or migraines. Often, Christina is so ill that she doesn't answer the phone. She has to live with her parents so someone can take care of her all the time. She had to quit a successful job. She's in financial disaster. But she has the joy of Christ. During those times when Christina can't leave the house, talk on the phone, or see her friends, she talks to God. Sometimes she'll spend literally all day praying. And her life reflects her powerful relationship with Christ.

Last week, Christina told me that she needed $2,500 to pay doctor bills and buy groceries. She couldn't go out and work for the money, so she prayed. A few days later, an anonymous letter appeared in the mailbox. It contained a check for $2,000. The other $500 came through anonymous mail during the rest of the week.

Christina's faith made the impossible a reality. She prayed that God would provide for her needs. More importantly, though, she *believed* that God could do what she asked.

Jesus told us that all we need is faith the size of a mustard seed for Him to work in our lives. Have you seen a mustard seed lately? It's a tiny little thing—about the size of a grain of sand. If you have just *that much faith*, Christ will move the obstacles, leap over the challenges, and meet your every need. That's His promise.

Discussion Starters:

1. What does the tiny size of a mustard seed reveal about faith?
2. What limitations does the world put on you? Are you facing a challenge that seems impossible to handle? Explain.
3. Name someone you know who has great faith. Why is his or her faith so big?
4. What does today's verse tell you about the power of God?

Lifeline:

God plants the seeds of faith. A strong family keeps them watered with encouragement.

DO YOU TRUST HIM?

"And [He] said, 'Truly I say to you, unless you are converted and become like children, you will not enter the kingdom of heaven. Whoever then humbles himself as this child, he is the greatest in the kingdom of heaven.'"

⟿ Matthew 18:3-4

My college football coach and his seven-year-old son, Lee, came to our sports camp one summer to help lead our staff. Shortly after they arrived, Coach Utley, Lee, and one of the campers, Chad, went water skiing. Coach drove the ski boat while Chad, a 220-pound football player, skiied behind. But soon after Chad got up on the slalom (single) ski, he lost control. Chad crossed the wake—the wave path behind the boat—too quickly and leaned hard on the tow rope. The boat flipped instantly, throwing Coach and Lee into the cold waters. Coach swam desperately around the boat to find Lee. He panicked—the little fellow was nowhere to be found. Several minutes passed. In final desperation, Coach ducked under the overturned boat and found Lee treading water and breathing in the air pocket created by the "turtled" boat.

"I knew you'd be here, Daddy," were Lee's first words. He never doubted for a second that his daddy would rescue him.

Little kids have great faith! They believe in people with all their hearts. They trust their parents, teachers, and God. Their love is pure and whole-hearted. Children find joy in little things. They don't worry much about the next day of school or what they're going to have for lunch. They believe that those things will be provided for them.

Jesus knew what He was talking about when He said we should become like little children. He's more impressed with the simple love of a child than with the theological doctrines and doubts of an adult. Jesus wants us to let go of our worries and skepticism. He wants us to quit saying, "Prove it, God!" and start declaring, "I believe it, God!"

Discussion Starters:

1. Why do we lose our childlike faith as we grow up?

2. Why does Jesus want us to have the faith of a child?

3. How can we have faith when we haven't seen Him yet with our own eyes?

Lifeline:

Discuss a situation in which your family needs to have childlike faith.

THEY'RE EVERYWHERE

"'For where two or three have gathered together in My name, I am there in their midst.'"

⟿ Matthew 18:20

You can find them in the most amazing and unusual places. They're in adobe huts in Mexico, igloos in Alaska, prison cells in Siberia, Amazon villages in South America, and in homes across this nation. What are they? Groups of believers gathered together in twos, threes, and fours to worship in the name of Christ. It might seem odd or even impossible to have such a small body of worshipers, but Jesus promised that it only takes you and one other person to have Christ in your midst.

He's with your family right now.

As you read Scripture, pray, and talk about Jesus, you might as well put one more place setting at the table—for Him. Maybe you can't see Him, and maybe He seems quiet, but Christ is with you just the same. Through His Holy Spirit, Jesus keeps you coming back to devotions time and again. He helps you understand God's Word as it is read. He gives meaning and purpose to your discussion. He even helps you to remember and apply His instructions and promises to your life.

How would your life change if you never once forgot that Christ is with you? How would your family devotions improve? Would you let your mind wander during prayer? Would you look over at your brother and think about getting back at him? Would you find more meaning in reading the Bible?

Next time you pray with a friend or family member, seeking the Lord's presence, praising Him, and asking for answers, keep in mind that He's already there. He's listening, and He's nearer than you think. But don't take my word for it—take His.

Discussion Starters:

1. What would you call a gathering of believers? A church? A Bible study? Explain your answer.

2. Christ is here in your family worship time. How does that affect you?

3. How can you include Him more in your discussion?

4. When are you most aware of Christ's presence? Why?

Lifeline:

How should you treat one another, knowing that Jesus is watching and listening?

ADAM AND WHO?

"And He answered and said, 'Have you not read that He who created them from the beginning made them male and female, and said, "For this reason a man shall leave his father and mother and be joined to his wife, and the two shall become one flesh"? So they are no longer two, but one flesh. What therefore God has joined together, let no man separate.'"

↪ Matthew 19:4-6

"And I now pronounce you husband and…husband?"

Wait a minute. Doesn't that seem a little strange? It does to me—especially when I consider that the most valuable expression of God's craftsmanship was His creation of Adam and Eve. The two were made "in God's own image." Adam and Eve were designed distinctly male and female for an incredible marriage relationship built to last a lifetime. Sexual intimacy was God's gift for the husband and wife to enjoy with each other and nobody else, for their entire lifetime. In that way, marriage is set apart from every other relationship.

I know it's different from what you hear in the media, but God didn't make the first couple Adam and Steve. Nor did He create one-night stands. There is no provision in the Bible for homosexual relationships, premarital sexual relationships, or extramarital sexual relationships. The Bible repeatedly says that all sex outside of marriage is dead wrong.

A lot of people will tell you otherwise, though. *Time* magazine recently reported that since we evolved from apes and apes are unfaithful, it's okay for us to be unfaithful, too![7] Nothing could be further from the truth. Married partners should save their affection for each other. Unwed people should save their affection for their future spouses.

My friend Davis recently married. He and his wife, Sarah, waited to have sex until they married. They'll tell you it was hard. Their hormones often felt out of control. But on their wedding night, Davis and Sarah were able to love freely, without comparing themselves or each other to past sweethearts. Now it's easier for them to be vulnerable with one another because they built trust and respect by not pushing any God-given boundaries.

Wait to give yourself to your spouse. It will be well worth it.

Discussion Starters:

1. Why did God invent marriage?
2. Why is it so hard to remain sexually pure?
3. Why did God tell us to wait for sex until we're married?

Lifeline:

Parents, encourage each child to make a commitment to sexual purity. Then talk about how your family can promote abstinence and healthy dating.

I'LL GIVE YA ALMOST ALL MY HEART

"The young man said to Him, 'All [your commandments] I have kept; what am I still lacking?' Jesus said to him, 'If you wish to be complete, go and sell your possessions and give to the poor, and you will have treasure in heaven; and come, follow Me.' But when the young man heard this statement, he went away grieving; for he was one who owned much property."
↪ Matthew 19:20-22

Girls, imagine the finest boy you ever laid eyes on. He's cute, smart, funny, popular—and he's in love with you. Sound good? Well, let's say he asks you to marry him (after you've dated for a while). He promises to be absolutely faithful to you... 364 days out of the year. On his bended knee, the guy then says he loves you with *almost* all his heart—but he has this small crush on Jenny, whom he wants to save his affection for just one day out of the year. What would you say? Would you marry him? Or what flavor of pie would you smash in his face?

Guys, how about you? The gorgeous babe you've secretly liked since kindergarten suddenly decides she wants to share *almost* all her life with you. She tells you that she'll be loyal most of the time, but she says she can't promise that you'll always be her number one man. She's got a thing for guys with blond hair, and yours is brown. But she claims she still loves you. How would you respond? Would you give her a wedding band? (If you say yes, we'd better talk!)

I'm sure you would never make a lifelong commitment to someone who was even a tiny bit wishy-washy about you. Jesus is the same way. He saw through to the rich young man's heart and knew he wasn't totally sold on Him. We might read this scripture and think, *That's pretty harsh. The young man did almost everything right, and Jesus still turned him away.* But if we wouldn't accept anything less than complete commitment from someone, why should He?

Jesus knows exactly what keeps us from loving Him fully. He realized the rich young man loved money more than he loved Him.

What's keeping *you* from making a total commitment to Christ?

Discussion Starters:

1. What things are getting in the way of your relationship with Christ?
2. Why did the young man walk away?
3. Why does God want all of our hearts?

Lifeline:

Encourage one another to make a sincere, total commitment to God.

PREMEDITATED SACRIFICE

" 'Behold, we are going up to Jerusalem; and the Son of Man will be delivered to the chief priests and scribes, and they will condemn Him to death, and will hand Him over to the Gentiles to mock and scourge and crucify Him, and on the third day He will be raised up.' "

⮌ Matthew 20:18-19

Little Lori Ann was 14 when she slipped into the back row of our rowdy, fun, and growing youth group. The patch over her eye immediately gave away her condition when I saw her precious, innocent face. Lori had facial cancer. Doctors had removed her eye to try to save her life. But her illness was growing—and fatal. Over the next two years, the cancer spread throughout her face and neck. Amazingly, as she walked steadily toward death, Lori's faith grew stronger. She and I became close and talked as a father and daughter would about death, heaven, and Christ's provision for eternal life. Lori grew to love her Savior.

The week before her death, her doctor came into her room and told her that they had done all they could. The medicines weren't working. Soon the tumors would take over. With the faith of an 80-year-old saint, Lori looked at her doctor and bravely said, "I appreciate all you've done, but don't worry, I won't die when the medicine runs out—I'll die when Jesus takes me home."

As I stood by her hospital bed, I realized that Lori was facing her death the same way Jesus faced His...with courage, grace, and dignity. In fact, Lori's last words before she closed her eyes for the last time were to her unsaved mom. Lori softly whispered, "Mom, I hope some day you'll know Jesus like I do."

Lori was able to face pain and death without fear because she knew God's plan for her eternal life. Christ knowingly endured incredible suffering because He knew God was in control as well. Do you?

Discussion Starters:

1. If Jesus knew when and how He'd die, why didn't He change the plan and run?
2. What do you think His disciples thought when He told them the fate that was ahead of Him?
3. How can a 16-year-old like my friend Lori have such great faith?

Lifeline:

Lori was an amazing witness to her mom. How can your family allow trials to make you all better witnesses for Christ?

WHEN IN DOUBT, SERVE

" 'It is not this way among you, but whoever wishes to become great among you shall be your servant, and whoever wishes to be first among you shall be your slave; just as the Son of Man did not come to be served, but to serve, and to give His life a ransom for many.' "

⌁ Matthew 20:26-28

How often do you sit around the house and just "veg" with nothing to do? What do you do when you come home from school or work? Watch a little TV? Plug in your Walkman? Skim the newspaper? Lounge on the couch? Do you want to make life at home really fun and dynamic and surprising—anything but boring? Then adopt Jesus' motto. He always said, in effect, "When in doubt, *serve.*"

Seriously! It probably sounds backward to you because our society likes to indulge. We treat ourselves to movies, dessert, and reclining chairs. When we're bored, we usually sit. But Jesus told us how to best spend our time when He said, "Do you wanna be great or be fulfilled? Then serve!"

We have fun with the "serving motto" at my house. Our family found that serving others brings harmony to our home, brings smiles to faces, and kicks life in the funny bone. Whose job is it to wash the dishes? Mine. Who's supposed to take out the trash? Me! Who tries to do whatever needs doin'? Me! Why waste all that time and energy arguing about who's supposed to do what? It's much easier to serve.

If your family has trouble letting go of grudges, arguing, or having touchy feelings, I suggest you adopt the "when in doubt, serve" philosophy. If each person joyfully serves one another with Christ's love, in 30 days there will be peace. Servanthood will wave the magic wand of love—Christ's love—throughout your home.

Is someone in your house hurting? Rub his shoulders or send some encouraging words his way. Is your mom tired? Fold her laundry or put gas in her car. People appreciate even the smallest things you do for them.

Jesus hit the nail right on the head! Do you wanna be the best you can ever be? Become an expert in other people's needs, find joy in meeting those needs, and that's exactly what you'll become!

Discussion Starters:

1. Why is the greatness/serving paradox so true?
2. What would Jesus say about the present state of servanthood in your house?
3. What is one new way that you could be a servant to your family?

Lifeline:

Let serving begin with you!

MANGERS, DONKEYS, AND CROSSES

"'Say to the daughter of Zion, "Behold your King is coming to you, gentle, and mounted on a donkey, even on a colt, the foal of a beast of burden."'" And the disciples went and did just as Jesus had instructed them, and brought the donkey and the colt, and laid their coats on them; and He sat on the coats."

⟿ Matthew 21:5-7

He could have ridden a chariot into town...that's how the self-proclaimed gods of the Roman military made their arrival. He could have forced His followers to carry Him in a sedan chair. That's how Egyptian, Syrian, and Babylonian kings made their slaves carry them atop their shoulders. So what was this divine King doing on a donkey, a lowly beast of burden?

Jesus rode a donkey in fulfillment of prophecy (see Zechariah 9:9) and because He never intended to elevate Himself. He came to earth as a man to identify with your hurts and forgive your sins, not to bring Himself worldly glory.

My friend Andy lost his granddad to cancer yesterday. Jesus hurts for Andy. He knows how Andy feels because He saw the pain of the sick and diseased as well (see Matthew 8). Sandi lost her dad to alcoholism, and the next week her brother was killed in a drunk driving accident. Jesus sheds tears with Sandi. He's been there. He knows the pain of losing a dearly loved one. When His close friend Lazarus died (before Christ raised him from the dead), "Jesus wept," too (John 11:35).

Jesus even understands our temptations. Billy is torn, struggling like crazy because his friends are turning to pot and alcohol. He wants to be true to his parents and his personal convictions, but now he's losing his friends. Jesus sighs deeply. He felt the same pain as Judas walked out on Him and turned his back after years of friendship (see Matthew 26).

Jesus chose to be all man while being all God. He wanted to know first-hand how you feel. He wanted to participate in and understand your pain. So He came from a manger to a donkey to a Roman cross.

Next time you wonder, *Does anybody know how I feel?* you can bet your last penny that Somebody knows. Jesus, the One who loves you most, also understands you best. He knows, and He cares.

Discussion Starters:

1. What does it mean to you that Jesus shared in your humanity?
2. How do you think Jesus understands your pain right now?

Lifeline:

How can your family better empathize with one another's trials?

KIDS SAY THE NEATEST THINGS

"But when the chief priests and the scribes saw the wonderful things that He had done, and the children who were shouting in the temple, 'Hosanna to the Son of David,' they became indignant and said to Him, 'Do You hear what these children are saying?' And Jesus said to them, 'Yes; have you never read, "Out of the mouth of infants and nursing babies You have prepared praise for Yourself"?'"

⟿ Matthew 21:15-16

Dan Roberts, my country music songwriter buddy, absolutely loves his four-year-old son. The other day, Dan and his son, J. D., were saying how much they loved each other, and their comparisons grew more profound each time they spoke.

"Dad, I love you more than a car," J. D. said, his eyes big.

"J. D., I love you more than an 18-wheeler," Dan responded proudly.

J. D. knew just how to top that. He gleefully said, "Dad, I love you more than all the tables in McDonald's!"

Now, to a four-year-old, that's all the love imaginable. Kids just tell it like it is, don't they? We grown-ups get so stiff, prideful, and arrogant that we sometimes forget to say honest, simple things like "God is so good" and "Jesus loves me, this I know, 'cuz the Bible tells me so." Children embrace God's truth and His love, while adults usually reason their faith away. Kids could teach adults a thing or two by their trusting example.

Next Sunday at church, watch the four-year-olds' Sunday school class. Chances are, they'll come out of class proudly carrying an "I love Jesus" card or wearing a big heart with a cross in the middle.

Or take note of your younger brother or sister (or other little kids you know). Watch how easily they fold their hands to pray. Notice how quickly they accept that God loves them.

Kids aren't complicated. They don't argue over issues of faith. They believe God is good because it's in the Bible. They want to know Jesus, and they readily ask Him into their hearts. Kids are the best living examples of faith. That's why Jesus said, "Let the little children come to Me, for theirs is the kingdom of heaven" (see Matthew 19).

Discussion Starters:

1. Why did Jesus place such value on children?

2. How can we be mature and responsible and still have a childlike faith?

Lifeline:

As a family, write down several positive childlike characteristics. Then pray together that God would help your family to have a trusting faith.

ONCE UPON A ROCK

"Jesus said to them, 'Did you never read in the Scriptures, "The stone which the builders rejected, this became the chief corner stone; this came about from the Lord, and it is marvelous in our eyes"? Therefore I say to you, the kingdom of God will be taken away from you and given to a people, producing the fruit of it.'"

↜ Matthew 21:42-43

Ever notice that when you give your life over to God, things can get much easier? Often when you start tithing your money, your finances work themselves out. When you let go of a hurtful friendship, God will usually bring a better friend along. And when leaders place the nations they are guiding in the hands of God, God usually responds with blessings as well.

That's what happened in the United States. The nation was founded by serious Christians. America's early leaders sowed the teachings of God into its schools, laws, and cities because their faith was so important to them. And the nation was blessed because of it.

The first president, George Washington, wanted to glorify God as he led the nation. Washington said reverently, "O most glorious God in Jesus Christ, my merciful and loving Father, let me live according to those holy rules which Thou hast this day prescribed in Thy Holy Word."[8]

Alexander Hamilton, known as "the ratifier of the Constitution," signed the Constitution and then said, "I now offer you the outline of the plan they have suggested. Let an association be formed to be denominated 'The Christian Constitutional Society,' its object to be first: The support of the Christian religion. Second: The support of the United States."[9]

America was built on strong Christian principles, and as a result, God blessed her with more prosperity than any other nation in the history of the world. But now her federal government, media, and educational system are systematically and purposefully snuffing God out of the people's daily lives. America's soaring crime rate, divorce rate, and sexually transmitted disease rate stand testimony to the way the nation has willfully turned its back on Him.

Through prayer and the democratic process, you can make a difference in the world. What are you doing to help turn your country to God?

Discussion Starters:

1. What are some of the good things about your nation?

2. How can you help turn the anti-God trend in your nation?

Lifeline:

How can your family be an example in your community?

WEDDING CLOTHES

"'But when the king came in to look over the dinner guests, he saw a man there who was not dressed in wedding clothes, and he said to him, "Friend, how did you come in here without wedding clothes?" And the man was speechless. Then the king said to the servants, "Bind him hand and foot, and throw him into the outer darkness; in that place there will be weeping and gnashing of teeth." For many are called, but few are chosen.'"

⁓ Matthew 22:11-14

I love weddings. I always get a 50-yard-line seat (the best view) as the pastor—the guy lucky enough to help the bride and bridegroom "tie the knot." I've done $50,000 weddings and $50 weddings. (Actually, as long as you can say "I do" and stand by it for about 50 years, it doesn't really matter what the price tag is.) But no matter how much is spent, the most incredible moment is the second the bride enters the chamber adorned with delicate white lace. Guys, as you stand there waiting, it will make you faint in awe if you're not prepared. There is nothing on earth like a bride adorned for her husband. As my kids say, "It's awesome!"

Earthly weddings are beautiful and magical, but God's wedding feast will be even more special. In that union of God's children (the bride) to Jesus Christ (the bridegroom), God's true believers will adorn themselves with spiritual wedding clothes. The love, faith, and righteousness that we clothe ourselves in each day will shine brilliantly in heaven.

Just as earthly brides spend hours preparing for their husbands, so should Christ's children take the time to be ready for their awesome meeting with Him. Is there someone for whom you need to have more compassion? Are you being patient enough with your brother or sister? Does your head swell with every "A" you receive or each relationship you have?

On the fantastic day when you meet Jesus face to face, you'll be blown away by His glory and majesty. But God makes it clear that the only ones welcome into His home are those clothed in Jesus' righteousness.

Would you be dressed appropriately for your Bridegroom if you saw Him today?

Discussion Starters:

1. What is God's criterion for His wedding guests?

2. Why does God compare our union with His Son to a wedding feast?

3. Are you dressed for the occasion? Why or why not?

Lifeline:

What would your wedding clothes look like if you met Him face to face right now? Discuss.

GIVE IT TO WHOM?

"[The Pharisees asked,] 'Tell us then, what do You think? Is it lawful to give a poll-tax to Caesar, or not?' But Jesus perceived their malice, and said, 'Why are you testing Me, you hypocrites? Show Me the coin used for the poll-tax.' And they brought Him a denarius. And He said to them, 'Whose likeness and inscription is this?' They said to Him, 'Caesar's.' Then He said to them, 'Then render to Caesar the things that are Caesar's; and to God the things that are God's.'"

↩ Matthew 22:17-21

Adolf Eichmann, a German officer serving under Adolf Hitler, was responsible for the extermination of several million Jewish citizens in World War II. He was apprehended, then tried and convicted in Jerusalem in 1961. There, Eichmann pleaded his alibi. He said, "I never did anything, great or small, without obtaining in advance express instructions from my superiors. I was in the iron grip of orders." Eichmann, maintaining his innocence, repeated, "I had to obey the rules of war and my flag."[10]

He rendered to Hitler and ended up killing countless innocent people.

Maybe Eichmann was following Hitler's orders, but there is always a higher law that rules when issues of right and wrong are at stake.

As a young person living in a society which has become more hostile to God, you, too, will have to decide where your loyalties lie. For instance, many schools now forbid organized prayer meetings on campus. Other schools teach only evolution and won't hear of presenting creationism. What will you do when you're confronted with situations like these? Where will you place your loyalties?

There are times when we must follow the law and "render to Caesar," but God is our ultimate authority. No matter what the cost, we're supposed to stand up for Him and His Word. This calls for submission and courage. Do you have the strength of character to render yourself to God when He asks you for obedience?

Discussion Starters:

1. How can you apply Jesus' parable to your life?

2. How can you discern when it's appropriate to submit to God rather than the law?

3. Describe a time in your life when you should have obeyed God but instead rendered your loyalty to Caesar (meaning, the government, the world, etc.).

Lifeline:

How can you better obey God's authority in your life?

I'M THIRD

"One of them, a lawyer, asked Him a question, testing Him, 'Teacher, which is the great commandment in the Law?' And He said to him, '"You shall love the Lord your God with all your heart, and with all your soul, and with all your mind." This is the great and foremost commandment. The second is like it, "You shall love your neighbor as yourself."'"

↪ Matthew 22:35-39

Plain and simple, it's the key to happiness. You want to enjoy life? Put God first. You wanna enjoy it greatly? Put others second. You wanna enjoy it to the max? Put yourself third. At our sports camps, we call it "I'm Third." It's our motto.

Johnny Ferrier was a longtime family friend. This pilot bravely chose to guide his crippled Air National Guard jet into a backyard garden in the center of a heavily populated suburb, where he stayed with the plane and died on impact. Johnny could have bailed out to save himself, but he knew that leaving the plane unguided could have resulted in the death of many innocent civilians. To his last breath, he lived placing himself third.

God is the best! He rules. And when you let Him rule your priorities, you place Him first. If you're wondering whether you need to adjust your priorities, take this quick test. Ask yourself, "Where do I spend my money? What takes up most of my time?" How you answer those questions will show you if you're putting other things or people before God.

You place others second by loving them, serving them, and putting their needs ahead of your own. Look at the people around you. How well do you serve your family? Do you consider their needs, too?

How can you put yourself third? By loving yourself—treating your body as a temple of the Holy Spirit, not using alcohol or drugs, and not filling your eyes and ears with impure sights and sounds. God commanded us to love others as we love *ourselves*. Low self-esteem isn't for children of God. Love yourself the way God commands you to love others.

Jesus. **O**thers. **Y**ourself. That formula spells "joy." And if you follow the two greatest commandments, that's what you'll have.

Discussion Starters:

1. How will you put God first in your life today?
2. What are some specific ways you can practice "I'm Third" throughout this week?

Lifeline:

An "I'm Third" home is a great place to live.

LEAD, DON'T MISLEAD

"Then Jesus spoke to the crowds and to His disciples, saying: 'The scribes and the Pharisees have seated themselves in the chair of Moses; therefore all that they tell you, do and observe, but do not do according to their deeds; for they say things and do not do them.'"

⤴ Matthew 23:1-3

Governor Spencer endorses abortions and then tells Americans that she's going to be tough on criminals.

Dan boasts of his great accomplishments in football as he buys his little brother, Tommy, beer for a Saturday night party.

Mr. Owens punishes his daughter Amy for cheating on a test while he cheats on his tax report to the I.R.S.

Jana scolds her son for talking back at the kitchen table while she dominates her husband, Marty, and undermines his authority at home.

Bobby runs for student council president at his Christian high school as he continually pushes his girlfriend, Lesley, to have sex.

Samantha parties on Friday and Saturday nights and then carries her Bible to Sunday school and church leadership meetings.

Hypocrisy... it's the antithesis of leadership. It confuses, misleads, and destroys.

Brad showed up at my door, heartbroken. His high school youth leader, the one who led him to Christ and discipled him, had turned his back on God. Brad couldn't understand how someone who always appeared so confident in his faith, so on track with God, could become involved in drugs. "How can I ever trust anyone again? Is Christianity just a big joke?" Brad asked, wondering how to put his faith back together.

True leadership is consistent. You must be able to trust the one you follow. Jesus was a true leader, an example for others. His actions always mirrored His words, and He condemned those who said one thing and then did another.

But Jesus also forgave those inconsistencies, our tendencies toward hypocrisy and judgmentalism. Have you confessed yours?

Discussion Starters:

1. Whom do you lead? Who follows your example?

2. How can you demonstrate consistent leadership?

3. Who are you following? What kind of a leader is he or she? Explain.

4. Why was Christ the best example of a leader?

Lifeline:

Home is the place to forgive inconsistencies. It's also the place where we should strive to be more faithful to our calling to be Christlike examples.

HOUSE PAINTING

"'Woe to you, scribes and Pharisees, hypocrites! For you clean the outside of the cup and of the dish, but inside they are full of robbery and self-indulgence. You blind Pharisee, first clean the inside of the cup and of the dish, so that the outside of it may become clean also. Woe to you, scribes and Pharisees, hypocrites! For you are like whitewashed tombs which on the outside appear beautiful, but inside they are full of dead men's bones and all uncleanness. So you, too, outwardly appear righteous to men, but inwardly you are full of hypocrisy and lawlessness.'"

↩ Matthew 23:25-28

My brothers and I were always so excited to do yard work. (Right!) But when Dad said, "Do it, boys," we were left with no choice. So we told our friends we'd play baseball later and worked to make our house shine like new. We mowed the grass, weeded the flowerbed, painted the house, and watered the trees. It was hard work, but when we were done, our house looked great on the outside.

It was even more important, though, for our family to ensure that the inside of our house was *spiritually* clean. It was everybody's job to make our home a happy place to live, a place that honored God. We worked, sweated, and spent the time to clean up that Texas home. Now, the inside view didn't always look as good as the outside view. But God knew we were working on it. And fortunately, He isn't nearly as concerned about the kind of grass growing in the front yard or the shade of paint on the door as He is about the length of our arguments or the thoughts in our hearts.

Cleaning up the inside of your home is a daily job. How do you clean? By praying consistently and truly forgiving those who've let you down. By saying "I'm sorry" and deciding to follow Christ more diligently tomorrow.

Jesus wasn't just telling the Pharisees to clean *their* thoughts and insides. He meant *you* (and your family), too. Are you painting the walls of your heart with faithfulness and weeding the bitterness out of your mind?

Discussion Starters:

1. What can you do today to help beautify the outside of your home? The inside?

2. How clean is your house on the inside? Are you focusing too much on the yard?

Lifeline:

Ask God to show your family the areas in your lives that need more housecleaning.

FOLLOW THE (RIGHT) LEADER

"Then if anyone says to you, "Behold, here is the Christ," or "There He is," do not believe him. For false Christs and false prophets will arise and will show great signs and wonders, so as to mislead, if possible, even the elect. Behold, I have told you in advance.' "

⮑ Matthew 24:23-25

Follow the wrong crowd to a party and you're liable to get into serious trouble with alcohol or drugs. Follow the wrong boy or girl on a date and you might get incredibly hurt. Follow the wrong spiritual leader and you just might wind up in hell.

Almost 10 million misled Mormons follow the lead of the late Joseph Smith. This man, who grew up in a Christian home, believed that all denominations of the Christian faith are wrong and that God would set up the only true Christian denomination through him.[11] Joseph Smith taught that God was once a man who progressed to be a God and that "man is co-equal to God himself."[12] That's certainly not what the Bible says.

Charles Taze Russell began the Jehovah's Witnesses in 1870. Today two million people align themselves with this cult. It denies every cardinal belief of traditional Christianity, including the doctrine of the Trinity, the divinity of Jesus Christ, His bodily resurrection, salvation by grace, and the eternal punishment of the wicked.[13]

The New Age movement is even more prevalent. Its philosophy includes reading palms and tarot cards, consulting psychics, doing Eastern meditation, and channeling with crystals (basically, spirit possession). Horoscopes are also part of the growing New Age movement—millions of people read them in the newspaper each day.

The Bible warns against cultic beliefs and practices for a reason. The beliefs are not only completely opposed to the principles Jesus taught, but they are also extremely enticing. Many people will start out "dabbling" in cultic ideology and end up full-fledged cult members—often without realizing what they've done. There are an estimated 700 to 5,000 false religions in America to watch out for. Don't follow any of them. Let only the real Jesus of the Bible lead you. Your eternity depends on it!

Discussion Starters:

1. What is a cult? What are the characteristics of a cult?

2. What should you do when you encounter false christs or cult members?

Lifeline:

How can you help one another to distinguish between false christs and the real Christ?

DADDY'S HOME!

"'And then the sign of the Son of Man will appear in the sky, and then all the tribes of the earth will mourn, and they will see the Son of Man coming on the clouds of the sky with power and great glory. And He will send forth His angels with a great trumpet and they will gather together His elect from the four winds, from one end of the sky to the other.'"

↩ Matthew 24:30-31

It's my job to travel and recruit Christian athletes for our sports camps. I love sports and working with students, but I hate leaving home. Chuck Swindoll says, "Happiness is seeing anything but home in the rearview mirror of my car"—and I agree. Unfortunately, however, I'm on the road 40-50 days a year.

Now, there's nothing special about the White *house*, but the people in it—my wife and kids—are the strongest magnets I've ever known. I'll drive a million miles if that's what it takes to be home when my kids wake up in the morning. When they were small, sometimes after I'd been gone a week or two, I'd be greeted with "DADDY'S HOME" and "WELCOME HOME, DAD" banners and posters strung all over the house. Back then, I would bring home little gifts for all the kids.

"Dad, what did you bwing me?" little Cooper would always ask.

"I brought you...me!" I'd reply, grinning.

"I know dat, Dad, but what did you *really* bwing me?"

I'd smile, bend down, and pull out from behind my back a small present. Cooper would excitedly throw his little arms around my neck.

After one particularly long trip, I arrived home late one night and found one of my little girls asleep with her blanket by the front door. She didn't want me to miss her. I joyfully picked her up and carried her to her room, cuddling her lovingly to my chest.

My homecomings are a blast. But they're nothing compared to what Jesus' return to earth will be like. Scripture says that the Lord will return with power and glory. Trumpets will announce His arrival; angels will gather His children. And we will be joyfully united with Him as He takes us to our heavenly home.

Discussion Starters:

1. How do you know that Jesus will include you when He returns to earth?

2. Why do you think He's coming back some day?

3. What can you do to be as ready as possible for His return?

Lifeline:

Help your family get ready for Jesus' homecoming!

THE SECOND COMING

"'But of that day and hour no one knows, not even the angels of heaven, nor the Son, but the Father alone. For the coming of the Son of Man will be just like the days of Noah. For as in those days before the flood they were eating and drinking, marrying and giving in marriage, until the day that Noah entered the ark, and they did not understand until the flood came and took them all away; so will the coming of the Son of Man be.'"

↤ Matthew 24:36-39

Scripture is clear and history stands witness that Jesus Christ came once to planet earth as a lamb to be sacrificed for our sins. Scripture is equally clear that He will return again. Literally hundreds of passages in the Old and New Testaments state this. When will His return be? No one except God knows. Will it be soon? We hope so, because when He does come back, all murder, abuse, crime, and sorrow will cease for His followers.

There are many indications that Christ's return could be soon.

According to the books of Daniel, Isaiah, and Revelation, the nation of Israel will be intact when He returns. That was impossible from A.D. 67, when Israel was destroyed, until May 14, 1948, when Israel was restored as a nation. Today, the tiny, turbulent country is poised for His return.

According to Revelation 13:17, a world leader will emerge who will control all world purchasing through one system. Only those people who have this leader's approval (the mark of the beast) will be allowed to buy or sell. The emerging World Wide Web, scanners, and electronic banking have only recently made such a system feasible.

There's more. Revelation 9:16 states that a 200-million-man army will come from the land east of Israel (India, Japan, China). This was impossible until recently. Today, China boasts of an army of 200 million.[14]

Although Christ gave a ton of references to His second coming, He was discreet about the details to ensure that "no man knows the hour" (see verse 36). But He spoke about His return with certainty to give us hope and to encourage us to live for His coming every day of our lives.

Discussion Starters:

1. If Jesus were returning today, would you live differently? If so, how?

2. What do you picture when you hear the phrase "Daddy's coming home"?

3. What will you say when you first meet Jesus face to face?

Lifeline:

What other signs does the Bible give that point to the time Jesus will return?

ETERNAL INVESTMENTS

"'For it is just like a man about to go on a journey, who called his own slaves and entrusted his possessions to them. To one he gave five talents, to another, two, and to another, one, each according to his own ability; and he went on his journey. Immediately the one who had received the five talents went and traded with them, and gained five more talents.... Now after a long time the master of those slaves came and settled accounts with them. The one who had received the five talents came up and brought five more talents, saying, "Master, you entrusted five talents to me. See, I have gained five more talents."'"

↪ Matthew 25:14-16,19-20

Who you are is God's gift to you. What you do with it is your gift to God.

On September 19, 1967, Jim Abbott was born with only one hand. When he was in grade school, he didn't stand a chance when baseball season came around and all his friends went out to play catch and hit the ball. But Jim had a dream and the courage to back up his dream. He later pitched for the USA Olympic team and helped win them the gold medal. As a New York Yankee, he stunned the world by being the first one-handed pitcher to throw a no-hitter in a professional baseball game.[15]

Ludwig van Beethoven, the great composer, became hearing impaired. But his deafness didn't keep him from writing music. He wrote some of his best compositions—music that broke with tradition and made history—*after* he turned completely deaf. Beethoven is universally recognized as one of the most brilliant composers who ever lived.

The pages of history are literally packed with men and women who the world said "had no talent," "didn't stand a chance," and "could never make it." But instead of believing that they'd never go anywhere in life, these "untalented" people invested and used their God-given gifts every day until their dreams came true. And that's what Jesus wants us to do—use our talents for His glory.

Discussion Starters:

1. What is your dream? What talents did God give you that can help you achieve that dream?

2. How can a weakness actually help you realize your dream?

3. What is the greatest gift God has given you? How can you invest this gift to its fullest?

Lifeline:

Encourage one another to reach your dreams!

HAVE YOU DONE IT FOR THEM?

" "Then the King will say to those on His right [the sheep], "Come, you who are blessed of My Father, inherit the kingdom prepared for you from the foundation of the world. For I was hungry, and you gave Me something to eat; I was thirsty, and you gave Me something to drink; I was a stranger, and you invited Me in; naked, and you clothed Me; I was sick, and you visited Me; I was in prison, and you came to Me." ...[Then] the King will...say to them, "Truly I say to you, to the extent that you did it to one of these brothers of Mine, even the least of them, you did it to Me." ' "

⇝ Matthew 25:34-36,40

Poor people starve. Most rich people throw food away.

Elderly people lie in their hospital beds or nursing homes and wish for attention. Young people waste an average of three to five hours a day in front of their TV set, video games, or CD player.

Mentally and physically challenged people long for the opportunity to have a friend in school. The athletes, whiz kids, and popular people pass them by in the hallways without even a hello or a smile.

Fortunately, lots of Christians reach out to the less fortunate and sacrifice to give to the poor. In this passage, Jesus was clear that if you love Him, you'll do just that...you'll take your time, your talents, and your possessions and give them away. If you do, you're what He calls a "sheep," and He is well pleased with you. If you don't, you're a "goat," and your faith is questionable (see Matthew 25:41-46).

A few years ago when our kids were all at home, we had a piggy bank at our breakfast table. In order to get breakfast every morning, each family member had to bring a coin to put in the bank, which we used to sponsor urban kids to Kanakuk-Kanakomo Kamps. Whenever *anyone* in the house made any money, no matter how much or how little, the first portion always went to some work God was doing around the world.

You don't need to be ashamed of your blessings. But you do need to share them. It'll show God where your heart is and where you stand with Him. How much of your time and resources do you give to His children?

Discussion Starters:

1. What are some ways you can give back to Jesus?
2. Who are some less fortunate people you know who would benefit if you shared your time, heart, and resources?
3. Who gets the most when you give? Why?

Lifeline:

Giving is often a trademark of legitimate faith!

DEDICATION OR DESERTION?

"A woman came to Him with an alabaster vial of very costly perfume, and she poured it on His head as He reclined at the table.... [And Jesus said,] 'When she poured this perfume on My body, she did it to prepare Me for burial. Truly I say to you, wherever this gospel is preached in the whole world, what this woman has done will also be spoken of in memory of her.' Then one of the twelve, named Judas Iscariot, went to the chief priests and said, 'What are you willing to give me to betray Him to you?' And they weighed out thirty pieces of silver to him. From then on he began looking for a good opportunity to betray Jesus."

↪ Matthew 26:7,12-16

Scholars suggest the vial of perfume could have been the poor woman's most valued possession. Perhaps she had been saving it since her 18th birthday, planning to give this treasured gift to the man who would be her husband. But whatever the woman's aspirations, it's obvious she admired the Savior and would sacrifice any of her possessions to show her family and friends that she was a devoted follower.

Two thousand years haven't erased the story of her great dedication.

Judas Iscariot walked with the Savior for three wonderful years. He watched this God-Man heal outdoor hospitals full of people with debilitating diseases. He saw the Messiah reach out and touch the hearts of the poor and lonely, value children as heavenly treasures, and elevate women to their proper place of dignity and honor. Judas walked with Jesus as He introduced grace to this world and literally brought God's mercy from heaven, showing the almighty Creator's amazing love for His children. Yet Judas couldn't resist the bribe and sold his soul for a bag of silver.

Two thousand years haven't erased the story of his great desertion.

You, too, have been exposed to the Savior. You also have seen His love and mercy. How are you going to respond? You will either embrace Him or betray Him by your choices and actions. Will you sacrifice for Jesus, or will you be swayed by money and the moment and lose the best Friend you've ever had? What story will you leave behind?

Discussion Starters:

1. What would you give Jesus if He came to your home today? Why?

2. It's easier to deny Jesus than to sacrifice for Him. What things in your life (or in the culture) deny Jesus? In what ways do you sacrifice for Him?

3. Practically speaking, how can you live in a way that honors Him today?

Lifeline:

Honor Jesus by honoring your family.

THE BLOOD COVENANT

"While they were eating, Jesus took some bread, and after a blessing, He broke it and gave it to the disciples, and said, 'Take, eat; this is My body.' And when He had taken a cup and given thanks, He gave it to them, saying, 'Drink from it, all of you; for this is My blood of the covenant, which is poured out for many for forgiveness of sins.'"

↜ Matthew 26:26-28

"I promise." "Let's shake on it." "I guarantee it!" "Trust me."

Jesus didn't have to say all those things to seal His covenant with us. He simply held up the loaf of bread, ripped it in half, and in so many words said, "Friends, tomorrow they're going to do this to My body. Eat this, and remember Me." He poured out the wine and affirmed, "My blood will pour out for you until My heart bleeds to death. It's proof positive that I love you. I came for this purpose. Drink this and remember My love for you."

Jesus' death created an even stronger covenant with His children. He, being a man, made a blood covenant promise with God on behalf of all men. And He, being God, the Creator of all people, was able to forgive you and me when He took the nails in His wrists and died so that you and God could be bonded forever.

We break our word as easily as chefs crack eggshells in restaurants on Saturday morning.

But Jesus keeps His. The term He used, "covenant," means a promise, and biblical blood covenants are never, ever broken. Period. On the day of the cross, Jesus sealed a friendship between God's kids and Himself that makes communion the most important banquet you'll ever attend. The Bible calls it, in effect, a covenant meal. Discover now in your family discussion the full impact of this "commitment feast" between you and God.

Discussion Starters:

1. What did Jesus mean when He said, "This cup...is the new covenant in My blood" (Luke 22:20)?
2. How does His pledge give you freedom?
3. Why was the shedding of blood necessary in this covenant between God and man?
4. Why is it important to take communion regularly?

Lifeline:

Write a covenant that states your family's commitment to God and your love for Him.

THE NIGHT SORROW MASTERED THE MASTER

"Then Jesus came with them to a place called Gethsemane, and said to His disciples, 'Sit here while I go over there and pray.' ...Then He said to them, 'My soul is deeply grieved, to the point of death; remain here and keep watch with Me.' And He went a little beyond them, and fell on His face and prayed, saying, 'My Father, if it is possible, let this cup pass from Me; yet not as I will, but as You will.' ...He went away again a second time and prayed, saying, 'My Father, if this cannot pass away unless I drink it, Your will be done.'"

⌒ Matthew 26:36,38-39,42

I cried pools of tears when my older daughter left home for a college far, far away. I miss her beyond description. Her genes are half me! I poured all that I had into her for 18 years. We're best friends and mutual admirers. I have more sweet memories of her than I can count.

Jesus also felt deep sorrow. He knew the night before His crucifixion that a torturous death awaited Him. I've often wondered which part of the ordeal He dreaded the most. The flogging? The public ridicule? The fists in His face? The crown of thorns? The grueling walk to Golgotha? The crucifixion?

As the father to my four best friends (outside of my wife), I know that one of life's greatest agonies is being separated from those you deeply love. I believe that as Jesus agonized in the Garden of Gethsemane, His greatest anxiety was knowing that in a few short hours His close bond with His Father would be ruthlessly—even if only for a short while—broken. As He looked ahead to the next day, He could see Himself becoming the curse of sin. His holy Father would turn His head and for the first time ever, Jesus would be fatherless—desperately alone—and the thought crushed Him.

Jesus' grief was deep, but His obedience to the Father ran deeper. Even under terrible sorrow and anxiety, Jesus was able to say, "Not My will, but Yours be done."

Discussion Starters:

1. Kids, describe the importance of having a close relationship with your parents (even if you don't always feel like it). Parents, describe your love for your kids.

2. How do you think Jesus was feeling that night in Gethsemane?

3. How does Jesus' statement to His Dad, "Your will be done," inspire you today?

Lifeline:

Parents need to be careful in giving commands to their kids, and kids need to make sure they respond with respect and obedience.

A DISTANT FOLLOWER

"But Peter was following Him at a distance as far as the courtyard of the high priest, and entered in, and sat down with the officers to see the outcome.... Now Peter was sitting outside in the courtyard, and a servant-girl came to him and said, 'You too were with Jesus the Galilean.' But he denied it before them all, saying, 'I do not know what you are talking about.' When he had gone out to the gateway, another servant-girl saw him and said to those who were there, 'This man was with Jesus of Nazareth.' And again he denied it with an oath, 'I do not know the man.' A little later the bystanders came up and said to Peter, 'Surely you too are one of them; for even the way you talk gives you away.' Then he began to curse and swear, 'I do not know the man!' And immediately a rooster crowed."

               ⮌ Matthew 26:58,69-74

The pressure was as intense as it gets. Peter's hero was being whipped, stripped, spit upon, and beaten like a rabid wolf. The trial was merciless, and the Roman cross awaited Him. The Jewish leaders were in a rage. Peter saw his own impending death flash before him. He had followed Jesus for three life-changing years. Peter had hungrily sunk his teeth into every word He spoke. Now, afraid and timid, Peter followed at a distance. The distance made him question. The distance made him curse. The distance made him forget that Jesus could overcome any obstacle.

The distance made him deny the One he loved most.

Your eighth grade friends like heavy metal music. Your best friend slips a pack of cigarettes into your backpack. That gorgeous cheerleader with the bad rep wants you to ask her out. Everybody cusses, so why can't you? You haven't been invited to a party in weeks because you're a "Jesus freak." The popular kids are asking you for take-home test answers. You look pretty weird carrying a Coke at a keg party.

Pressure. Peter felt it, and every teenager alive feels it. Sometimes it gets too hot to handle during those turbulent growing-up years. When you desire to have a close relationship with Jesus and you live with a constant awareness of His presence in your life, it's easier to do the right thing. But when you follow Him at a distance, denying Him is as natural as breathing.

Discussion Starters:

 1. Why do you think Peter denied Jesus? From fear? Embarrassment?

 2. Why do distant followers fall?

 3. What temptations cause you to fall?

Lifeline:

How can your family follow Him more closely?

THE SACRIFICE

"Now at the feast the governor was accustomed to release for the people any one prisoner whom they wanted.... But the governor said to them, 'Which of the two do you want me to release for you?' And they said, 'Barabbas.' Pilate said to them, 'Then what shall I do with Jesus who is called Christ?' They all said, 'Crucify Him!' ...Then he released Barabbas for them; but after having Jesus scourged, he handed Him over to be crucified."

↜ Matthew 27:15,21-22,26

Within a matter of minutes, the run-down New York apartment building went up in flames. Firemen rushed to the scene, futilely shooting water into the mountain of fire and smoke. The crowd looked on in horror as Sharon, one of the residents, stood by and called out in fear, "My baby, my baby! Someone save my baby!" In a burst of great courage, Fireman John leaned his tall ladder into the inferno on the second-story balcony, scurried to the top, and disappeared into the smoke. The astonished crowd cheered wildly as John reappeared with Sharon's baby in his arms, wrapped safely in her nursery blankets. The building collapsed just as John pitched the baby into the soft safety net outstretched below. Overcome with emotional gratitude for the stranger and his dying act of heroic sacrifice, Sharon cried wild, happy tears as she cuddled her child to her breast.

Seventeen years later, Alisa, a tall, sober, teenage girl, stands next to a granite tombstone. She stares intently at the hand-hewn figure carved into the stone—a fireman with a baby in his arms. As she places fresh-cut flowers next to the grave, a passerby asks, "Are those for your father?"

Alisa tenderly wipes the tears from her cheeks with the back of her hand, swallows the lump in her throat, and replies, "No, I never knew him, but he's my friend. See, this man died for me."

And another man—Jesus—died for *you*.

Discussion Starters:

1. How do you think Barabbas felt as he walked away from prison a free man that fateful crucifixion day?

2. Describe your emotions as you read these two stories. How does the story of Barabbas affect your life?

3. How do you feel about "the Man who died for you"?

Lifeline:

As we serve and sacrifice for each other in the home, we more fully appreciate Jesus' sacrifice for us.

AN R-RATED DEATH

"They stripped Him and put a scarlet robe on Him. And after twisting together a crown of thorns, they put it on His head, and a reed in His right hand; and they knelt down before Him and mocked Him, saying, 'Hail, King of the Jews!' They spat on Him, and took the reed and began to beat Him on the head. After they had mocked Him, they took the scarlet robe off Him and put His own garments back on Him, and led Him away to crucify Him."

↜ Matthew 27:28-31

It looks too easy when you see it in the movies and on carved statues in churches. If the crucifixion were pictured accurately, Hollywood wouldn't be able to film it, and no one would buy a ticket to watch the horrible human sacrifice. The statue would be far too graphic to place in our churches.

No, folks, it wasn't Hollywood, and it didn't look like the romanticized pictures that hang on museum walls. The Roman cross and the scourging that led up to it were the most cruel human torture ever committed.

He endured it for you. He loved you that much.

He knew we'd end up in hell if He didn't die for us. It was too much for Jesus to imagine His precious children hurting, so He allowed Himself to suffer through it so that by believing in and receiving Him, we might never know the pain of hell.

Read Isaiah's words as he prophesied about Jesus' death 1,500 years before it took place: "But He was pierced through for our transgressions, He was crushed for our iniquities; the chastening for our well-being fell upon Him, and by His scourging we are healed" (Isaiah 53:5).

Imagine standing on a platform in front of your entire school while your friends and enemies shout insults at you and other people kick and punch you until all your strength is gone. That would be awful.

But what Jesus went through was far worse.

Next time you read about His death in the Bible, let the words sink in. Christ was humiliated, physically and emotionally stripped naked, beaten mercilessly, and *nailed* to a cross. And He endured it all for you.

Discussion Starters:

1. Why do we so often ignore or glamorize Jesus' death on the cross?
2. What does Jesus' act of sacrifice reveal about His character and His relationship with His children?

Lifeline:

How can your family learn to more fully appreciate Jesus' death and sacrifice on the cross?

GROUNDS FOR RESURRECTION

"Now on the next day...the chief priests and the Pharisees gathered together with Pilate, and said, 'Sir, we remember that when He was still alive that deceiver said, "After three days I am to rise again." Therefore, give orders for the grave to be made secure until the third day, otherwise His disciples may come and steal Him away and say to the people, "He has risen from the dead," and the last deception will be worse than the first.' Pilate said to them, 'You have a guard; go, make it as secure as you know how.' And they went and made the grave secure."

↝ Matthew 27:62-66

Jesus' physical resurrection gives the greatest evidence that He is "God in the flesh." No *other* religious leader in history was resurrected. Because He rose from the dead, your faith is as real as the food in your cupboard. But critics say it was a hoax, so how do we know it's historical fact?

• *The Roman guards*—Jesus' tomb was guarded by Roman sentries. Roman soldiers were highly trained and able to defend their ground against many times their number of enemies. If they retreated, slept on the job, or defected, they'd be subject to gruesome execution.[16]

• *The Roman seal*—In his book *Evidence That Demands a Verdict*, Josh McDowell wrote, "Considering in like manner the securing of Jesus' tomb, the Roman seal affixed thereon was meant to prevent any attempted vandalizing of the sepulchre. Anyone trying to move the stone from the tomb's entrance would have broken the seal and thus incurred the wrath of Roman law."[17] If you were caught breaking the seal, you might have been crucified yourself.

• *The stone*—In keeping with Jewish tradition, a one- to two-ton rock was rolled up against the tomb entrance. One man could never move the stone by himself. But eyewitness accounts documented in the gospels indicate the stone was removed completely away from the entire tomb.[18]

• *The appearances*—The books of John and 1 Corinthians document that Jesus appeared alive and well to the apostles and 500 others.

No one could've stolen Jesus' body. No one could've broken into the tomb. The only way Jesus could have left His grave was if He'd supernatually risen from the dead. And we have evidence to prove He did.

Discussion Starters:

1. Do these historical facts change your views on the resurrection? Explain.

2. Why is the resurrection so important?

Lifeline:

Christians can look forward to eternal life together in heaven because Jesus is risen.

THE GREAT COMMISSION

"But the eleven disciples proceeded to Galilee, to the mountain which Jesus had designated. When they saw Him, they worshiped Him; but some were doubtful. And Jesus came up and spoke to them, saying, 'All authority has been given to Me in heaven and on earth. Go therefore and make disciples of all the nations, baptizing them in the name of the Father and the Son and the Holy Spirit, teaching them to observe all that I commanded you; and lo, I am with you always, even to the end of the age.'"

⟿ Matthew 28:16-20

Imagine you have a million dollars for yourself and a million dollars to give away to a friend who is penniless. Now picture your friend opening the suitcase to discover all that money inside. Wouldn't it be amazing to see the look of happiness and astonishment on his face? Wouldn't that be a fun and rewarding thing to do?

Now envision this: You're standing with a friend you've witnessed to at the gates of eternity. Heaven is on the right, and hell is on the left. You both joyfully run through heaven's gates, praising God. Imagine how grateful your friend would be to you for leading her to eternal salvation and telling her about having a relationship with Jesus Christ.

Doesn't one scenario strike you as much more fulfilling, important, and lasting than the other? Folks, Jesus admonishes us to understand and hold on to our faith, to live the Christian life to its fullest, and to talk about Him everywhere we go!

When I accepted Christ into my heart as a 17-year-old, my first prayer was about how to share it with my brother and my best friend, Wade. Being nervous about this new adventure and scared of rejection, I prayed and prayed. Well, God answered those prayers. He had prepared both of them to hear what I wanted to say. They were open, ready, and eager to know Him, too.

Witnessing to my loved ones was one of the best events of my life. I challenge you to be Christ's messenger to an unbeliever. The experience is more valuable than all the money in the world.

Discussion Starters:

1. Read verses 18-20 again. What do they say to you?

2. What people do you know who need Jesus? How and when would it be appropriate to discuss Him with them?

Lifeline:

The family is the best place to encourage one another in carrying out the Great Commission.

Luke, the "beloved physician," contributed this super-accurate, historical document in his effort to reach the Greek culture—the Gentiles—with the good news of God's saving grace. Luke is noted for his attention to detail and his concern for the hurting, the brokenhearted, and the lost. In this gospel, Luke made it clear that Christ was born to save true believers who are from all the world's nations—Jesus didn't die just to save the Jewish people. The gospel of Luke is also unique because while Luke recognized Christ's deity, he emphasized Christ's humanity—showing us His compassion and empathy for us in our earthly struggles.

OLD MEN AND RIVERS

"But [Zacharias and Elizabeth] had no child, because Elizabeth was barren, and they were both advanced in years.... And an angel of the Lord appeared to him, standing to the right of the altar of incense.... But the angel said to him, 'Do not be afraid, Zacharias, for your petition has been heard, and your wife Elizabeth will bear you a son, and you will give him the name John [the Baptist].' ...Zacharias said to the angel, 'How will I know this for certain? For I am an old man, and my wife is advanced in years.' The angel answered and said to him, 'I am Gabriel, who stands in the presence of God, and I have been sent to speak to you and to bring you this good news.'"

🕮 Luke 1:7,11,13,18-19

Some people are late bloomers.

My father started kayaking at 70 years old. He liked it so much, he couldn't keep it to himself. Dad made his kids all try it. "We Whites get our feet wet together," he said.

So we took the plunge. Most of us have become decent at the sport. Still, we marvel at Dad's ability to paddle circles around his family.

In '88, Dad kayaked the Grand Canyon. He made it through in two weeks with a bunch of yuppies half his age. When he finished, they hoisted him up on their shoulders and marched him around like a king.

Old men like Dad aren't supposed to do that stuff. Old men sit in rocking chairs, snoozing with their feet up and their newspapers spread across wide expanses of cotton pajamas. Old men order oatmeal in restaurants and drink Milk of Magnesia. Old men play Scrabble.

Old men are supposed to do tame things, not be out conquering the 10 hardest rivers in America, rubbing shoulders with baby boomers in the wilderness, telling jokes, and doing calisthenics. But Dad's no ordinary man.

In some ways, my dad reminds me of Zacharias, who, in the twilight of his life, fathered the prophet John the Baptist. In Zacharias's case, however, God chose him to be John's father and did it through His power.

If you're facing formidable circumstances, don't stress. As He did with Zacharias's situation, God can easily turn your impossibility into a reality.

Discussion Starters:

1. When did you last face an impossibility? How did God work through it?
2. What does Scripture say about impossible situations (see Matthew 19:26)?

Lifeline:

Have each family member describe a time in which God helped him or her overcome hopeless circumstances.

SIGN OF THE TIMES

"Mary said to the angel, 'How can this be, since I am a virgin?' The angel answered and said to her, 'The Holy Spirit will come upon you, and the power of the Most High will over-shadow you; and for that reason the holy Child shall be called the Son of God. And behold, even your relative Elizabeth has also conceived a son in her old age; and she who was called barren is now in her sixth month. For nothing will be impossible with God.' And Mary said, 'Behold, the bondslave of the Lord; may it be done to me according to your word.' And the angel departed from her."

↜ Luke 1:34-38

"Live a little," said the bright billboard.

Our local Dairy Queen meant no harm when it erected the thing 15 years ago. The message was intended to say, "Come in. Get out of the heat. Forget your diet." Problem was, the sign was located next to a cemetery.

Folks depend on signs for direction in life—where to go, what to do, who to believe. Sometimes people depend on signs too much. Zacharias did, as we saw in the preceding devotional.

The angel Gabriel said to him, "Your wife Elizabeth is going to have a baby." Zacharias answered, "How do I know you're not pulling my leg? Elizabeth and I are old!"

It wasn't enough to be chatting with an angel. He wanted proof to convince him that two old people could still be parents. Zacharias was preoccupied with signs, so Gabriel gave him one—muteness.

Not so with Mary, the mother of Jesus. Sure, she didn't know how she'd conceive a child. She said to Gabriel, "But...I'm a virgin." When Gabriel explained that Jesus would be conceived by the Holy Spirit, though, she yielded. It didn't matter to Mary that no one might believe her—she believed the angel of the Lord. She simply said, "If God says so, then okay."

God's word wasn't enough for Zacharias. He wanted a sign. But after Mary understood what was to happen in her, she believed God's word. She didn't need a sign.

Sometimes we're just supposed to take things—especially God's promises to us—on faith.

Discussion Starters:

1. Zacharias's questioning seemed so innocent. Why was Mary given God's approval while he was struck mute?

2. God will have His way whether we're miserable in the meantime (like Zacharias) or not. How have you resisted God these last few weeks?

3. How might you be blessed if you quit resisting?

Lifeline:

Pray for your family to submit (like Mary) to God and His will for your life.

ENGAGED AND WITH CHILD

"Joseph also went up from Galilee, from the city of Nazareth, to Judea, to the city of David which is called Bethlehem, because he was of the house and family of David, in order to register along with Mary, who was engaged to him, and was with child."

↬ Luke 2:4-5

Engaged and with child. That sounds like an oxymoron if I've ever heard one.

If you're a little taken aback by Mary's condition, think how Joseph felt. Understandably, he wanted to send her away for nine months so she—and probably, he—wouldn't be publicly embarrassed. But God said, "The baby is Mine. Marry her and raise that child as if He were your own" (see Matthew 1).

Joseph swallowed his pride and did exactly what God commanded.

Mary and Joseph most likely were subject to a bunch of gossip, rumors, and accusations. But they trusted and obeyed God. The Lord had told them it was necessary that Jesus be born of a virgin. Prophets had proclaimed that the Messiah's mother would be a virgin, which would make God the Father of His Son—in every sense of the word.

A couple of things come to mind when I think about the virgin birth. First, virginity was important then, and virginity is important now. Sex was meant for marriage back then, and sex is still meant only for marriage. Second, the fact that Mary was a virgin shows just how powerful God is. Just as God created Eve from Adam's rib, so He created a tiny baby in Mary's womb.

The miracle child of Bethlehem is still the miracle child. God is still omnipotent. And if He could create a child in a virgin womb, He can turn your life around.

There's just one catch. You, like Joseph and Mary, must be obedient and let God do things His way.

Discussion Starters:

1. Why was it important for Mary to be a virgin?

2. Could you have been as obedient to God as Mary and Joseph were? How do you think they dealt with the scorn and humiliation they undoubtedly faced?

3. In what ways do you need God to work a miracle in your life today? Do you believe He can do it? Why or why not?

Lifeline:

A miraculous God can build a miraculous family. How can your family be more obedient to God and allow Him to build you up together?

NAMELESS IN NAZARETH

"And when eight days had passed, before His circumcision, His name was then called Jesus, the name given by the angel before He was conceived in the womb."

↜ Luke 2:21

You may not realize this, but God once went a week without a name.

Look for yourself. It's there in print. Luke 2:21 tells us, "And when eight days had passed, before His circumcision, His name was *then* called Jesus, the name given by the angel before He was conceived in the womb" (emphasis added).

God without a name. What a tragedy! Here's the ruler of the universe, lying around in diapers with all the relatives calling Him "the baby." Like the rest of the boys in the neighborhood, God had to wait eight days for His name. Then when His parents, following Jewish custom, named Him at His circumcision, they gave Him the most popular name in Israel.

"Jesus." It was every mom's choice back then. They'd have called him "Justin" or "Jeremy" if He were born today. There were probably 50 others with His name around town. I can just imagine roll call in the synagogue.

"Abram?" *"Here."* "Benjamin?" *"Here."* "Eli?" *"Here."*

"Jesus?" *"Uh, do you mean the one from Jericho? Or the weaver's son? Or the one whose mom said she was a virgin?"*

"Now, class..." the rabbi would say, attempting to stop the laughter.

Think how embarrassed our Lord may have been while growing up. How common and ordinary He may have felt! I think that's how He planned it, though. And I think that's what Luke intended to capture for us in chapter 2. Jesus came into this world just like you and me. He cried, sucked His thumb, wet His bed, and slowly grew to manhood. That's part of why I love Him. He spent some time on my level before He died for me.

I suppose it's all right that Jesus began His life on earth without a name. In the end, He had a slew of them: Wonderful Counselor. Prince of Peace. Lamb of God. Holy One. The Christ. Alpha and Omega. The Almighty. King of kings. Lord of lords.

Not bad for a no-name kid from Nazareth.

Discussion Starters:

1. Of all the names given to our Lord, what's your favorite? Why?

2. What does your own name mean? (Parents should take the time to find this out in advance.) What is one way you can live up to your name?

Lifeline:

Although it was common, the name Jesus means "savior." Parents, relate your story of salvation.

REPENT!

"And he came into all the district around the Jordan, preaching a baptism of repentance for the forgiveness of sins."

↪ Luke 3:3

Copernicus, the founder of modern astronomy, put scientists and clergy into an uproar when he said the earth circled the sun. Einstein, an internationally famous physicist, developed the theory of relativity. Susan B. Anthony led the women's suffrage movement, which gave women the right to vote. Michael Jordan of the Chicago Bulls has led his team to several national titles and is widely regarded as one of the best basketball players of all time.

These men and women have all shaped our lives in some way. We recognize their names, and in some cases, read about them in school.

But when it comes to salvation, your name and your accomplishments are not enough. You've got to repent and accept Christ to enter heaven.

In a loud voice, John the Baptist told his audience those same things. He said, "It's not enough to call yourself a Jew! Your name and heritage alone won't get you into heaven! You've got to shape up and fly straight before the wrath of God comes upon you!"

Whoa! Those are fightin' words.

They're also *impossible* words. After all, who of us is good enough to gain eternal life? Not me. Nevertheless, John roared on. "Repent and be baptized!" he shouted. "Stop doing bad things! Start doing good!"

It wasn't popular, but he preached it. He was showing the world its need for a Savior, paving the way for Jesus to come and die for those of us who just can't seem to be perfect.

Jesus is coming back some day. He'll leave His awesome home up in heaven and come to interrupt our lives. The thing is, He won't care what a big shot you are. It won't matter if you're smart, rich, funny, or popular. Jesus will only be impressed with eternal things. He'll stride right up to Michael Jordan (or whoever happens to be MVP of the universe at the time) and say, "Nice jump shot. But did you repent?"

Discussion Starters:

1. What do repentance and baptism have to do with salvation?

2. Is repentance a one-time thing? Why or why not?

Lifeline:

Have every family member make a list of the things they're ashamed of. Then, without reading the lists, gather together, silently confess your sins to God, ask His forgiveness, and burn the lists in the fireplace.

CANOE TRIPS IN MAY

"When He began His ministry, Jesus Himself was about thirty years of age, being, as was supposed, the son of Joseph, the son of Eli, the son of Matthat, the son of Levi, the son of Melchi, the son of Jannai, the son of Joseph..."

↩ Luke 3:23-24

"Nathan...David...Jesse...Obed...Boaz...Sala...Nashon...*zzZZZ...zzZZZZ...zzZZZZ...*"

I'll bet you've been tempted to skip over the genealogy sections of the Bible, too. Why read a bunch of names? Well, I think I understand partly why the scribes kept all that mumbo-jumbo in the Bible. They were tracing the Messiah's family line all the way through the Old Testament.

Lineage—family—is important.

One May, I went down the Buffalo River in northwest Arkansas on a father and son "experiment." The men and boys were pumped. But the women weren't happy about the outing.

"It's too cold. They're only four years old," the moms said before we plunged into the first rapid, vowing each life jacket would stay on until we returned. "Can't you wait until July when the water's lower?" they pleaded.

Well, the moms were right. Our first evening out was spent drying Batman sleeping bags. But when the stars appeared and our boys were finally asleep, we fathers began to do what psychologists say we never do.

We began to talk.

That night around the campfire, one father, Chuck, confided in me. He said he expected too much from his son, Treven.

"It's driving both of us crazy," he concluded.

But the next morning, when Chuck capsized in white water and Treven was pulled under the canoe, Chuck wasn't so concerned with his son's IQ or batting average. He was groping wildly for a tiny hand beneath the waters. When he finally pulled the shivering child to his chest, a new relationship formed before my eyes.

Thank You, Lord, for families. Thank You for Luke's cumbersome river of names. And thank You for canoe trips in May. They always remind me of what's important.

Discussion Starters:

1. Give five reasons why your family is important to you.

2. Why are family times significant? What's your favorite family tradition?

Lifeline:

Plan to start a new family tradition or memory. Then do it!

85

MASTER OF THE MOMENT

"Jesus, full of the Holy Spirit, returned from the Jordan and was led around by the Spirit in the wilderness for forty days, being tempted by the devil. And He ate nothing during those days, and when they had ended, He became hungry. And the devil said to Him, 'If You are the Son of God, tell this stone to become bread.' And Jesus answered him, 'It is written, "Man shall not live on bread alone."' ...When the devil had finished every temptation, he left Him until an opportune time."

↩ Luke 4:1-4,13

Diets come and go in the White house (the White house of Missouri, that is). Jogging regimens begin, then come to a standstill. New Year's resolutions turn to faint memories by Valentine's Day.

Jesus understands. He was tempted to break His diet (and give in to the devil) once. It was a "slimmer than slim" fast in the desert of the Dead Sea region. He went there to get wisdom. He had some important decisions to make and didn't want His stomach to interfere with His brain.

Forty foodless days and nights dragged by. On the 41st morning, the devil'd had enough of discipline, so he offered the Lord a stone sandwich.

"Here," he said with a nasty grin. "Have a bite. A month and a half of being good is bound to make a man hungry."

But Jesus didn't budge. His resolution didn't become a faint memory because He knows a thing or two that you and I don't. He knows the power of the moment. He understands the way it can defeat our promises. He realizes the devil never takes a day off and that Satan can pinpoint just when we're ready to give up—pouncing on our moments of weakness.

Jesus must have been thin as a rail that morning when He looked the devil in the eye and told him to get lost. The devil slinked away, defeated. And Jesus, with His mind made up, marched straight back to Galilee and chose His disciples.

Satan may be the master of temptation...but Jesus can help us master those weak moments. With Him, we *can* make our goals a reality.

Discussion Starters:

1. What resolution is hardest for you to follow through on?
2. How does Satan usually tempt you?
3. How can God's Word help you say no to Satan when you're tempted?

Lifeline:

Outline how you individually can reach an important resolution. Then as a family, pray that God would help you in those moments when you're tempted to give up.

CLOSE TO HOME

"And all were speaking well of Him, and wondering at the gracious words which were falling from His lips; and they were saying, 'Is this not Joseph's son?' And He said to them, 'No doubt you will quote this proverb to Me, "Physician, heal yourself! Whatever we heard was done at Capernaum, do here in your hometown as well."' And He said, 'Truly I say to you, no prophet is welcome in his hometown.'"

⮑ Luke 4:22-24

Jon, a former programs director at Kanakuk Kamp, was bringing his sweetheart home from college to meet his folks. The two had gotten out of the car and were walking up the sidewalk when suddenly Jon panicked.

He'd forgotten his girlfriend's name.

Fifty feet stretched between Jon and disaster. He stopped to tie his shoe, scrolling mentally through the alphabet, hoping to land on the correct initial. The method failed. They walked closer to the door. He tried to picture her signature at the bottom of notes she had written him. No luck.

Desperate, Jon asked his sweetheart if she didn't think it might be better to postpone the introduction until another night.

She answered, "Tonight is fine. Why? Is something wrong, Jon?"

"I just wanted to be sure you're ready to meet my folks," he said.

When they finally reached the porch, Jon had an idea that saved him. He asked to see his girlfriend's driver's license. "My dad doesn't believe that you and my mom have the same birthday. I need to prove it," Jon explained to her. He glanced at her license quickly and sighed in relief.

Annemarie. How could I forget?

Sometimes familiarity causes amnesia. Those we claim to know the *most* are often the ones we know the *least*. That's how it was with Jesus in His hometown. The people looked at Him as Joseph's son but couldn't see that He was the Son of God. Sadly, "Christian amnesia" still exists today, even among the most religious people. Those Christians claim to know Jesus, but they really only know *of* Him. Christ doesn't live in their hearts.

What about you? Do you *really* know Jesus?

Discussion Starters:

1. Why do you think it was so hard for the people of Nazareth to accept Jesus?

2. Why might it be difficult for some churchgoers to really know Him?

3. What does it mean to "know Jesus"? How can you improve your friendship with Him?

Lifeline:

Set a place for Jesus at your table tonight. You'll be surprised how different your prayers are when you remember your Friend is present.

BOOTFISH AND THE BELIEVER

"When He had finished speaking, He said to Simon, 'Put out into the deep water and let down your nets for a catch.' Simon answered and said, 'Master, we worked hard all night and caught nothing, but I will do as you say and let down the nets.' When they had done this, they enclosed a great quantity of fish, and their nets began to break; so they signaled to their partners in the other boat.... And they came and filled both of the boats, so that they began to sink."

↩ Luke 5:4-7

The back of the menu at the Reservoir Cafe in Deckers, Colorado, reads, "If ya want whiskerfish, go to Walsenburg." My friend Barry, who was about to dine there, considered the advice, then looked at his young waiter. "You're not going to believe this," said Barry, "but I caught a seven-pound cutthroat at Spinney Lake today. Want to know how I caught him?"

The boy nodded, his mouth hanging open. Barry went on. "I had just fallen in the inlet at Spinney. My waders (fishing pants) were almost filled with ice cold water. I was shouting, and all the fellas on the shore were laughing at me. So do ya know what I decided to do?"

"No, sir. What's that?" asked the boy.

"Pray," said Barry. "I said, 'Lord, I've been out here since five o'clock this morning, and I haven't caught a thing. I'd be ever so thankful if You'd treat me like You did Peter on the Sea of Galilee and give me one big, fat fish that I can tell my friends about back home.'

"Well," Barry continued, "I walked about five feet, saw a huge cutthroat caught in the shallows, kicked him up onto the grass, put him in my net, and walked off. But then I threw him back in the river."

"Yeah, right," mumbled the young waiter. "So what'll it be, sir?"

"Nothing, thanks," said my friend as he closed the menu and smiled. "I think I'll go to Walsenburg for the whiskerfish."

Why do folks have such a hard time believing God blesses His children? God is the great gift-giver. And if you don't believe me or Barry, look in the Word. Simon Peter has an even better fishing story than Barry.

Discussion Starters:

1. When were you surprised by one of God's blessings?
2. The book of John tells us 153 fish were caught that morning (21:11). When God gives so extravagantly, what does that tell us about Him? What kind of attitude should we have toward Him?

Lifeline:

Keep tabs on God's blessings today. Share your findings at family devotions tomorrow.

A CHILLING PROPOSAL

"And some men were carrying on a bed a man who was paralyzed; and they were trying to bring him in and to set him down in front of Him. But not finding any way to bring him in because of the crowd, they went up on the roof and let him down through the tiles with his stretcher into the middle of the crowd, in front of Jesus. Seeing their faith, He said, 'Friend, your sins are forgiven you.'"

↶ Luke 5:18-20

Kris loved Diane enough to freeze his backside off. Literally.

With a sign in one hand and a spool of twine in the other, he carefully climbed the ski lift pole at Breckenridge, Colorado. Wind whipped his naked face. Snow collected inside his jacket and melted, tracing two wet paths down Kris's legs, soaking his socks. Pneumonia was a distinct possibility.

At the top, Kris wrestled the sign onto cold steel and squinted toward the top of the mountain. Kris tied one last knot and threw a prayer toward heaven. "Dear God, thanks for Diane," he shouted to the wind. "Please let her say yes. And please let this marriage last!" Then he came down from the sky, took his three other signs, hung them on three other poles, and waited for morning.

At noon the following day, Diane took a fairy tale ski-lift ride. With that trademark sparkle in her eyes, she read the words: "Little Mo...you're sooper dooper...will you be...Mrs. Cooper?"

And Diane said yes!

Since then, I have often thought that any other fool would've found a safer way to ask for a woman's hand in marriage. My friend Kris, though, is not just "any other fool." He was and still is a fool for Diane.

Sometimes the greatest love is one that's willing to play the fool. The paralytic's friends had that kind of love for him. They were willing to climb the building where Jesus was preaching and lower their friend through the roof. They loved him so much and wanted him healed—physically and spiritually—so much that they were willing to look silly. Jesus looked at their foolish love and rewarded them for being faithful.

Oh Lord of the sky, snow, and wind, let our love for You be foolish.

Discussion Starters:

1. What was so amazing about the men's love for their paralyzed friend?
2. What are you willing to do to see your friends come to Jesus?

Lifeline:

Have each person write down the name of one pre-Christian friend. Then pray for those friends, and think of one way to show Jesus' love to them.

THE RIGHT-HANDED MAN

"On another Sabbath He entered the synagogue and was teaching; and there was a man there whose right hand was withered."

⌒ Luke 6:6

Doctors notice things. You can go see them for a sprained ankle and leave with allergy medicine. They spend about 10 minutes checking you and about 15 minutes asking you questions. Doctors are thorough. They don't want to miss anything.

Luke was a doctor. More than any other New Testament writer, he chronicled the details of disease. Men with withered right hands in other gospels might as well have taken a number and stood in line for sympathy. (Notice that the books of Matthew and Mark don't note which hand was deformed as Luke does.) But Doctor Luke eyed the patient and said, "Aha! Now, that man's *right hand* is withered!"

Okay, so it's a minor detail. But if it was *your* hand being operated on, wouldn't you want the doctor to know the difference?

God notices the details of our lives even more. Nothing slips by the Great Physician. To God, I'm not just the man in Branson who's having a good or bad day. To Him, I'm Joe White, husband, father of four, financer of two college students, director of seven camps, manager of a thousand employees, zookeeper of countless pets, man prone to exhaustion...and coincidentally a right-handed, beloved member of His kingdom.

God knows what makes us happy and why we get miffed. We can't do anything, say anything, or think anything without His knowledge (see Psalm 139). Growing up is often tough. Sometimes we can't even comprehend ourselves. But God can, and when you pray to Him, He'll understand what you need—even before you ask.

That thought is comforting to me. It makes me happy to know that some day when God calls me up from the dugout, He'll know which side of the plate I like to bat on.

Discussion Starters:

1. What things would you like to be known for in your family? Why?

2. How can it change your prayer life to realize that God knows about all your needs?

3. What does it do for your self-esteem to know that God cares about the details of your life?

Lifeline:

Take some time to praise one significant characteristic of another family member.

TWO HEARTS?

" 'The good man out of the good treasure of his heart brings forth what is good; and the evil man out of the evil treasure brings forth what is evil; for his mouth speaks from that which fills his heart.' "

↬ Luke 6:45

Pay attention and read closely, 'cause I'm going to tell you something you probably didn't hear in biology class.... Did you know you have two hearts? You do! Your first heart pumps blood. If it quits, your body dies. But the "heart" the Bible talks about the most is your personality, your spirit. If it quits, your soul dies.

Your heart reflects who you are, what your character is. It's your decision-making, emotional side. If your heart and thoughts are centered on Christ, your actions and words will reveal Him living in you. If your heart is focused on junk, your actions and words will show it, too. Make no mistake about it: Every TV show, movie, magazine, and CD you see and hear programs your heart. Even the kinds of friends you associate with will have a deep impact on you.

Ally, a young friend of mine, tells me that she stopped buying fashion magazines at the grocery store last year. "I used to spend hours reading them," she says, "but then I realized that I always felt bad about myself afterward. I thought my clothes were too ugly and my body was too fat. I got so obsessed with myself, I couldn't even focus on God."

The kind of stuff you put in your heart will determine who you become.

If you feed your body only junk food and candy, you'll eventually get sick. Your hair will lose its shine, your teeth will rot, and you'll get tired more quickly. The same principle applies to your heart. If you feed it rotten entertainment and expose it to friends who are bad influences, your heart will get spiritually sick.

Take some time to evaluate whether your heart is getting enough spiritual nourishment. It's important—what you put in it will either draw you close to God or take you far from Him.

Discussion Starters:

1. How well is your heart getting fed these days? Explain.
2. Why is it so important to consider what you put in your heart?
3. Why does the Bible talk so much about the heart?

Lifeline:

Evaluate whether your hearts are getting enough spiritual nourishment.

LONG-DISTANCE LOVE

"And a centurion's slave, who was highly regarded by him, was sick and about to die. When he heard about Jesus, he sent some Jewish elders asking Him to come and save the life of his slave.... Now Jesus started on His way with them; and when He was not far from the house, the centurion sent friends, saying to Him, 'Lord, do not trouble Yourself further, for I am not worthy for You to come under my roof; for this reason I did not even consider myself worthy to come to You, but just say the word, and my servant will be healed.' ...Now when Jesus heard this, He marveled at him, and turned and said to the crowd that was following Him, 'I say to you, not even in Israel have I found such great faith.'"

⌒ Luke 7:2-3,6-7,9

Every year at Christmastime, Will and Cindy save all their Christmas cards and put them in a basket. They keep the basket on a shelf next to the dining room table, and each night at dinner, they select a card and pray for the person or people who sent it.

"Dear God, help Johnny in his dental practice in Oregon."

"Lord, comfort Ted and Ginger as they make their move from Boise."

It didn't take too long for word to get out concerning Will and Cindy's basket. Now people send them Christmas cards throughout the year just so they can be on the prayer list.

Do you see what's happened here?

Prayer is effective whether it is long distance or as close as a touch. Jesus prayed for people no matter where they were, and the results were amazing! Jesus didn't even have to touch the centurion's slave to heal him. The Lord just prayed for him—long distance (see verse 10).

Prayer is powerful. One July, Will was sent another Christmas card. It was in the heat of summer, when all us Ozark people are nothing more than muffins in an oven. Will opened the letter and read, "Just praying that God relieves you of this heat. Love, Todd—in cool Colorado." Will told me that at that moment, a breeze blew across his face. And he said he may be mistaken, but he thought he could smell just a hint of pine in it.

Prayer across the plains. It's long-distance love, and it works!

Discussion Starters:

1. Why did the centurion's faith get results?

2. When and how has Jesus most powerfully answered your prayers?

Lifeline:

Make a family prayer basket and lift your friends and relatives up in prayer.

MOVE OVER, SAINT MARY

"When the men came to Him, they said, 'John the Baptist has sent us to You to ask, "Are You the Expected One, or do we look for someone else?"' At that very time He cured many people of diseases and afflictions and evil spirits; and He gave sight to many who were blind. And He answered,...'Go and report to John what you have seen and heard: the blind receive sight, the lame walk, the lepers are cleansed, and the deaf hear, the dead are raised up, the poor have the gospel preached to them. Blessed is he who does not take offense at Me.'"

↜ Luke 7:20-23

My friend Dave, a youth pastor, pulled into the gas station for one last stop. "We're going to St. Mary's glacier," Dave informed the attendant. "I don't need a map. I've been there a half dozen times before."

He paid up, hopped back in the van—which carried a dozen teenagers—and drove on. Confident of the direction he was heading, Dave parked and led his group up the mountainside. They were pumped. In July, there's no better place to go snow sledding than St. Mary's. But it's not great for hiking, and the heat that day was brutal. After three hours of hiking to find the glacier, the teens demanded an explanation.

"Dave! I thought we were gonna go sledding!" one boy complained.

"Where's the snow, Dave?" said another. "You need snow to sled."

Dave turned red and defensive. "I'm sure we came the right way. It's got to be here," he insisted.

"Look!" said a girl in the back of the crowd. She pointed way below to a tiny patch of white on a distant ridge. Dave's heart sank as he realized his mistake. He covered his head as the mob dog-piled on him.

Fortunately, Dave and his group found other snow that day and ended up having a blast. But after hearing Dave's story, I couldn't help but wonder, *How could a youth leader miss something as big as a glacier?*

In the same way, how can we as Christians fail to recognize our Lord? We often look right past Jesus, the most important Person in our lives. We can't identify His voice. Or His direction. Or His love. We say we know Him, and then we don't notice Him and His work in our lives.

Can you recognize Jesus in your daily experiences, or do you constantly stumble over Him?

Discussion Starters:

1. Why was John anxious to confirm Jesus' identity?
2. What do you think Jesus meant in verse 23?

Lifeline:

What things has God been doing in your life that you might have missed?

93

TUNING OUT

"When a large crowd was coming together, and those from the various cities were journeying to Him, He spoke by way of a parable.... As He said these things, He would call out, 'He who has ears to hear, let him hear.' His disciples began questioning Him as to what this parable meant. And He said, 'To you it has been granted to know the mysteries of the kingdom of God, but to the rest it is in parables, so that seeing they may not see, and hearing they may not understand.'"

⟿ Luke 8:4;8-10

As a young man, Arthur was devastated when a short stint of navy navigation ruined his hearing. Eventually he grew bitter. Often, he cursed the cannons that had blasted him into near silence. He'd never again hear a bluebird, a tractor, or the sounds of farm life without his hearing aids. In time, though, Arthur grew to love his hearing aids because he found power in them.

Slowly, Arthur began to abuse that power. If Martha, his wife of 43 years, wanted him to help can fruit, he'd simply turn the dial down on his hearing aids and tune her out. If she needed eggs fetched, he'd casually reach behind his ear, pretend to scratch his head, and *presto!* Martha was gone. If Arthur didn't feel the urge to help that day, well, the dial was always close at hand. But Martha wasn't fooled.

Fortunately for Arthur and his marriage, his ways came to a smoking halt one hot August night. Martha had just asked Arthur to help with the dishes when she heard sirens. She looked out the kitchen window and saw an ominous glow. Martha looked at Arthur in his easy chair, acting oblivious to her request. Casually, she walked over to him and knelt down.

"Arthur?" she said, mouthing the words without a sound.

Arthur turned his volume up just a hair.

"Arthur?" she mouthed again.

When she finally got his full attention, Arthur's eyes grew round and wild. That's because Martha leaned close to her husband's cheek and shouted, "In case you're interested, Arthur, *the barn is on fire!*"

"He who has ears to hear, let him hear!"

Discussion Starters:

1. What did Jesus mean when He said, "Seeing they may not see, and hearing they may not understand" (verse 10)?

2. Is God trying to tell you something? If so, what?

3. How do you tune Him out? How do you tune others out?

Lifeline:

How can you as a family help each other better listen to God?

A TIME FOR MUSIC

"But as He went, the crowds were pressing against Him. And a woman who had a hemorrhage for twelve years, and could not be healed by anyone, came up behind Him and touched the fringe of His cloak, and immediately her hemorrhage stopped. And Jesus said, 'Who is the one who touched Me?' ...When the woman saw that she had not escaped notice, she came trembling and fell down before Him, and declared in the presence of all the people the reason why she had touched Him, and how she had been immediately healed. And He said to her, 'Daughter, your faith has made you well; go in peace.'"

↤ Luke 8:42-45,47-48

Often, as in today's passage of Scripture, God's timing surprises us. A man named Winn would tell you he certainly found that to be true.

Winn's guitar was his prized possession. He loved it more than anything—except his wife, Sarah. One August, the insurance premium came due on Sarah's Corvette. For days, Winn prayed to find money to pay the debt, but nothing came. Winn dreaded Sarah's inevitable solution.

"You know, Winn," Sarah said one morning, "we *could* sell your guitar to pay the bill." She waited nervously for Winn's response.

Winn fought it, but he knew Sarah was right. They sold the guitar and settled the account. And something wonderful happened that winter. When the music died, Winn's obsession with his talent faded, too.

In the spring, Sarah's Corvette was pummeled by a hailstorm. The insurance check soon arrived in the mail. But rather than fix her car, Sarah took the check to a guitar shop and bought Winn the best guitar there.

"I believe God says the time has come again for music in our home," Sarah told a beaming Winn when he asked her why she'd done it.

As Winn found, God's timing is unexpected.

I'll bet the hemorrhaging woman would agree. She'd been bleeding for 12 years, but as soon as she touched Jesus, *poof!* her illness was gone.

Why didn't He heal her before? we might wonder.

We don't know the answer. But we do know the Lord always has a plan and a reason for His ways—and His timing is perfect.

Discussion Starters:

1. At first, what did you think of God's timing with the hemorrhaging woman? How did everything work out for the best?

2. How do you usually respond to "lousy timing" in your life?

Lifeline:

Pray the Lord's Prayer together. When you reach the part about "Thy will be done," consider what this means concerning His timing in your life.

BIG THINGS ... SMALL PACKAGES

"An argument started among them as to which of them might be the greatest. But Jesus, knowing what they were thinking in their heart, took a child and stood him by His side, and said to them, 'Whoever receives this child in My name receives Me, and whoever receives Me receives Him who sent Me; for the one who is least among all of you, this is the one who is great.'"

↜ Luke 9:46-48

Lyle is some rascal! He once talked a friend of mine, Bill, into getting on a bull. Now, Lyle must have done some smooth talking because Bill had never ridden anything fiercer than a 10-speed. Nonetheless, Bill stood in the arena and watched as Lyle brought the animals out, stampin', snortin', and starin' at Bill as if they'd like to stomp out his tastebuds.

"Dear God," Bill prayed in a whisper, "don't let that one with the broken horn be mine. And that one in the middle looks like he could cough up bigger things than me."

Then Lyle called for a little, tiny bull way back in the corner of the holding pens. He chuckled to himself as the animal was brought forward.

"This one oughta do it," said Lyle as Bill climbed aboard. "Oughta be just your size. Puny little cow like that can't be too hard to ride."

"Don't they come any larger than this?" spouted Bill, relieved enough now to poke fun at the beast.

"Sometimes big things come in small packages," said Lyle, smiling.

Six seconds later, Bill was on his back, picking mud from his teeth. The bull, Thunderbolt, star of the movie *My Heroes Have Always Been Cowboys,* snorted once and trotted back to the pen.

"Why don't *small* things ever come in small packages?" Bill groaned.

I think Jesus would've gotten a chuckle out of Bill's story. Like Bill, His disciples also had a hard time believing those who were small and unassuming—"the least of these"—could be great. Jesus had to bring over a little child so the disciples would get it. Bill had to be thrown from a puny bull. But the point was made: Those who appear weak or small are often the strongest and greatest—both in the bullring and in the kingdom of God.

Discussion Starters:

1. Why were the disciples arguing over who was greatest among them?
2. What types of things do you argue about in your family?
3. What did Jesus mean by saying, "Whoever is least among you is the greatest" (see verse 48)?

Lifeline:

Discuss what things make a person "great" in your family.

REVENGE OF THE FLATTENED PARAKEET

"And a lawyer stood up and put Him to the test, saying, 'Teacher, what shall I do to inherit eternal life?' And He said to him, 'What is written in the Law? How does it read to you?' And he answered, 'You shall love the Lord your God with all your heart, and with all your soul, and with all your strength, and with all your mind; and your neighbor as yourself.'"

⇝ Luke 10:25-27

Ty knew and understood the Golden Rule. But he chose to ignore it when it came to practical jokes—especially when his friends were getting married. It seems Ty had played one too many wedding tricks on pals who preceded him in matrimony...and maturity. Ty had done it all: Written "Save me" in white polish on the bottoms of the bridegroom's shoes (for the congregation to read when the couple knelt at the altar). Fired cap guns during solemn vows. Stuck a melted candy bar down the bridegroom's pants while the couple kissed. The list goes on and on.

So when Ty's turn came to tie the knot, the masses were ready to retaliate. On the morning of his wedding, his friends "did unto him as he had done unto them" and pretended to throw him a handyman shower. "You shouldn't have," said Ty to his grinning groomsmen. In the end, he wished they wouldn't have. Instead of tools, Ty got some interesting pets. Here's a short list of the gifts he opened that day: a rabbit, a squirrel, a cat, and a mouse. All of them stiff. And from the best man, Ty got a paper-thin parakeet, too flat to hold a tune.

Now, I don't mean to imply that practical jokes are sinful. My point in telling you this story is simply this: Love other people the way you want to be loved. If you don't want your sister to read your diary, stop prying the lock off hers. If you don't want people to gossip about you, stop broadcasting your friends' stories to the entire school. If you want to be heard, listen to what others say and don't interrupt them.

What you do for others is as powerful as what you don't do. If you want to successfully follow God's greatest commandment, decide how you want your family and friends to treat you and love them that way first.

Discussion Starters:

1. There are active and inactive components of God's command. In other words, proper love involves doing and not doing. Give examples of both.

2. Who is your neighbor?

3. Name one thing you do to others that you wouldn't want done to you.

Lifeline:

Keep one another accountable for changing the way you treat others.

BEEF JERKY FROM HEAVEN

"Jesus replied and said, 'A man was going down from Jerusalem to Jericho, and fell among robbers, and they stripped him and beat him, and went away leaving him half dead.... [A priest and a Levite passed the man by without helping him.] But a Samaritan ... felt compassion, and came to him and bandaged up his wounds, pouring oil and wine on them; and he put him on his own beast, and brought him to an inn and took care of him.... Which of these three do you think proved to be a neighbor to the man who fell into the robbers' hands?' And he said, 'The one who showed mercy toward him.' Then Jesus said to him, 'Go and do the same.'"

↪ Luke 10:30,33-34,36-37

It was raining when Dennis slowed to pick up the old hitchhiker on I-35 (though picking up hitchhikers is not usually a good idea).

"Wow, Den! He's dirty as tar," said a buddy as they drew near. "What if he pulls something funny? Let's go—I'm starving. I'd kill for some jerky."

Dennis listened but still braked his Buick to a halt. The man raced to catch his ride. Inside the car, Dennis's friends jeered at the spectacle. "Wouldn't it be funny to burn rubber right when he got to the door?"

"Yeah! Yeah! Fling gravel everywhere. C'mon, Den, we're hungry. This geezer will probably want us to drive clear across the state."

"Shhh," Dennis said. The door opened, the backseat got quiet, and a handsome old man climbed inside, wringing wet and very grateful.

"Lawd, it's a soggy day in paradise," said the man, offering something to the guys. "Any you boys want a piece o' jerky?"

"Yes, sir," said Dennis. "We were just saying how nice that'd be. Weren't we, guys?" Dennis grinned and looked at his red-faced friends. Then he got back on the road and took the man as far as he needed to go.

As Dennis discovered, it's difficult to be a "good Samaritan." It takes time, patience, and sometimes money. It also takes guts. Your friends might laugh at you or even snub you. Other people won't understand. But Jesus calls us to show mercy to others, regardless of how dirty, poor, and unattractive they are; regardless of how little time or money you have.

How can you be a good Samaritan today?

Discussion Starters:

1. Why didn't the "holy men" help the man in Luke 10:30-37?

2. What compelled the Samaritan to help the man?

3. How can you serve others this week?

Lifeline:

Take 15 minutes of your time today or tomorrow to help someone.

"GODDA SKRATE"

"It happened that while Jesus was praying in a certain place, after He had finished, one of His disciples said to Him, 'Lord, teach us to pray just as John also taught his disciples.' And He said to them, 'When you pray, say: "Father, hallowed be Your name. Your kingdom come. Give us each day our daily bread. And forgive us our sins, for we ourselves also forgive everyone who is indebted to us. And lead us not into temptation."'"

↪ Luke 11:1-4

Do you ever wonder if God laughs when kids pray? I think He might. After all, some of what they say is pretty funny. One father told me of a conversation he had with his five-year-old, Ashley, the other day.

"Dad?" Ashley asked.

"Yeah, pumpkin?"

"Who's Howard?"

"Howard who?"

"Daaad! You know...the Howard-be-Thy-name Howard. That's who."

See what I mean? Some of this stuff is stand-up material. How could God *not* laugh?

Ed told me of the prayer his nephew Timmy prayed during the debate over abortion laws in the beginning of Bill Clinton's presidency.

"Dear God," Timmy said, "thank You for this day. Thank You for Mommy and Daddy and Uncle Jim and Aunt Carolyn and all my friends at school. And God, please...please don't let Bill Clinton get an abortion."

Okay. That one probably brings a tear as well as a smile. At any rate, here's the point: "Godda skrate" and "Godda skood" (that's five-year-old talk for "God is great" and "God is good"), no matter how anyone prays it.

It doesn't matter so much what your prayers sound like.... God cares more about having you come to Him honestly and regularly, with love and honor. And He always hears you.

Have you come to Him lately?

Discussion Starters:

1. The disciples had probably prayed all their lives. So why did they suddenly come to Jesus, asking Him to teach them how to pray?

2. Some say the Lord's Prayer is a how-to model. What does it teach us about the practice of prayer?

3. Why does God want His people to pray?

Lifeline:

Set aside a time each day to pray together individually and/or as a family.

MORE LIGHT!

" 'The eye is the lamp of your body; when your eye is clear, your whole body also is full of light; but when it is bad, your body also is full of darkness. Then watch out that the light in you is not darkness. If therefore your whole body is full of light, with no dark part in it, it will be wholly illumined, as when the lamp illumines you with its rays.' "

↪ Luke 11:34-36

Lots of kids run away at least once in their lives. Bonnie did when she was eight. From her point of view, the problem started with spinach.

"I'm not gonna eat it!" said Bonnie.

"You most certainly are!" her mother stated.

"I'll run away if you make me!"

"I'll help you pack," said Bonnie's father. And up the stairs they went to find the suitcase. Ten minutes later, Bonnie's parents continued their reverse psychology at the front door.

"It might be kind of scary out there," Bonnie's father warned. "And it's cold and dark. But if you've got to go, you've got to go."

"I'm not afraid!" said Bonnie, hungry for independence but not for spinach. With suitcase in hand, she crept to the edge of the porch, stopping where the light from inside the house ended.

"I want more light!" she demanded.

Her father switched on the porch lamp, and Bonnie ventured out into the yard, where once again the light melted into the shadows.

"More light!" she said again.

"That's all there is," said Bonnie's father.

For a brief moment, Bonnie considered the darkness. Then she shrugged her shoulders, came back inside, and ate her spinach—cold.

Like Bonnie, we should also be leery of the darkness—spiritual darkness. That kind of darkness will blot out God's light and lead us in the wrong direction. Next time you encounter spiritual darkness, turn the other way and walk back, as Bonnie did, toward the light.

You'll be glad you did.

Discussion Starters:

1. What is spiritual darkness?

2. How can this darkness enter a person or a family?

3. How can we get rid of darkness and bring more light to our lives?

Lifeline:

Does your family have "cracks" that allow darkness to creep in? If so, what are they? How can you plug up those cracks?

TREASURES

"Then He said to them, 'Beware, and be on your guard against every form of greed; for not even when one has an abundance does his life consist of his possessions.' And He told them a parable, saying, 'The land of a rich man was very productive. . . . [And the man said to his soul], "Soul, you have many goods laid up for many years to come; take your ease, eat, drink and be merry." But God said to him, "You fool! This very night your soul is required of you; and now who will own what you have prepared?" So is the man who stores up treasure for himself, and is not rich toward God.'"

↩ Luke 12:15-16,19-21

In our Ozark mountain hometown each Friday night, our friends and neighbors pack the grandstands like sardines in a tin can to cheer wildly for the heroes of the gridiron (that's hard-core football talk for "football field"), the Branson Pirates. My son, for better or for worse, is an outside linebacker who would rather run into a stadium wall than open his English book. He tells me the loud and rather obnoxious football crowd gives him tremendous energy that he discharges with every leather-cracking tackle.

I love watching my son play. But I'm still a little puzzled by his team name. People cheering for the *Pirates*? It seems odd to scream and yell for a name that represents a team of thieves, murderers, and rebels.

Pirates were greedy guys. Those swashbucklers were known to do anything to get treasure. They blew up and raided ships, robbed people blind, and invaded homes to obtain and hoard their fortunes. Gold, jewelry, diamonds, silver, rubies, and pearls filled their chests of sordid gain.

We desire treasures, too. A lot of us place too much value on popularity, athletic skill, sex appeal, fast cars, trendy clothes, or money.

Jesus said, "Where your treasure is, there your heart will be also" (Luke 12:34). If anything is more important to us than God, it's a problem. If you're unwilling to talk about Jesus with others, that's a problem. If you think about something other than Him too much or it becomes a source of pride, it's a problem.

Store your treasures in heaven. That's where you'll find real wealth.

Discussion Starters:

1. According to the parable, what is the definition of greed? Can a person be financially wealthy but not greedy? Explain.

2. What does it mean to be "rich toward God"?

Lifeline:

Decide upon the richest couple you know—people who seem to be "rich toward God." Then invite them over for dinner and ask what their secret is.

ON CAT'S FEET

"'Be like men who are waiting for their master when he returns from the wedding feast, so that they may immediately open the door to him when he comes and knocks.... You too, be ready; for the Son of Man is coming at an hour that you do not expect.... The master of [a disobedient] slave will come on a day when he does not expect him and at an hour he does not know, and will cut him in pieces, and assign him a place with the unbelievers.... Be dressed in readiness, and keep your lamps lit.'"

↪ Luke 12:36,40,46,35

Catherine was a tenured, experienced schoolteacher—until she had her own kids. Now she's a stay-at-home mom. Her kids sure don't get away with anything, though. Catherine already knows every trick in the book.

Most teachers are like that—goof-proof, eagle-eyed, always waiting for trouble to materialize, and hoping to catch students causing problems. Catherine was *exactly* like that. She told me a story that proves my point.

"Edward, one of my students, was a good kid," she assured me. "But he had a sweet tooth that made him a thief."

Every day when Catherine went to turn in attendance, Edward would sneak to the top drawer of her desk, steal her breath mints, and pass them out to the class. Then, somehow he'd always hear her and be back at his desk before she discovered him.

"I finally caught him red-handed one day," Catherine told me. "You should've seen his face."

"How'd you do it?" I asked. "Didn't he hear you coming?"

"It was nothing special," she said, smiling. "I just took off my shoes."

Edward got lazy and overly confident. He took it for granted that he'd be able to detect his teacher's footsteps. And he was caught unawares.

Jesus similarly warns us to be ready for His return. We won't hear footsteps, and we don't know when He's coming back, so we'd better live all the time in a way that glorifies Him—and not just when we think someone's looking.

Our souls are too important to play games with the Teacher.

Discussion Starters:

1. Why do you suppose people do bad things while Jesus is away?

2. Is it possible to do good in His absence—for the wrong reasons? Why?

3. If you knew Jesus were coming back tomorrow, would you live differently? If so, how?

Lifeline:

Determine as a family to live every day as if He's returning tomorrow.

HAIL TO THE BAND-AID

"And there was a woman who for eighteen years had had a sickness caused by a spirit; and she was bent double, and could not straighten up at all. When Jesus saw her, He called her over and said to her, 'Woman, you are freed from your sickness.' And He laid His hands on her; and immediately she was made erect again and began glorifying God."

⟿ Luke 13:11-13

Band-Aids fascinate me. They do! I mean, who could have guessed that Band-Aids would end up being so important, effective, and necessary? Since Earl Dickson invented the first Band-Aid in 1921, millions of people have used them. I know—I've used them countless times on myself and my kids. Even now, a tiny bandage stares at me from my index finger. The funny thing is, I've forgotten why it's there.

But looking at it reminds me of how often we take healing for granted.

I read recently that initial sales of the Band-Aid were so low the product was almost canceled.[1] Isn't it odd how sometimes we reject the things that are intended for our own good?

Jesus understands such rejection. His healing was severely criticized (see Luke 13:14-17). You would think that healing someone who had been sick for 18 *years* would have caused the people to throw Jesus a party, close down the town, and celebrate the miracle. But the synagogue official got legalistic on Jesus. He didn't care that the woman was healed from a life of pain.

We often take the Lord's healing for granted, too—even His spiritual healing. Why don't we tell our friends and fellow church members when God has released us from a sinful habit? Why don't we proclaim it from the rooftops when Christ heals our hearts and eases our suffering?

And why don't we ask Him for healing more often? God is still as powerful as He was in biblical times. He *can* heal your heart and body.

Fortunately, the story will change some day. Men and women will reach for the Savior. People will bring their hurts to God. Jesus will bind up every wound and dry every tear (see Revelation 21). And all of heaven will say thank You to the great and glorious Healer.

Discussion Starters:

1. Why did the synagogue official in verse 14 respond the way he did?

2. How did the woman respond to her own healing?

3. Tell about a time when you've seen God heal.

Lifeline:

Develop the habit of praying for family and friends who are sick. Then watch for God to work.

A TIGHT SPOT

"'Strive to enter through the narrow door; for many, I tell you, will seek to enter and will not be able.'"

Near Cricket Creek in southwest Missouri is a mud cave. It's full of thick, red, sloppy mud—the kind that never, ever comes out of your mother's carpet if you're unfortunate enough to bring it in on your shoes.

In that cave, there's a narrow tunnel that leads from one room to the next—"the birth canal." It's about the size of a chubby sixth grader.

A long time ago (when I was in sixth grade myself), some friends and I explored that mud cave. Harry, one of the boys, thought he was a real explorer. He entered the cave, bragging loudly to the other guys about his earlier adventures in other caves.

"This cave ain't nothin'," Harry boasted, walking behind me. "I'm bored. The other caves were tons better. I hope we meet a bobcat or a bear or a badger or somethin'. Did I tell you I fought off a snake the last time I went cavin'?—" He stopped, his eyes wide.

We had just reached the birth canal. Embarrassed, Harry knew it'd be no picnic trying to squeeze himself through that tunnel. Well, we pulled while Harry squawked, squirmed, and rearranged himself. When we were done, a more humble Harry came out of the birth canal. And that was the last we heard about Harry's more exciting, previous adventures.

I like to tell that story because it makes me think about the way we become born again as Christians. When Jesus said the path to eternal life is through the narrow door, He wasn't kidding. Sometimes it's a little painful, kind of a tight squeeze. Some people want to go an easier way and try to get around it, but there's only one correct route.

In the cave, to get from one room to the other, you have to go through the birth canal. In life, to get from death to eternal salvation, you must enter through the narrow door—and the only way to do that is to accept Jesus Christ as your Lord and Savior.

Discussion Starters:

1. What is the "narrow door" that Jesus spoke of in verse 24?
2. How do you enter through that door?
3. Have you walked through that door yet? If so, when? If you haven't, why not?

Lifeline:

How can your family introduce people to Christ? What steps will each family member take to follow through on doing that?

THEY'LL BE WATCHING YOU

"It happened that when He went into the house of one of the leaders of the Pharisees on the Sabbath to eat bread, they were watching Him closely."

⤸ Luke 14:1

Mother Teresa once said, "Witness always. Use words when necessary."

Did you know you can be an evangelist for Christ without ever opening your mouth? It's true. Why? Because people who don't know Christ are more likely to notice His love when they see it *demonstrated*.

Every day I look around and see people showing God's love through their actions. I see staff workers at Kanakuk tying little boys' shoes and making them laugh. I see friends drying friends' tears, teenagers taking the time to smile at and greet the elderly, and parents leaving work early to see their kids' games and recitals. Those acts of kindness are remembered because love is powerful. Loving people through your actions melts boundaries, brings forgiveness, builds trust and credibility, and reveals Jesus Christ.

Like it or not, the unbelieving world is watching you closely. They see your bowed head in restaurants, your breaking of bread with others, your joyful conversation and encouragement, your hugs and handshakes, your extra-large tip for the worn-out waitress. They'll call you a hypocrite if you cut people off on the road or roll your eyes at the slow cashier in the grocery store. If your actions don't line up with what you profess, if you aren't consistent, your words will be meaningless.

If you love Jesus, you must be accountable for your actions. It's not always easy to live as a witness for Christ, but it's important. Your loving actions could cause someone to desire a relationship with the most loving One of all—Jesus.

Discussion Starters:

1. What can you do at work, school, or home to be a witness for Christ?

2. Have you ever damaged your witness by something you've done? How can you resolve this?

3. What's the difference between loving others through our actions and trying to be saved by our works?

4. The spoken message is important, too. When and how should words be used in expressing our faith?

Lifeline:

Discuss together how each one of you will aim to show Christ's love. Then during your next devotional time, describe your results.

THE FATTENED RUFFLES BAG

"And He said, 'A man had two sons. The younger of them said to his father, "Father, give me the share of the estate that falls to me." ...And not many days later, the younger son gathered everything together and went on a journey into a distant country, and there he squandered his estate with loose living. Now when he had spent everything...he began to be impoverished.... So he got up and came to his father.... And the son said to him, "Father, I have sinned against heaven and in your sight; I am no longer worthy to be called your son." But the father said to his slaves,..."Bring the fattened calf, kill it, and let us eat and celebrate; for this son of mine was dead and has come to life again; he was lost and has been found."'"

↝ Luke 15:11-14,20-24

The problem with prodigals today is that none of them want to leave. They want their inheritance, and they want to keep their bedroom, too. They want all the benefits of the "distant country" (their independence) right there in the den—with the TV, the CD player, and a big bowl of potato chips to fill their stomachs. They want cash, no curfews, and maid service.

Parents of these prodigals contribute to the problem. They're not like the father in Jesus' parable who let his son walk away so he'd grow up. Today's parents sigh and fill the potato chip bowl again. They nag, scold, and plead for change. But they don't draw any lines. And in failing to do so, they don't prepare their kids for the distant country of adulthood.

Friends of mine recently told their prodigal, Sherry, to "hit the road." When Sherry smirked at them, they sent her out, duffel bag in hand, with no clue where to go. She went to the library and lasted about 12 hours.

Sherry returned that night with a humble attitude; a smile instead of a smirk; and a "sir," a "ma'am," and a "please." She realized that the life of a prodigal is not all it's cracked up to be.

"Praise God!" said her parents. "Our daughter has come home! Quick! Go fetch the fattened Ruffles bag." And they celebrated long into the night.

Discussion Starters:

1. Why do today's prodigals hang around instead of leaving?

2. How can parents prepare their kids for the distant country of adult life?

3. Why are rules and discipline important?

Lifeline:

Ultimately, every child must move away from home. Use this story as an opportunity to talk about what skills kids need to learn for adulthood.

BIG BROTHER IS WATCHING YOU

"'Now his older son was in the field, and when he came and approached the house, he heard music and dancing…. He became angry and was not willing to go in; and his father came out and began pleading with him. But he answered and said to his father, "Look! For so many years I have been serving you and I have never neglected a command of yours; and yet you have never given me a young goat, so that I might celebrate with my friends; but when this son of yours came, who has devoured your wealth with prostitutes, you killed the fattened calf for him."'"

⮌ Luke 15:25,28-30

On a beautiful stretch of land near my midwestern hometown, the Brown brothers battle a constant war with one another. Both are wealthy. Both live in fabulous mansions. It seems they should both be happy. But they aren't. Why? Because neither brother wants the other to be happy.

The older brother, Jim, built his house first. It was huge, with wall-length windows and a fountain in front. But soon after, the younger brother, Joe, struck it rich and built an even bigger—and more lavish— home. Jim added a wing to his house; Joe put a pool in the backyard. Jim poured a tennis court; Joe installed a top-of-the-line entertainment system.

This game Jim and Joe play has gone on for years. It's all very entertaining to the neighbors. But I can't recall even a single time when I've driven by and seen either one of them enjoying all that "stuff."

The prodigal's brother also struggled with being competitive. He couldn't look past himself to rejoice in his sibling's warm welcome. He thought he deserved much more than his wayward brother.

We are all like the prodigal son who ran from his father, but we are also like his older brother. We, too, struggle with envy and bitterness. I challenge you to release your jealousy and give it to God. When you do, I can guarantee that it won't matter as much who's wearing what or which neighbor has more money. By His grace, God will enable you to become more content with what you have.

Discussion Starters:

1. Why was the brother's response (in Jesus' parable) so sad?
2. How are you most like that older brother?
3. We're never told, but what do you think might have become of the older brother? Why?

Lifeline:

Rather than focus on what you don't have, be thankful for God's blessings. Write a list together of the things for which your family is most grateful.

IT'S THE LITTLE THINGS
THAT MAKE THE DIFFERENCE

"'He who is faithful in a very little thing is faithful also in much; and he who is unrighteous in a very little thing is unrighteous also in much. Therefore if you have not been faithful in the use of unrighteous wealth, who will entrust the true riches to you? And if you have not been faithful in the use of that which is another's, who will give you that which is your own?.'"

✍ Luke 16:10-12

Before Joseph Lister pioneered sanitary operating conditions in the nineteenth century, as many as 90 percent of some hospitals' patients died after surgery. When he first presented his views on germs, Lister's fellow doctors laughed at him.[2]

"You're kidding," they scoffed. "Germs are too tiny to cause infection!"

But Lister remained faithful to his theories. He pressed on, telling anyone who would listen that "it's the little things that can make the difference." Soon surgeons began to employ his methods of cleanliness. Before long, they reported fewer infections and higher survival rates.

I believe that's how it works in life as well. When we pay attention to the seemingly trivial parts of our friendship with God—like tithing, praising Him, praying regularly, and studying His Word—the other things always seem to fall into place.

God wants to be Lord over your whole life. He wants you to follow Him through to the last detail. How you handle the small stuff reveals your character and shows how obedient you are to Him. That little white lie does matter to God. Taking that dollar from your friend is a big deal. Spending tithe money on new clothes *really* bothers God.

At the same time, the good things we do for Him—no matter how small—are significant, too. That kind word is noticed by Jesus. Your feeble prayers for your unsaved friend *always* matter. The offering you give from your small allowance is a lot to give.

Jesus made a good point when He said, "Why should I trust you with eternal things when I can't trust you with worldly details?" (see verse 11).

You can take a chance and ignore these little things if you want. But if you ask me, that's bad medicine.

Discussion Starters:

1. Can you think of a time when you were faithful with a "little" and the Lord entrusted you with "a lot" as a result? If so, what happened?

2. What will you do to be more faithful with the small things?

Lifeline:

What little things can you improve in your relationship with God?

SERVING IN GOD'S COURT

" 'Now the poor man died and was carried away by the angels to Abraham's bosom; and the rich man also died and was buried.' "

↪ Luke 16:22

A friend of mine promises this story is true. And since I trust my friend, I'll pass it on to you.

Carolyn and her seven-year-old daughter, Stephanie, were walking down a steep hill to a tennis court one early autumn evening. Suddenly, Carolyn caught her toe on the root of an elm and tumbled forward.

"Owww!" she exclaimed when she finally stopped. "I think I've broken my ankle."

Stephanie was too small to support her mother's weight and too young to find help alone, so the two of them huddled in the chilly evening and prayed for somebody to come along. As they prayed, they heard voices. They looked up and saw two men dressed for tennis, carrying rackets. When the men saw Carolyn, they rushed to her aid. One of them got Carolyn to an emergency room, while the other called her husband.

During the ride to the hospital, Carolyn learned from her rescuer that he and his friend belonged to her church's singles' group. But the next Sunday, when Carolyn tried to hunt them down for a proper "thank you," no one in the church seemed to know who she was talking about, which was rather unusual for a small-town church.

To this day, their identities remain a mystery to Carolyn.

Now, I know you can't believe everything you hear, but I do believe God works in strange ways—and maybe sometimes He uses angels. After all, the Bible is full of them. God sent angels to speak His messages to people (see Luke 1), to reveal things to people (see Genesis 31), and to protect and help people (see Matthew 4). Even today's Scripture mentions that an angel carried the poor man into heaven.

Hmmm. With what the Bible says about angels, I'm inclined to believe there were two angels, ready to play tennis that day, sent to help my friend Carolyn. I'll bet their game would've been an overhead smash.

Discussion Starters:

1. Jesus said He could call upon a multitude of angels to help Him (see Matthew 26). Do you think God uses them to protect us today? Explain.

2. Why wasn't God more specific about angels in the New Testament?

3. What do you know of angels? Who were some other angels in the Bible?

Lifeline:

Thank You, Lord, for sending Your angels to help us in times of need!

"49PLUS"

"'Be on your guard! If your brother sins, rebuke him; and if he repents, forgive him. And if he sins against you seven times a day, and returns to you seven times, saying, "I repent," forgive him.'"

↪ Luke 17:3-4

Jennifer loves deciphering license plates, so much so that she writes those clever logos down and keeps them in a scrapbook.

"4U2NV," "SAY-AHH," "2COOL4U," and "2CCME" (To see, see Me) are some of the good ones she has seen. But it's not easy to collect them. "It's dangerous business," she told me once after a particularly interesting run-in with another motorist.

Jennifer was driving to work one afternoon when she spotted a blue Volkswagen with the license plate "49PLUS." Speeding up to get a better look, she got a little too close. All of a sudden, *wham*! their bumpers met.

Oh, no! thought Jennifer. *How am I ever going to explain this*?

"Good morning," the other driver said calmly as he got out of his car. The man wore a bright smile even though all around them cars were beginning to honk.

"Look, mister, I'm really sorry," Jennifer began.

"Relax," the man said. "It's okay. I'm just glad nobody's hurt."

They traded insurance information, and when they parted, the man waved to Jennifer as she climbed back into her car.

Afterward, the incident—the message "49PLUS" and the man's kindness —kept playing through her mind. She couldn't get over the driver's attitude toward her, and his license plate added to the mystery. But the next morning during her devotions, Jennifer came across Luke 17:4 and clasped her hand over her mouth in surprise.

Jesus said we're to forgive others 49 times and more, she realized.

"49PLUS" wasn't just a snappy license plate message on the man's car. It was obviously his motto for living life.

Do you forgive others in the same way?

Discussion Starters:

1. Why is it so important for Christians to forgive others?

2. Why was Jesus the best person to talk to us about forgiveness?

3. What happens when people hold a grudge? How do they feel? How do others view them?

4. Are you holding a grudge? How can you release your resentment?

Lifeline:

If there's someone in the family you need to forgive—or ask forgiveness from—go to that person in private today and do it.

CAN YOU TAKE THE HEAT?

"'But on the day that Lot went out from Sodom it rained fire and brimstone from heaven and destroyed them all. It will be just the same on the day that the Son of Man is revealed.'"

⟿ Luke 17:29-30

Kyle and Sharon had saved a long time to build a house. When it was finally done, the place was beautiful—big, airy windows; rich wooden floors; French doors; and a big, long redwood deck that wrapped around the house. They'd been in it no more than six months when their son, Stephen, came in from the yard one day covered with seed ticks.

"Here," Sharon said, grabbing a rag. "Let me wipe those nasty things off you."

When she was finished, Sharon lit the rag on fire and let it burn until she was sure the ticks were gone. Then she stomped on the rag and threw it in the trash can, thinking the fire was out.

It wasn't.

A few minutes later, Sharon and Kyle smelled smoke. And it wasn't coming from the oven. Their dream home burst into flames, and the fire began to consume everything in sight. The heat was incredible.

They called me, and I helped battle the flames and move furniture until my skin was red, my hair was singed, and our efforts were halted by the danger at hand. In the end, it was a total loss.

Since then, Kyle and Sharon have rebuilt their home. Still, every time I drive down their road, I can't help but remember that devastating fire and the terror, pain, and loss it brought. As awful as it was, though, I believe that fire was only a glimpse of what hell will be like.

I know it's unpopular today to speak of fire and brimstone. I'm not comfortable with the way some preachers use it to scare folks, but I don't believe we should ignore it, either. Jesus talked about hell a lot. Obviously He thought it was important. Do you?

Discussion Starters:

1. Why do you think many people are reluctant to admit God will one day punish sin?

2. Hell is real, and sin is serious. What do *you* think about God's coming judgment of sin? Does it scare you? Will you be ready? Explain.

3. How can you convey the truth of God's judgment without sounding judgmental yourself?

Lifeline:

Together, thank God for His forgiveness and for saving you from hell.

BUGGING DADDY

"Now He was telling them a parable to show that at all times they ought to pray and not to lose heart.... [And God said,] 'Now, will not God bring about justice for His elect who cry to Him day and night, and will He delay long over them? I tell you that He will bring about justice for them quickly. However, when the Son of Man comes, will He find faith on the earth?'"

Luke 18:1,7-8

Kids have the gift of persistence. They know exactly how to wear down their parents until their folks buckle and give in.

My friend Will could tell you about that. One summer day, his three-year-old, Wesley, bugged him 47 times for a Coke.

"I was painting the bedroom when I heard the refrigerator door open," Will told me. "I knew something was up when I saw Wes coming down the hallway with his hands behind his back. He had deliberately disobeyed me. Believe me, when he saw the look in my eyes, he knew he was history. I was serious when I told him, 'No pop before dinner.'"

"And?" I asked.

"Well, the little guy thought fast," said Will. "He pulled that bottle of Coke from behind his back and said, 'Happy birthday, Daddy!' But I didn't let him get away with that. My birthday was still a month away.

"So," Will continued his story, "I took that Coke and started chugging, just to show him I meant business when I said no. But then—" Will cleared his throat, "—well, then he sorta gave me that cute grin of his and said, 'It's my birthday, too.'" Will looked sheepish. "So I gave him the last sip," he said, shrugging his shoulders.

Okay, Wesley was being devious. But he was persistent—he didn't give up, and eventually his dad granted his request.

Similarly, Jesus told us in Luke that we must be persistent with our heavenly Father. If you have a request, don't abruptly stop asking. God always hears your prayers. Have faith—your heavenly Father loves you more than your earthly father ever could. God *will* answer your prayers.

Just be persistent.

Discussion Starters:

1. Why does God want us to pray "at all times"?
2. Have you ever lost heart over a prayer request? When? How can you keep from getting discouraged in your prayer life?

Lifeline:

Pray persistently as a family for those requests that haven't been answered right away. Then wait and watch for God's hand to work.

GOOD DOGGIES

"A ruler questioned Him, saying, 'Good Teacher, what shall I do to inherit eternal life?' And Jesus said to him, 'Why do you call Me good? No one is good except God alone.'"

↪ Luke 18:18-19

Next time you hear someone calling his dog, listen to the choice of words. Often the person will say, "Here, Spot! Come here, Spot! Yeah. That's a good doggie!"

A "good" doggie? There's no such thing as a good doggie. Why, if I committed one-tenth of the crimes ol' Spot does on the neighbors' lawns, or stayed out all night, or jaywalked, or chewed a hole in my wife's favorite sweater, you'd be hard pressed to find somebody who'd call me "good."

Last Christmas, I visited a neighborhood manger scene, complete with hay, glittering angels, and kids dressed like wise men. It was peaceful. But in the midst of it all, I started thinking about the fact that we all need a Savior—even those cute kids. *I'm so thankful Jesus was born and came to die for our sins,* I thought. Just then, the "good" doggies of Kanakuk Hill arrived suddenly, disturbing the peace and interrupting my thoughts.

At least one dog in the 15-member gang was not in the Christmas spirit, because a nasty fight began. It took 10 minutes to separate the combatants and a good deal longer to calm the kids. When it was all over, I heard one dog owner who had the audacity to call his animal a "good doggie." *If good doggies ruin the neighborhood manger scene and cause a fight, I don't want to know what bad doggies do,* I thought, irritated.

Jesus was also careful in using the word *good.* When the ruler addressed Him as "good Teacher," Jesus pointed out that only God is good. He said, in effect, "You must know I'm God since you're calling me good. Everyone else is sinful."

It's easy to misuse the word. Often we'll say people are good if they stay out of trouble and are nice to be around. But no matter how good we think they are, they're still sinful inside—still in need of a Savior.

Discussion Starters:

1. At first glance, Jesus seemed to be disagreeing with the man's assessment of His "goodness." But what was His real point?

2. Why is it not enough to call Jesus a "good teacher"?

3. Don't misunderstand—many Christians are good people. But where does that goodness come from?

Lifeline:

Discuss the difference between believing Jesus is a "good teacher" and following Him as your "good Master."

THE STONES

"As soon as He was approaching, near the descent of the Mount of Olives, the whole crowd of the disciples began to praise God joyfully with a loud voice for all the miracles which they had seen, shouting: 'Blessed is the King who comes in the name of the Lord; peace in heaven and glory in the highest!' Some of the Pharisees in the crowd said to Him, 'Teacher, rebuke Your disciples.' But Jesus answered, 'I tell you, if these become silent, the stones will cry out!'"

⮑ Luke 19:37-40

If you haven't already noticed, cave exploring is one of my favorite things to do. And near Branson, Missouri, there is a cave worth visiting. The original concept behind Talking Rocks Cavern was this: Let the rocks speak for themselves, and the beauty of nature will tell its own story.

When the cave was first opened, you could press a button and listen to a deep, booming voice describe the world of stalactites and the influence of a trillion drops of water on a boulder. Now the tour is led by guides.

I miss the old days when you could hear the rocks talk.

Nature reveals God's awesome handiwork and power. With all we do, our work doesn't even come close to His. We construct buildings; God creates mountains. We build speedy cars; God pours fast-moving rivers. We paint pictures of flowers; God fills the earth with wildflower meadows.

God cares for all of His creation—especially for His people (see Matthew 6). But we've become, as C. S. Lewis stated, "the silent planet." We've become a largely praiseless people, afraid of vocal worship. How often do you say, "Lord, You've done a great job" or "You're amazing, God!"?

I think we usually get too caught up in what we've done and dismiss what God does for us. The Pharisees were like that. They didn't want swarms of people praising Jesus. But Jesus said that even if the Pharisees stopped the people from giving thanks to God, He would still be glorified through nature (see verse 40).

Fortunately, there will come a time when *all* of God's creation praises and glorifies Him. Until then, I challenge you to exercise those God-given vocal cords. Spiritual laryngitis is unhealthy for your soul.

Discussion Starters:

1. Why did the Pharisees want to silence the people's praise?

2. Have you ever been too timid to praise God? Why?

3. How can you be more vocal about your love for God?

Lifeline:

Read Psalm 33 together, then discuss one thing for which you can each thank God.

THE ROBBERY OF RELIGION

"Jesus entered the temple and began to drive out those who were selling, saying to them, 'It is written, "And My house shall be a house of prayer," but you have made it a robbers' den.' And He was teaching daily in the temple; but the chief priests and the scribes and the leading men among the people were trying to destroy Him."

↪ Luke 19:45-47

Until you've experienced it, you can't imagine what it's like to be robbed.

"It's shocking," a friend of mine said. "You come home expecting your house to be just as you left it. Instead, you find that someone snuck inside and threw your things all over the place. When you discover that some of your most prized possessions are missing—like a graduation ring or the tennis racket you used to win your high school state championship—well, it makes you just want to sit down and cry."

Robbery is like that. It takes away that for which someone has poured out sweat and effort. It takes without a second thought or even a backward glance at the trouble it has caused. It takes and walks away.

Legalistic religion is like that, too. It takes the free gift of salvation, for which Jesus poured out blood, and puts a price on it. It claims that grace isn't enough—that you have to work your way to heaven. Religion takes the peace of a believer and replaces that peace with guilt. It takes and walks away.

Rule-based religion made Jesus mad. He couldn't stand the legalistic Pharisees telling people (step by step) how they could be saved. He got furious when He saw the hypocrisy in the Jewish temple—so mad, in fact, that He grabbed a whip and drove the "robbers" out of His presence. Religion made Jesus angry because it robs people of intimacy with God. Fortunately, true Christianity, which focuses on having a relationship with the Lord, recovers the stolen goods.

And it's a relationship that can never be taken away.

Discussion Starters:

1. In biblical times, men sold sacrificial animals for an enormous price, right there in the temple. Why did this anger Jesus?

2. It's disturbing to see our Lord so angry. Yet what does this passage reveal about God's view of "religion" as opposed to a "relationship"?

3. Are there other times when anger is appropriate? When?

Lifeline:

When something is free, you might wonder if the product is inferior or damaged. How could this mentality affect your view of God's grace?

THE FLIP OF A COIN

"They questioned Him, saying, 'Teacher, we know that You speak and teach correctly, and You are not partial to any, but teach the way of God in truth. Is it lawful for us to pay taxes to Caesar, or not?' But He detected their trickery and said to them, 'Show me a denarius. Whose likeness and inscription does it have?' They said, 'Caesar's.' And He said to them, 'Then render to Caesar the things that are Caesar's, and to God the things that are God's.'"

↩ Luke 20:21-25

"Heads, you win. Tails, you lose."

Jesus grew up during a time when people believed major decisions should be made by the gods. Consequently, they devised tons of methods by which they could persuade the gods to give a definite yes or no.

That's how the coin toss got started.[3] With the flip of a silver piece, great tracts of land were bought, criminals were indicted, marriage partners were chosen, and crops were planted. The people revered the gods (and Julius Caesar, whose head appeared on all the money in the land) so much that they were willing to stake their futures on whichever way a coin landed in the sand.

So when the Pharisees asked Jesus whether it was lawful for them to give back to Caesar, their question was gun-barrel loaded.

Jesus didn't flinch, though. I love the way my Lord answered those weasels who tried to trick Him into making some negative statement about the law. He simply said, "By all means, pay the man! His head's on the coin, isn't it?" But then, with a little twist they hadn't counted on, Jesus said to them, "But whatever has God's picture on it belongs to God." In one swoop, Jesus affirmed both the government's leadership and God's authority.

I believe Jesus would offer the same advice to twentieth-century people. He'd say, "If you want to be good citizens, don't cheat on your taxes. And if you want to be on good terms with God, give to Him the things that bear His image—namely, your life, your soul, yourself."

Discussion Starters:

1. How were the Pharisees trying to manipulate Jesus?

2. What was Jesus' attitude toward authority? What is your attitude?

3. What does it mean to bear the image of God?

Lifeline:

Make a list of some leaders in your community. Then, as a family, decide how you can honor God's command to submit to those leaders and render the appropriate things back to them. For example, police officers enforce the speed limit. You can honor God and your local officers by not speeding.

THEY SAY . . .

"Now there came to Him some of the Sadducees (who say that there is no resurrection).... [And Jesus said, 'The sons of this age cannot] die anymore, because they are like angels, and are sons of God, being sons of the resurrection. But that the dead are raised, even Moses showed.... Now He is not the God of the dead but of the living; for all live to Him.'"

⮌ Luke 20:27,36-38

It's funny how we live our lives by what "they" say without even knowing who "they" are or how "they" got their information. Nevertheless, for successful living, it's important for you to know a few of these "theysayisms." For instance...

"They say you should wait 30 minutes after eating before you get back in the pool." (What would happen if you got back in after 29?)

"They say you should drink eight glasses of water a day." (Why not nine?)

"They say a swallowed piece of gum takes seven years to digest." (How do they know that?)

"They say more people die every year in automobile accidents than in airplane crashes." (This last one does nothing to comfort me, especially since I know that when my plane lands, I have to take the freeway home during rush hour. Besides, it's no wonder more people die every year in automobile accidents. Who can afford to fly?)

As it is, we treat this information like gospel, don't we? We live and breathe and make decisions as if "they" wrote the book on life.

It's hard to overlook what "they" say, especially when you're growing up. But while what your friends say is important, what God says is *truth*.

Next time you're confronted with what "they" say, remember what Jesus did under peer pressure. Whenever He was presented with a theysayism, He always responded with a "Word-of-Godism." And when He did, "they" usually had very little to say in return.

Discussion Starters:

1. Like the Sadducees, there are many in this world who will urge you to live according to some code besides the Bible. How will knowing the Bible help you resist their advice?

2. One of the clearest modern examples of a faulty theysayism is this: They say, "Everyone is doing it." Why is this wrong? How could you answer this statement with Scripture?

Lifeline:

Discuss your favorite "Word-of-Godism" with your family.

EIGHT SECONDS TO SUCCESS

"And He looked up and saw the rich putting their gifts into the treasury. And He saw a poor widow putting in two small copper coins. And He said, 'Truly I say to you, this poor widow put in more than all of them; for they all out of their surplus put into the offering; but she out of her poverty put in all that she had to live on.'"

╰⌒ Luke 21:1-4

Lyle's been the best in America in his sport more than once.
He makes his living on the back of a snorting beast.
He goes to work in jeans and steps in piles of manure at the office.
He eats power lunches with tobacco-spitting cowboys.
He pays his entry fees with the money he earned shoeing horses.
He gets on.
He rides.
He falls.
He lands on his head.
The next time he rides, he's wearing a neck brace.
This time he stays on.
Sometimes he works all night and comes home poor and dirty.
His wife, Kathy, and his daughter, Sasha, adore him.
Lyle loves riding bulls, but he loves Jesus more.
Lyle lives life eight seconds at a time.

Sometimes success is measured in small increments. The widow in Jesus' parable gave her "all" even though she had only a few meager coins. My friend Lyle, as a professional bull rider, gives his all in the ring, even if only for a few seconds at a time. If each one of us gave of ourselves and loved God with the widow's and Lyle's intensity, we'd all be closer to Him.

Love God with 100 percent of your heart. Although it's important to give to Him and spend time with Him, God doesn't measure our faithfulness in quantity. He cares more about the level of devotion, the quality of our relationship with Him. Sometimes small things are the greatest measuring sticks of our inner character.

Discussion Starters:

1. Why was the widow's gift of two small copper coins so significant?

2. What are some various ways Christians can give their all for Christ?

3. How can you give 100 percent to God?

Lifeline:

Have each person write "100" on a slip of paper. Then carry it around for a few days as a reminder to give God your all, in everything you do.

DOUG AND THE VOLCANO

"[He said], 'There will be great earthquakes, and in various places plagues and famines; and there will be terrors and great signs from heaven. But before all these things, they will lay their hands on you and will persecute you, delivering you to the synagogues and prisons, bringing you before kings and governors for My name's sake.... But you will be betrayed even by parents and brothers and relatives and friends, and they will put some of you to death.... Yet not a hair of your head will perish. By your endurance you will gain your lives.'"

⤶ Luke 21:11-12,16,18-19

Being a camp director, I hear some wild stories. But Doug's volcano story was the strangest—so crazy that at first I thought it was a hoax.

"You're kidding," I said to Amy, who was waving her hands frantically, telling me the news. "Doug was in a volcano? The same Doug who used to be a Kanakuk counselor in cabin 13? No way."

But it was true. Several other Kanakukers were with him, too, singing and praising God on top of Mount Merapi on a clear summer's day in 1992.

They'd been told it was safe.

"The mountain hasn't erupted in 16 years," said some of the locals.

So with confidence, Doug and his friends neared the rim and sat on the rocks to worship God. Suddenly, the mountain gurgled and spewed hot lava everywhere. It was probably the shortest worship service in history.

"It's sorta hard to keep singing 'Kumbaya' when you're running for your life. Anyway, it's nice to still have all my hair," Doug told me when we finally talked. He paused and touched the scar on his head, then added, "I believe God has more plans for me on earth."

I believe that, too. And I believe that some time in life, we all will go through our own fiery ordeals. We'll be tested, tried, and persecuted. But don't fear it. God assures, "Not a hair of your head will perish" (verse 18).

Some day, the things Jesus predicted will come to pass. Are you ready for your own Mount Merapi?

Discussion Starters:

1. What fiery ordeals has the Lord already seen you through?
2. What fears do you have about the end times?
3. Scripture says that during the end times, not a hair on our heads will perish. It also says that some of us will die. In what sense is each of these statements true?

Lifeline:

Jesus said that in the end times some family members will betray one another. Make a pact that such betrayal will never happen in your family. Write it down and sign it. Perhaps you can even display it in your home.

EGG ON OUR FACES

"Then came the first day of Unleavened Bread on which the Passover lamb had to be sacrificed. And Jesus sent Peter and John, saying, 'Go and prepare the Passover for us, so that we may eat it.'"

⟿ Luke 22:7-8

In the "old days" of Oklahoma City, they had a tradition at John Marshall High School called the "Senior Egg Fight." It was a nasty event. Well, somehow 12-year-old Randy decided to sneak into his neighbor's garage and steal the rotten ammunition, which was being saved for that blessed day. One spring midnight, Randy took those eggs and shared them with his neighbors—and their cars, driveways, roofs, sheds, shrubbery, lampposts, and latticework. Unfortunately for Randy, about 154 eggs later, he stepped on a cat's tail. The cat went public with its pain, complaining so loudly that several porch lights winked on.

Randy took off. "God, help me!" he prayed, hearing heavy footsteps behind him. He ducked into a side yard, crawled inside a trash can, pulled the lid down quietly, and held his breath. The footsteps stopped, then passed on in the night. Relieved, Randy pressed his hand against his heart, forgetting the last egg was in his shirt pocket. *Splat.* His hand was covered, but it didn't matter. He was free! He grinned all the way home.

The next morning, however, Randy wasn't smiling. That Sunday in church, the preacher spoke on the Passover and what it means to Christians today: "We celebrate the Passover because it reminds us of God's mercy on His children. The Lamb's blood marked on the Israelites' doors saved them from death, and Jesus'—the Lamb's—blood will save you from death. You're all sinful—" he stopped and looked in Randy's direction "—but if you accept Christ, His blood will wash away, or pass over, your sins." The preacher paused. "Anyone want to ask Christ into his or her heart today?"

Surrounded by his neighbors, Randy meekly stood up, prayed, and confessed his "rotten" sin. And much to Randy's relief, Christ washed away his sins long before he finished washing the egg from the neighborhood.

Discussion Starters:

1. State one thing you know about the Passover.
2. What heavy footsteps would have caught up with us if Christ, the Passover Lamb, had not died for our sins?
3. As sinners, we all have some "egg on our faces." What's one way you can thank God today for passing over your sins?

Lifeline:

Read Exodus 12:1-36. Study it together as a family. Then make plans to prepare a true Passover meal the next time the date is celebrated.

NOT ME!

"'But behold, the hand of the one betraying Me is with Mine on the table. For indeed, the Son of Man is going as it has been determined; but woe to that man by whom He is betrayed!' And they began to discuss among themselves which one of them it might be who was going to do this thing."

⤷ Luke 22:21-23

On a hill about 300 yards from Kanakuk Kamp sits a residential treatment center for teenagers. It's so close that I could probably take a bow and shoot an arrow to its doorstep. But I wouldn't. Some of those kids can't have anything that sharp. They are troubled kids—the kind parents usually have in mind when they say, "No kid of *mine* will ever act like that." Parenthood, however, has a way of changing our thinking.

Vince and Marie really believed their daughter Tiffany was an angel. So when Tiffany's first-grade teacher called them in for a conference, they were stunned. Tiffany had been bullying the other kids? Never!

"The other kids must have been really mean to her. Tiffany would never start a fight," her parents protested.

The teacher just shook her head.

It's easy to think like Vince and Marie. Often, we don't want to accept responsibility. We say, "I would never do such a thing. Not me." We reason, *The preacher is speaking to that guy over in pew 47. He's not looking in my direction. Sure, I'm a sinner, but look at the Smiths. They're worse.*

We don't like to admit that we (or our kids, friends, or family) are capable of sin because it's uncomfortable. But we are very capable.

Look at Judas. I'm sure he never wanted (in the beginning, at least) to betray Jesus. Well, I don't want to turn my back on God, either. But I have this haunting feeling that if I'd been in Judas's shoes way back then, I might have done the same thing he did.

So instead of arrows, I shoot prayers at that little center on the hill. I know that in spite of my own daily betrayals, God looks at me and says, "There's Joe White. I'm proud he's a kid of mine"—and I am so thankful.

Discussion Starters:

1. Judas wasn't the only disciple who turned on Jesus. Who else did? Why?

2. Jesus knew who was going to betray Him, but He still broke bread with the traitor. What does that say about Him?

3. What is one way *you* have betrayed Jesus? How have you experienced His forgiveness?

Lifeline:

Thank the Lord that He loves you, even when you betray Him.

LIVING TOMBSTONE

"And He withdrew from them about a stone's throw, and He knelt down and began to pray, saying, 'Father, if You are willing, remove this cup from Me; yet not My will, but Yours be done.'"

↪ Luke 22:41-42

If Jesus had wanted something inscribed on His tombstone, I'll bet it would have been, "He did His Father's will."

What do you want written on yours some day? It's helpful to think about the message you want to leave to the world and then try to live in a manner consistent with that. My gran'ma took this idea of living with the "end" in mind to an unusual level.

Sixty years ago, Gran'ma bought a marker for her own grave. She got it for a good price and has taken it with her on countless moves. To my knowledge, she has never regretted the extra weight.

It's a sturdy stone—like the lady whose name is already on it. It's gone with her so many places that the stone has become chipped and flecked with rain.

I believe my grandmother's habit of carrying death around like a suitcase is noble. It makes her appreciate life more fully, breathe more deeply, kiss more babies, and plant more flowers.

Sometimes when I look at Gran'ma's stone, I wonder what we'll write there in that little space left purposely blank beneath her name. She hasn't told us yet what *she* wants it to say. But whatever it is, I know she will have lived up to it.

Somewhere out there is a stone that will bear *your* name one day. What will be written on that piece of granite? For what do you want to be remembered? Will people say that you, like Jesus, did your Father's will?

Discussion Starters:

1. How did Jesus' willingness to do His Father's will influence everything He did?

2. How did Jesus feel about His upcoming crucifixion?

3. As He wept in the Garden of Gethsemane, what do you think Jesus wanted us most to remember about His life and ministry? Why?

Lifeline:

Discuss: What's the one thing you'd like others to remember about you? About your family?

ROLL CALL AT THE TOP OF THE WORLD

"And [the thief] was saying, 'Jesus, remember me when You come in Your kingdom!' And He said to him, 'Truly I say to you, today you shall be with Me in Paradise.'"

⸺ Luke 23:42-43

Joey is a fierce competitor. As a former Athlete in Action, he has played hard all his life. He has won frequently, lost graciously, and always, always given 100 percent in everything he does.

That's why he got up at 3:00 A.M. with 15 other men and boys one day to climb one of Colorado's tallest, toughest peaks. With his hands in his pockets and his breath puffing white, Joey gazed at the renowned Diamond Face on the east side of Long's Peak.

The mountain is a jewel in the crown of creation, with rock that changes colors as the day goes by and a surface as smooth as ice. That's why they call it Diamond Face.

It's beautiful at the top. But it costs a lot to get there. Men have died on that face—slipped clean off the top, like snow from a high church steeple. For a thousand feet they are black, falling specks against a hard background. Then they are gone.

It was exactly the kind of challenge Joey likes.

I'd love to tell you that Joey conquered Long's, but he didn't. An hour into the 12-hour trek, Craig, one of the boys, got sick. Joey stayed with Craig, and he accomplished something far greater than reaching the peak. He led Craig to Christ!

Joey's name is on the registration sheet anyway, rolled up in a metal canister at the top of Long's Peak. His friends signed him in, knowing full well he probably would've beaten them all to the top. But since Joey stayed behind, Craig's name is on a more important roll—heaven's.

Some day, Craig will be with Christ in paradise, thanks to Jesus and to Joey.

Discussion Starters:

1. The thief on the cross never did anything to earn eternal life. What does that tell you about salvation?

2. Jesus said, "*Today* you shall be with Me in Paradise" (verse 43, emphasis added). What does that reveal about the passage from death to life?

Lifeline:

If you're a Christian, write your name in the margin next to today's verse. It'll remind you that your name is on the roll in heaven.

A GIVER OF LIFE

"And Jesus, crying out with a loud voice, said, 'Father, into Your hands I commit My spirit.' Having said this, He breathed His last."

↬ Luke 23:46

Steve and Julee were barren for almost a decade. The doctors told them they had little to no chance of ever having children. So the couple saved, sacrificed, and spent thousands of dollars just to hear the words, "You're pregnant."

Then one day, their dreams came true. *Doubly* true.

The twins, Justin and McKenzie, began to grow inside Julee. Steve and Julee were ecstatic. They painted the baby room, had baby showers, and read up on child rearing.

Soon, however, tests showed that only McKenzie was developing. Justin was stunted and deformed, not at all what my friends had hoped for in a son. Still, they prayed.

Improperly attached to his mother's placenta, Justin hung on—but only by a thread. While he took little nourishment for himself, McKenzie fed and thrived. At birth, Justin barely weighed a pound. Still, he escorted his sister into the world; visited earth for a brief, shining moment; breathed, cried, waved his tiny hands good-bye at McKenzie; and flew up to heaven.

The mood in the surgery room was bittersweet.

Later, his parents found out exactly what had happened. According to their doctors, if Justin hadn't at least partially attached his umbilical cord to his mom's placenta, he would have been spontaneously aborted—which would have led to McKenzie's abortion as well. So because Justin clung to the placenta, both children remained in the womb. And since Justin took only a little nourishment from the placenta, he left the lion's share for McKenzie.

In other words, he gave himself—his food and nourishment—so that she might have life. Does that sound familiar?

Discussion Starters:

1. The crucifixion was Jesus' payment for your sins, once and for all. How does it feel to know your penalty has been lifted forever?

2. Why did Jesus die for you?

3. How can you live today in light of Jesus' great gift on the cross?

Lifeline:

Press your wrist where your pulse is normally taken. That's exactly where a spike was driven into Jesus. Now, with a ballpoint pen, make a tiny dot there on your wrist. Allow this to remind you of God's great love for you.

A GRAVE MATTER

"And they found the stone rolled away from the tomb, but when they entered, they did not find the body of the Lord Jesus. While they were perplexed about this, behold, two men suddenly stood near them in dazzling clothing; and as the women were terrified and bowed their faces to the ground, the men said to them, 'Why do you seek the living One among the dead? He is not here, but He has risen.'"

↪ Luke 24:2-6

Two old bums wandered into a graveyard one night and got separated. Unaware that his friend had fallen into an open grave, the first bum, Fred, found his way out the other side. He had just given Charlie up for lost when he heard a noise.

"Helllp!" came Charlie's mournful voice. "Helllp! It's cold down here."

Fred went stumbling back to have a look around. He searched in the bushes. He poked around in the tall grass. Then suddenly, he heard the voice again. It was coming from a nearby hole in the ground.

"That sounds like Charlie over thar," Fred mumbled to himself as he ran to the lip of the grave. "Charlie? Charlie? That you?"

"Helllp!" said the pitiful voice. "Helllp! It's cooold down here."

Unfortunately, Fred, being a man of some honor—but few brains—made a sad miscalculation. "If dead folks cain talk," he said in the direction of the grave, "then I'm leavin'!" Fred turned on his heel.

Just then, Charlie cried out for help again, shivering in the cold.

"O' course it's cold down there!" said Fred, peering into the darkness. "Ya done kicked all yer dirt off!"

It's a silly story, but it illustrates a good point. Fred was right—it's ridiculous to look for the living among the dead. That's precisely why the women who visited Jesus' grave were so stunned. They didn't expect Him to be up and at it. He was supposed to be in His tomb, resting in peace.

Fortunately for us, Jesus isn't dead. His resurrection transformed history and countless lives. How has your life changed since "He has risen"?

Discussion Starters:

1. Why is Jesus' resurrection so important to the Christian faith?

2. Why do you think it's so hard for people to believe in the resurrection?

3. Will we have bodies when we're resurrected? (Read the rest of Luke 24.)

Lifeline:

As a family, visit the grave of someone who was a Christian. Thank God that this friend is in heaven—and that some day all Christians will be there.

A DATE WITH PAIN

"And He said to them, 'Thus it is written, that the Christ would suffer and rise again from the dead the third day.'"

↪ Luke 24:46

"A little rain never hurt anyone," Will's dad used to say. So Will took that advice to heart and to an extreme. In one naive move, he lumped all elements of weather together in that "nonhurtful" category and went headlong into life with his magical raincoat on.

Fog? "No problem," Will would say. "Just turn the fog lights on and drive a little faster. We'll be out of it soon."

Tornado watch? "Super day for a kite!"

As one might guess, problems were bound to arise for Will. Take, for instance, his first date with Cindy. The weatherman couldn't have given a more thorough prescription for disaster. It was snowing. Will was lovestruck. He drove too fast on an icy bridge and lost control. His truck skidded into oncoming traffic and collided with a semi.

Will and Cindy's first date lasted a little longer than he had planned. It took six weeks for them to (partially) recuperate from the terrible accident and even longer to finish the physical therapy. But, according to Will, all that pain was worth it. When he and Cindy finally left the hospital, they'd developed a special—if unique—relationship. And after that, Cindy had no choice but to marry the guy.

Now and then, I see the two lovers in my hometown. He's the one with the grin and the T-shirt on in January. She's the one on his arm, shaking her head and happily providing the warmth her husband needs.

If you talk to Will, he'll tell you the awful pain of that accident was worth it because that's what brought him close to Cindy. I think Jesus would say the same thing about His pain on the cross—that it was terrible, but necessary. Because He suffered, we now have eternal life and are in a never-ending relationship with Him.

Sometimes pain is good for the soul. Wouldn't you agree?

Discussion Starters:

1. Whose idea was it for Jesus to endure the pain of the cross?

2. How could a Father allow such suffering in His Son's life?

3. What tremendous good came from all that pain?

4. Describe a time when God brought something good from your pain.

Lifeline:

Thank God now for any difficult suffering He is allowing you to experience. Then discuss with one another how you can cling to God in spite of these circumstances.

ONE WITH WHOM?

"In the beginning was the Word, and the Word was with God, and the Word was God. He was in the beginning with God. All things came into being through Him, and apart from Him nothing came into being that has come into being. In Him was life, and the life was the Light of men."

↪ John 1:1-4

People smile when Keith comes to town. Once a stellar wide receiver in the NFL, Keith now works with youth and celebrates every minute of it. His home base is Denton, Texas, but he spends a lot of time at the growing Church of Katmandu, a third-world, poverty-stricken church at the base of 29,000-foot Mount Everest in the Himalayas. When he goes, he takes deflated soccer balls, footballs, and basketballs...and a hand pump.

Recently, on his 26-hour flight there, Keith sat next to Rob, a New Age mountain climber. They started talking, and Rob mentioned to Keith that he was heading for Mount Everest to become "one with the mountain."

Keith chuckled. "One with the mountain?"

"Yeah," the searching climber said, "the mountain and I will become united like one and the same. It'll be an awesome feeling."

Keith pondered this for a while and thought, *How weird. You can become one with your spouse and, in some senses, one with God, but one with a pile of rocks?*

After a few hours, Keith looked at Rob carefully and asked, "How would you like to become one with the God who made the mountain? It's really possible if you have a personal relationship with His Son, Jesus."

Rob smiled and pondered this. "One with God? Hmmm...I didn't know it was possible. No one's explained it to me like that before," he said.

Now, don't misunderstand Keith's point. There is nothing "New Age" about the Christian faith. But when we're in a relationship with Christ, *His Spirit lives in us.* It's one of the best things about being a Christian because it enables us to know intimately the God who created everything.

How well do you know the Lord? Does His Spirit live in you, or do you, like Rob, aim to fill your soul with other things?

Discussion Starters:

1. Who is "the Word" in this scripture?
2. Where was Jesus when the universe was created? Why did He come to earth?
3. How is it possible to become "one with God" (see John 14:20)?

Lifeline:

Do you (individually *and* as a family) live as if Jesus' Spirit is in you?

TAKING A DIP

" 'I did not recognize Him, but so that He might be manifested to Israel, I came baptizing in water.' John testified saying, 'I have seen the Spirit descending as a dove out of heaven, and He remained upon Him. I did not recognize Him, but He who sent me to baptize in water said to me, "He upon whom you see the Spirit descending and remaining upon Him, this is the One who baptizes in the Holy Spirit." ' "

↩ John 1:31-33

Mrs. Cecily Simmons is 86 years old and still runs her kitchen as if she were a "young pup." Every holiday, the smells of pies cooking, cookies baking, and turkeys roasting permeate her house. But the rest of the year, she likes to can. And every summer, Cecily makes jars and jars of pickles to give her friends and neighbors.

"Picklin'" (as Cecily likes to call it) is such a big job that she's started to hire neighborhood kids to help with the process. Together, Cecily and her helpers will pick cucumbers; slice 'em; soak 'em in salt, dill, and vinegar; and can 'em. After it's all done, she'll drop off the finished product on people's doorsteps—and her pickles are so good that you'd never remember they came from her dinky little garden out back.

They're totally transformed from the original cucumbers. They smell different, taste different, and even look different.

Baptism is supposed to work the same way. The word *baptism* comes from the Greek word *baptizo*, which means "to place into." Baptism in water symbolizes the change that occurs in your heart when you accept Christ. But baptism in the Holy Spirit is what *actually happens* when you become a Christian. Christ's Spirit lives in you and influences your decisions, your thoughts, and your actions. When you commit your life to Him, you start out looking like yourself and (hopefully) end up looking and acting more like Jesus. Your life progressively changes.

Cecily's pickles can't claim to be cucumbers after she's done with them—and you shouldn't aim to be the same person after Christ enters your heart. Have you invited Him into yours?

Discussion Starters:

1. How is baptism in water like being baptized into Christ?

2. What properties or characteristics of Christ are we supposed to take on when we become believers?

Lifeline:

How can we help each other be more like Christ today?

DISCIPLES

"One of the two who heard John speak and followed Him, was Andrew, Simon Peter's brother. He found first his own brother Simon and said to him, 'We have found the Messiah' (which translated means Christ). He brought him to Jesus. Jesus looked at him and said, 'You are Simon the son of John; you shall be called Cephas' (which is translated Peter). The next day He purposed to go into Galilee, and He found Philip. And Jesus said to him, 'Follow Me.'"

⟋ John 1:40-43

"I just can't get my act together."

"I'm totally addicted to drugs."

"I need peace. I've got ulcers, and I'm having anxiety attacks."

"I'm doing stuff I never, ever thought I'd do."

"I can't sleep at night."

For 20 years, I've counseled thousands of hurting teenagers and adults. One of the things I've found is that almost all the people who get caught up in sin and, as a result, get badly hurt have decided not to follow anyone. They rebel, stop listening to their parents or to wise counsel, and make up their own rules. In the process, they quit following God.

The best decision you can make is to become a disciple of Christ—to follow Him, learn from Him, and model your life after Him. Trying to live by following someone or something other than Christ is like trying to find a contact lens in the dark. It's difficult, risky (because you might make a mess of it), and eternally unsuccessful. You need Christ to light your way through life.

The happiest people I know are followers—disciplined learners, that is—of Christ and His teachings. For three intense years, 12 men followed Jesus practically everywhere He went. They attended every lecture, heard every parable, and witnessed every healing. Jesus taught His disciples by word and example, and eventually they changed the world.

You can, too. Are you a disciple of Christ?

Discussion Starters:

1. What do the words *discipline* and *disciple* have in common?

2. What do you think Jesus was looking for when He picked His disciples?

3. What kind of disciple are you? Explain your answer.

4. How well do you know your Leader?

Lifeline:

Who is the most devoted disciple of Christ you know? Why? What qualities make that person an obvious follower of Christ?

OINOS

"And both Jesus and His disciples were invited to the wedding. When the wine ran out, the mother of Jesus said to Him, 'They have no wine.' ...Now there were six stone waterpots set there for the Jewish custom of purification, containing twenty or thirty gallons each.... And He said to them, 'Draw some out now and take it to the headwaiter.' So they took it to him. When the headwaiter tasted the water which had become wine, and did not know where it came from (but the servants who had drawn the water knew), the headwaiter called the bridegroom, and said to him, 'Every man serves the good wine first, and when the people have drunk freely, then he serves the poorer wine; but you have kept the good wine until now.'"

↳ John 2:2-3,6,8-10

When is alcohol bad for you? How much is too much? If Jesus turned water into wine, is today's wine okay to drink?

The Bible is clear that certain things are harmful to the body and a sin to indulge in. But would Jesus make something that God wouldn't like?

The New Testament was written in the colorful Greek language. The original meaning of each word makes these questions about alcohol easy to understand. Wine in the English language comes from one of two Greek words. Oinos (the kind of wine Jesus made) is a word for purified grape juice that was ½ to 1 percent alcohol. Oinos was always diluted by 20 times its amount with pure juice or water. Shekar, on the other hand, is a word for strong drink. It's roughly 3 percent to 12 percent alcohol. Getting drunk with shekar is condemned in the Bible. All American beer (5 percent), wine (more than 12 percent), and hard liquor (20 to over 30 percent) are made of shekar.

Shekar is the most destructive drug in America. It's responsible for more deaths, abuses, and broken homes than any other substance.[1] Proverbs sounds the warning: "Do not look on the wine when it is red, when it sparkles in the cup, when it goes down smoothly; at the last it bites like a serpent, and stings like a viper" (Proverbs 23:31-32).

Don't let the sting of alcohol destroy you!

Discussion Starters:

1. What are the dangers of alcohol?

2. Why are people so attracted to strong drink?

3. Why is getting drunk a sin?

Lifeline:

Alcohol can lead to a lot of trouble for many people. What should your family policy toward alcohol be?

RIGHTEOUS ANGER

"And He found in the temple those who were selling oxen and sheep and doves, and the money changers seated at their tables. And He made a scourge of cords, and drove them all out of the temple, with the sheep and the oxen; and He poured out the coins of the money changers, and overturned their tables; and to those who were selling the doves He said, 'Take these things away; stop making My Father's house a place of business.' His disciples remembered that it was written, 'Zeal for Your house will consume me.'"

↩ John 2:14-17

Anger is a sin... unless God's reputation is at stake. And in our society, His name is put down everywhere. If you're a Christian, you should be frustrated, angry, and upset that your Best Friend, Master, and Leader is so often belittled and blasphemed. I'm sure mad, especially at Hollywood. I wouldn't even think of watching a movie or TV show that takes God's name in vain. Unfortunately, almost all movies and TV programs do it repeatedly. So at my house, we've agreed to watch only one or two carefully selected shows a week on TV and just a few movies. We don't mind missing the other stuff. We'd rather not support an industry that degrades the God who is so faithful, loving, and generous to us.

But God's name isn't just demeaned in the entertainment industry. At school and work, people take His name in vain repeatedly as well. How often do you hear, "Oh, my God!" or "Jesus Christ!" from your friends or coworkers? Don't excuse those remarks. That's not just the way people talk nowadays. Those comments are hurtful to God, the One who created you.

That's why Jesus got mad in the temple. The moneychangers made the temple into a shopping mall, cheapening God and His house of worship. Everyone who loves God should get angry when His name is cheapened. Jesus said we're to love our enemies and pray for those who persecute us (see Matthew 5:44). But we're also supposed to love God with everything we've got (see Mark 12:30). When we love Him, we'll live for Him. And when we live for Him, we'll do anything to protect His name.

Do you take a stand when you see people tear down God's reputation, or do you stand quietly by and let others drag His name through the mud?

Discussion Starters:

1. What's the difference between having righteous anger (like Jesus') and just plain getting mad? When is it wrong to get mad?
2. Why is it wrong to take His name in vain (see Exodus 20:7)?

Lifeline:

Discuss what you can say in response to people who put down God.

PECKING AT THE SHELL

"Now there was a man of the Pharisees, named Nicodemus, a ruler of the Jews; this man came to Jesus by night and said to Him, 'Rabbi, we know that You have come from God as a teacher; for no one can do these signs that You do unless God is with him.' Jesus answered and said to him, 'Truly, truly, I say to you, unless one is born again, he cannot see the kingdom of God.'"

           ⌒ John 3:1-3

When my daughter Jamie was growing up, we raised geese, rabbits, squirrels, raccoons, dogs, deer, possums, and any other stray animal that found its way (or was brought by Jamie) to our door.

One spring, I was incubating some duck eggs and made an awful mistake. It takes a baby duck 28 days to hatch, and the last two to three days, he's busy pecking out of his shell. Although the ducks struggle during this time, the process helps them become strong enough to survive once they're out in the world. Well, I felt so sorry for one of the toiling little ducklings that I "helped" him out of his shell the day after he'd pecked a hole in the egg. He died that night. The other ducklings struggled on their own and were free of their eggshells by the third day. They all survived.

God's timing exists for a reason—for baby ducks and for baby Christians. Just as I hurt the duck by forcing an early hatching, so we can wound our friends or family by trying to "make" them ready to be born again. When you're witnessing to someone, the Holy Spirit must be leading you or your friend will never cross the line to eternal life. Why? Because God needs to work in her heart first. What you say will usually confirm what God is already doing inside her soul.

How do you know when the time is right for someone to be born again? Observe. Is your friend "pecking at his shell," asking questions, becoming curious about Jesus? Is he interested in spiritual things?

It's important that we witness to others about Christ. But we also must remember that we can't do anything without God's power and wisdom. God says it's "not by might nor by power, but my My Spirit [and in My time]" that miracles will happen (Zechariah 4:6). Wait on Him.

Discussion Starters:

1. What does it mean to be born again?

2. Why did Nicodemus (a very religious man) need to be born again?

3. Why do we need to depend on God's timing for others to be born again? In what ways do we try to "open the shell" too soon?

Lifeline:

Pray for Christ to work in the hearts of your pre-Christian friends.

THE GREATEST VERSE

"For God so loved the world, that He gave His only begotten Son, that whoever believes in Him shall not perish, but have eternal life."

↜ John 3:16

For God . . . . (the greatest lover)
so loved . . . . (the greatest love)
the world . . . . (the greatest need)
that He gave . . . . (the greatest gift)
His only begotten Son . . . . (the greatest life)
that whoever . . . . (the greatest offer)
believes in Him . . . . (the greatest faith)
shall not perish . . . . (the greatest death)
but have eternal life . . . . (the greatest place)

John 3:16 . . . . (*the greatest Bible verse!*)

This is probably the most memorized verse in the Bible, but as with all familiar things, sometimes we just mumble the words and forget that the meaning is life-or-death significant. In one powerful sentence, John 3:16 affirms that God loves you, and He sent Jesus to die for you so you can live with Him forever in heaven. It describes the whole New Testament—and possibly your future—in a nutshell. Amazing!

Discussion Starters:

1. Why do some people call John 3:16 the greatest verse in the Bible? What does it mean to you?
2. What does the word *whoever* mean?
3. What does the word *believe* in this verse mean?
4. What do you think it will be like to have eternal life?
5. Which other Bible verses lay out God's plan of salvation?

Lifeline:

First, memorize John 3:16. Then practice saying it to one another, but explain the verse in words that an unbeliever would understand. This will help prepare you to discuss it (and God's message of salvation) with your friends who don't know Him.

AUCTION OVER!

"'He who has received His testimony has set his seal to this, that God is true. For He whom God has sent speaks the words of God; for He gives the Spirit without measure. The Father loves the Son and has given all things into His hand. He who believes in the Son has eternal life; but he who does not obey the Son will not see life, but the wrath of God abides on him.'"

↞ John 3:33-36

Bradford Fowler, an upstate New York man, was exceedingly rich. His 100-acre estate was worth millions. He owned houses, land, antiques, and cattle. But although on the outside he had it all, he was unhappy on the inside. His wife, Kate, was getting older, and they were childless. Bradford's only wish was to have a son who could carry on the family legacy.

Almost miraculously, Kate became pregnant in her later years, and she gave birth to a baby boy. Although Benjamin was born severely retarded, Bradford loved him wholeheartedly. He took his son everywhere he could and taught Benjamin everything possible.

When Benjamin turned five, Kate died. Grief-stricken, Bradford drew even closer to his special son. But soon after Benjamin's 13th birthday, his birth defects cost him his life, and he passed away almost as suddenly as he was born. Bradford died six months later, brokenhearted.

With no family left to inherit his riches, Bradford had requested in his will that his possessions be put up for auction. So one blustery November day, hundreds of wealthy bidders gathered to buy the Fowler family's riches. The first item offered was a painting of Benjamin. No one bid. Instead, the people waited like vultures for the riches. Finally, the poor housemaid who had helped raise Benjamin offered five dollars for the picture and easily took the bid. To everyone's shock, the auctioneer ripped a handwritten will from the back of the picture. In it, Bradford had written, "To the one who thinks enough of my son to buy this painting, I give my entire estate."

"Auction over!" the auctioneer shouted. And the greedy crowd walked away, stunned and dismayed.

Discussion Starters:

1. How was that auction like God's offer to us?

2. What exactly does God offer?

3. Who will be disappointed when the "auction" is over?

Lifeline:

Does your family value one another as much as Bradford valued his son?

GOD'S THIRST QUENCHER

"There came a woman of Samaria to draw water. Jesus said to her, 'Give Me a drink.' ... Therefore the Samaritan woman said to Him, 'How is it that You, being a Jew, ask me for a drink since I am a Samaritan woman?' (For Jews have no dealings with Samaritans.) Jesus answered and said to her, 'If you knew the gift of God, and who it is who says to you, "Give Me a drink," you would have asked Him, and He would have given you living water.' ... [Then Jesus said,] 'Everyone who drinks of this water will thirst again; but whoever drinks of the water that I will give him shall never thirst; but the water that I will give him will become in him a well of water springing up to eternal life.'"

⤻ John 4:7,9-10,13-14

Thirst quenching drinks are everywhere. Coke, Gatorade, Quick Kick, Canadian Coolers, Dr. Pepper, and Snapple are just a few of hundreds on the market. These drinks are so popular that advertisers spend a ton of money on drink product commercials every year. Gatorade paid legendary basketball player Michael Jordan millions just to call him "Mike" in its new product-promoting commercial. Pepsi paid Jordan just as much to drink Pepsi in front of a TV camera.

Fluids are popular because they're necessary for survival. In fact, as I've mentioned before, we need eight glasses of water every day to keep ourselves hydrated! But while we need drinks to stay alive, nothing we drink can permanently quench our thirst.

Jesus' living water is the exception.

His water will quench your thirst for meaning and purpose in life. As He told the Samaritan woman at the well, you'll never thirst again when you continue to trust Jesus and live for Him.

Unfortunately, there are as many cults and God-seeking religions as there are soft drinks. Millions of people, thirsty for God, flock to false religions every day. Even more try to quench their thirst through other people and things. They fill their desert-dry souls with friends, sports, fashion, love, parties, and work—hoping to find satisfaction.

But unless they drink from Jesus' well, they will all die with parched lips.

Discussion Starters:

1. Why did Jesus call Himself "living water"?

2. Why do sincere followers of Christ never thirst for another drink?

3. How can someone get a drink of living water?

Lifeline:

How has Jesus quenched your family's thirst with His living water? Discuss.

THE ARRIVAL

"The woman said to Him, 'I know that Messiah is coming (He who is called Christ); when that One comes, He will declare all things to us.' Jesus said to her, 'I who speak to you am He.' ...[The woman left and told others about Christ's arrival] and they [said] to the woman, 'It is no longer because of what you said that we believe, for we have heard for ourselves and know that this One is indeed the Savior of the world.'"

↪ John 4:25-26,42

Imagine that your hero was coming to your hometown and staying at your house. You would probably spend weeks preparing for his or her arrival. What would you do to get ready for this person? Make up the best bedroom? Cook the best food? Clean the house from top to bottom?

Once you did that, you'd have to decide where you would take your hero. How would you entertain this person? What would you say?

Think about the impact your hero's visit would have on your life. You'd probably talk about the event until your friends turned purple.

That's how excited the Old Testament prophets were when they told people about Jesus' coming. For 1,500 years, those saints longed for and wrote details about the Messiah. Jesus was a hot topic. Even before He came, Christ provided hope for people. Whenever times got dark, the prophets reminded the people that they had Someone to look forward to, Someone who would bring light to their world.

The prophets did such a good job of preparing the people for Jesus' arrival that even slaves, women, and children (sadly, the least valuable people in society during biblical times) recognized Him and were able to accept that Christ was who He claimed to be—the Messiah.

Have you, like the prophets and the woman at the well, let others know about Jesus? Do you, like people in biblical times, take the time to make your heart and your home a place where Jesus would feel welcome?

Do you really believe Christ is who He says He is?

Discussion Starters:

1. Why was the Messiah's arrival so exciting to the prophets and biblical people?

2. If you had lived in New Testament times, would you have believed Jesus when He said He was the Christ? Why or why not?

Lifeline:

Get yourself and other people ready for the Messiah. He's the most important Person you'll ever entertain.

"THEY JUST DON'T GET IT!"

"For Jesus Himself testified that a prophet has no honor in his own country."

~ John 4:44

Brett came to camp one summer as a confident 14-year-old to become a better soccer player. He left as an improved athlete, but he also left as a different person. One evening, after a lot of thought and discussion, he accepted Jesus into his heart.

Brett was excited about his newfound faith, but he was a little nervous about what his friends would think. He and the guys had hung out together since kindergarten, but they had been into everything *except* church.

After becoming a Christian, Brett prayed that his friends would see a change in him and accept Jesus into their hearts, too. His first day back, hanging out with the guys, Brett nervously told his friends the news.

"Hey, uh, guess what happened to me this summer?" he asked.

"You met some cute chicks!" Mike guessed.

"Nah, I met Someone better—Jesus," Brett said and held his breath.

Brett didn't get close to the reaction he wanted. His friends laughed. And they laughed at him for three years. The whole time, Brett prayed, tried to love them, and sought support from his Christian friends. Finally, one day Mike, his best friend, approached him. Mike was hurting from a broken relationship and asked Brett how he could get peace. They talked for hours, and at last, Mike gave his life to Christ.

Brett and Mike are still praying for their other friends who haven't stopped laughing at them. But they aren't too discouraged. They know that even Jesus had a hard time sharing God's truth with the people He knew best. Even Jesus was laughed at and misunderstood.

God is powerful, though. And that fact gives Brett and Mike hope that someday, their friends' sarcastic laughter will turn into real God-given joy.

Discussion Starters:

1. Why did those who knew Jesus best (the people of Nazareth) misunderstand Him most?

2. Why is it so hard to live out your faith around your closest unbelieving friends?

3. How can you best be a witness to your friends who don't know Christ?

Lifeline:

It's admirable to have friends you want to lead to Christ, but it's essential to also make friends who know Him so they can encourage you and keep you on track. Thank God for your friends who know Him, and pray for the ones who don't.

DO YOU *WILL* TO GET WELL?

"A man was there who had been ill for thirty-eight years. When Jesus saw him lying there...
He said to him, 'Do you wish to get well?' The sick man answered Him, 'Sir, I have no man
to put me into the pool when the water is stirred up, but while I am coming, another steps
down before me.' Jesus said to him, 'Get up, pick up your pallet and walk.' Immediately the
man became well, and picked up his pallet and began to walk."

↪ John 5:5-9

Beth was a sweet, cute sophomore at Texas Tech University. She came to me confused and in need of counseling as I traveled through Texas to hire summer staff for our sports camps.

"I feel so awful these days," she said as tears threatened to fill her huge, brown eyes. "My relationship with God is going nowhere right now."

"What's going on in your life?" I asked, concerned.

"Well, there's this guy..." Beth began, nervously tapping her fingers.

We talked for a while, and she sobbed. She told me her boyfriend was taking advantage of her and drawing her away from God.

"I know I'm not making God happy, but I can't break up with my boyfriend. I've always dated someone. I don't want to be alone," she said.

"Beth," I said, "if you really want to make your heart and your relationship with God better, then you've got to give God your will."

She looked up, astonished. "How'd you know that? How did you know my boyfriend's name is Will?"

A lot of people want to solve their problems—but not enough to give those people and issues over to God. That's why Jesus asked the sick man if he *wanted* to get well. The man would have to believe that Jesus had the power to heal him. He'd have to surrender his will to God, no longer trying it on his own. The man did, though, so Jesus healed him. Beth, on the other hand, didn't really want God to heal her problem. She didn't want to give God either of her "wills" and tried instead to handle the situation herself.

It's hard to give your will up to God and say, "I want what You want. I believe You can heal me—I can't do it myself."

But if you are *willing*, He is able. He can heal you.

Discussion Starters:

1. What's the difference between *wanting* and *deciding* to do something?

2. What does it mean to have Jesus own your will?

Lifeline:

Are you willing to let Jesus take control and own your will? Discuss.

INSTANT REPLAY

"'For not even the Father judges anyone, but He has given all judgment to the Son, so that all will honor the Son even as they honor the Father. He who does not honor the Son does not honor the Father who sent Him. Truly, truly, I say to you, he who hears My word, and believes Him who sent Me, has eternal life, and does not come into judgment, but has passed out of death into life.'"

↜ John 5:22-24

The game was intense. The crowd was jeering. I was a college football player, facing a tough national championship team. And we were playing on their turf. At least 80,000 biased fans watched from the stands, and millions more were viewing the game on TV.

The pressure got to me, and I made an embarrassing mistake during the game. I was the quarterback and accidentally handed the ball off to an opposing defensive player, giving them possession of the ball. I tried to hide my number under the pile of players. The play went by fast. Since our coach couldn't see clearly from the sidelines, I hoped he hadn't noticed.

No such luck. Later, after we lost the game, the team gathered in the locker room, where our coach saw a film of the game. He zeroed in on my mistake immediately and played the tape over and over again.

"Hey, White," he bellowed, "do you realize what you did here? You didn't think. You're partly responsible for losing this big game!"

I felt as small as a squashed bug, standing in the film room with my teammates as we watched the replay on the screen. *If only I could've erased the film before he saw it!* I thought as my stomach dropped.

I think God is like a coach in some ways, too. He sees it all and knows it all. He has "filmed" every sin, every mistake, every failure. He's no fool. But when you meet Him face to face, the judgment scene will be different. If you've accepted Christ into your heart and asked Him to forgive your sins, you'll step over to God's right hand and enjoy eternal life. Your sins will be erased, your heart will be "white as snow," and Jesus will say, "This one is My child. Her sins are forgiven. I died to erase them."

Thank You, God, for deleting our mistakes and loving us in spite of them.

Discussion Starters:

1. Who sins? Why do we sin? How can Jesus erase our sinful pasts?
2. Why is God's forgiveness such a big deal?

Lifeline:

Your family members should be able to learn from their mistakes without being judged and ridiculed for mess-ups.

BEARING WITNESS

" 'There is another who testifies of Me, and I know that the testimony which He gives about Me is true. You have sent to John, and he has testified to the truth. But the testimony which I receive is not from man, but I say these things so that you may be saved.' "

↶ John 5:32-34

Little Emma had been blind since birth. Poverty-stricken and basically abandoned by her parents, Emma had to make a living on her own. Every morning at six, she bundled up and walked 10 blocks to the Chicago train station and sold pencils to buy food and clothing. Most people in the station rushed by her each day, hardly noticing her raggedy clothes and white cane. Occasionally someone would drop a quarter in her money box and grab a pencil to do a good deed for the day.

One winter morning, the station was unusually crowded. Emma could hear hundreds of thumping feet rush from train to train. She scooted her chair closer to the wall, trying to keep out of the way. But as the people dashed into the crowded trains, one careless businessman ran into the blind girl and knocked her out of her chair. Emma's coins and pencils flew across the floor. Desperately, she crawled around, feeling for her precious coins and pencils. As she sat on the cold ground, whimpering, an elderly man gently picked her up, gathered her pencils and coins, and helped her get started again. Then the man handed Emma a $20 bill and began to walk away.

Emma, wanting to know who her rescuer was, cried out, "Mister, are you Jesus?"

"No, honey, I'm just one of His followers," the man answered, smiling.

Tears fell from Emma's unseeing eyes as she cried, "I knew you had to at least be related to Him."

Being a witness for Jesus isn't that hard. There are people everywhere who need your help and love. All you have to do is pay attention. Do people know you're a member of His family?

Discussion Starters:

1. How do we bear witness for Christ?

2. Name one situation you were in yesterday where you had a chance to be a witness. Did you demonstrate Christ's love? Why or why not?

3. How can you be a witness for Jesus in your family?

Lifeline:

Home should be the first place you give witness of Christ's love. Let your family members see Christ in you today!

WHOM DO YOU PLEASE?

"'How can you believe, when you receive glory from one another and you do not seek the glory that is from the one and only God?'"

⟜ John 5:44

Leroy is a smart high school junior. Lately, his friends have been mad at him because he won't give them the answers to the history take-home tests. Every time they ask, he says no. Where does he get his courage? Leroy cares only about pleasing God.

Anne is 16 and still has virgin lips. Several boys have tried, but no one has been able to kiss her. She's waiting for the right guy, but it's not easy. She's always getting teased about her purity. Where does she get her conviction? Anne cares only about pleasing God.

If it's not G-rated or an extra-clean PG flick, Krista doesn't go to the movie. She's left slumber parties when the movie rental was inappropriate. Last week, Krista even pulled her date out of the theater because the movie made fun of her Christian beliefs. Where does she get her confidence? Krista cares only about pleasing God.

Scott is a professional jeweler. Nine out of 10 jewelers he knows lie about diamond purity to make more money. Last week, Scott turned down $20,000 profit on a diamond deal because it was dishonest. Where does he get his integrity? Scott cares only about pleasing God.

Theresa is a successful doctor. One day, while preparing for surgery with seven other doctors, the conversation turned to faithfulness in marriage. All the doctors were cheating on their spouses. Theresa stood alone, the only one who had remained happily committed to her husband. Where does she get her loyalty? Theresa cares only about pleasing God.

Following God is often difficult. But it's a lot easier to walk with Him when you're focused on Who's really important. What your friends, coworkers, and even family members say doesn't matter a hill of beans if their words aren't matching up with God's Word.

Work to gain God's approval. You'll gain an eternal reward that will far outweigh your friends' acceptance.

Discussion Starters:

1. What does it mean to work for God's approval and not people's?

2. In what ways are you living for God's blessings? How are you relying too much on what your friends think?

Lifeline:

It takes a strong person to focus on what God wants. Encourage one another to do that today.

BY HIMSELF

"So Jesus, perceiving that they were intending to come and take Him by force to make Him king, withdrew again to the mountain by Himself alone."

When I first met Sam, I thought his schedule was going to flatten him. Sam was a junior in high school, working to get into a prestigious college. He had a 4.0, ran track, played basketball, was vice president of his junior class, volunteered with his church's junior high group, and had a steady girlfriend. At first, Sam kept up his activities and friendships by living on adrenaline. But as time passed, I could see he was losing gas.

Sam stopped sleeping. *Resting is a waste of time. I have more important things to do and people to be with*, he thought.

Soon, though, Sam's head began to drop in calculus class. He got circles under his eyes and also started getting irritable, snapping at his girlfriend and losing it on the basketball court.

His relationship with God began to slide, too. Quiet times became a thing of the past.

One day, after Sam fell asleep in class for the hundredth time and his girlfriend told him to straighten up, he decided to make some changes.

"I picked up the Bible and asked God to tell me how I should live my life. So He showed me what Jesus did when He was busy. And I couldn't believe it...Jesus slowed down and rested," Sam explained to me.

Jesus knew the value of solitude. He sure needed it after He fed the 5,000. It had been a long, tiring day. He'd spent His time surrounded by people who were clamoring for His attention, hanging on to His every word, and nudging Him for another miracle.

Jesus needed time with the Father after that. He knew He needed to rest and rebuild His strength in the Lord.

Jesus was perfect, but even He still needed to slow down.

Jesus was popular, but even He knew He couldn't find fulfillment from the multitudes of people who always flocked to Him or from the miracles He performed.

Solitude is important. And if God needs it, you do, too.

Discussion Starters:

1. Why is it so hard to slow down? To be alone?
2. What are some other instances in which Jesus was alone?

Lifeline:

If you're always running around, you won't be able to hear God's voice. Encourage one another to stop occasionally and listen to Him.

WAKE-UP CALL

"'For I have come down from heaven, not to do My own will, but the will of Him who sent Me. This is the will of Him who sent Me, that of all that He has given Me I lose nothing, but raise it up on the last day. For this is the will of My Father, that everyone who beholds the Son and believes in Him will have eternal life; and I Myself will raise him up on the last day.'"

↩ John 6:38-40

A good friend of mine, Kyle Rote, Jr., won the "Rookie of the Year" award several years ago in professional soccer. Shortly thereafter, he received a call from the president of the United States. When Kyle picked up the phone, the president introduced himself. Kyle thought it was a prank call from a buddy who often called, disguising his voice as a famous person's.

Kyle muffled his laughter and said, "Sure—the president of the United States. You're a big fake, a fraud, and you're crazy if you think I'm going to believe something as stupid as this joke, *Donny*."

The president paused, cleared his throat, and said, "Kyle, this is the president of the United States—not Donny—and I want to invite you to the White House to congratulate you on your recent honor."

Kyle was embarrassed beyond words.

Imagine being invited to a famous person's home and, like Kyle, humiliating yourself by not giving that person the respect he or she deserves. Well, Jesus tells us that one day, we're going live in His home (if we're His child) after we pass away. If you don't know Him during this lifetime, it will be an awkward experience—you'll be sent away to hell. But if you do know Him, if you can recognize His voice, coming to His home will be wonderful—you'll live eternally with the Savior.

You need not fear going home to Christ. It'll be the most welcoming, joyful homecoming you've ever known. But you should ensure that you know His voice so that when He calls, you'll be able to answer.

Discussion Starters:

1. Why do most people fear death?
2. What do you think it will be like to pass away and wake up in Jesus' home?
3. Can you recognize His voice? Why or why not?

Lifeline:

Encourage each other with the hope that life ends with a wake-up call from the greatest man who ever lived—Jesus.

THE BATTLE BELONGS TO THE LORD

"And He was saying, 'For this reason I have said to you, that no one can come to Me unless it has been granted him from the Father.' As a result of this many of His disciples withdrew and were not walking with Him anymore. So Jesus said to the twelve, 'You do not want to go away also, do you?' Simon Peter answered Him, 'Lord, to whom shall we go? You have words of eternal life.'"

⌒ John 6:65-68

For decades, countless faithful American young men followed the pointed finger and expectant scowl of the Uncle Sam posters plastered on draft buildings from the Atlantic to the Pacific. "Uncle Sam Wants You!" the posters read, urging young men to join the military and fight for their country.

As a citizen, you have a responsibility to your country. But as a child of God, you have a responsibility to the Lord. God wants you to fight and win a different sort of war. His desire is that you will join His eternal army and fight to win the souls of everyone He puts in your path. That's His will for your life.

God asks us to tell others about Him, but He also wants us to remember that salvation is up to Him. You can witness to a friend, but whether or not she accepts Jesus is in God's hands.

Remember—*God* has words of eternal life. Your role is to be a tool, someone God can speak through. It's essential to "fight" for your friends and relatives who don't know God. But only God can win the ultimate battle.

Discussion Starters:

1. How do we know that true Christians go to heaven?
2. What role does God's army play in bringing people to salvation? How can you, as a member of His army, fight for Him?
3. In order to be part of the battle to win others over for Christ, you'll have to put on God's heavenly armor (see Ephesians 6). In what ways are you donning the armor of God in school? At work? At home?

Lifeline:

Have someone in your family tell about a time he or she led someone to Christ. Answer: What was the experience like? How was God working in that person's life before he actually accepted Christ? What was your role in the experience?

A NEVER-ENDING CLASS

"But when it was now the midst of the feast Jesus went up into the temple, and began to teach. The Jews then were astonished, saying, 'How has this man become learned, having never been educated?' So Jesus answered them and said, 'My teaching is not Mine, but His who sent Me. If anyone is willing to do His will, he will know of the teaching, whether it is of God, or whether I speak from Myself. He who speaks from himself seeks his own glory; but He who is seeking the glory of the One who sent Him, He is true, and there is no unrighteousness in Him.'"

~ John 7:14-18

You're going to be in school for your entire life.

Now, before you panic, let me explain. Everything in your environment teaches you something. You learn from the TV set, your cassettes and CDs, and magazines and books. The 10 billion cells in your brain take in every sound you hear and sight you see. Those sights and sounds, which are stored in your subconscious, are recalled later.

Jesus knew learning is important—it affects who you become.

The first American teachers, in every school, taught the Bible. For America's first 100 years, *The New England Primer* showed every American kid how to read. The alphabet was taught like this:

A—"A wise son makes his father glad" (Proverbs 10:1).

B—"Better is a little with the fear of the Lord" (Proverbs 16:8).

C—"Come unto Christ all you who labor" (Matthew 11:28).

Kids back then spent hours reading Bible-based material, but now we spend most of our time in front of the TV. God's prescription for living is certainly not found there, though. I challenge you to turn off the TV once in a while and involve yourself in activities that would make God smile.

For instance, try to relate what you're learning in school to God's Word. Discuss current events or issues with your family—they'll help you figure out how to take a biblical stand. Learn to critically evaluate the media. What are they pushing? Do your values agree with their agenda?

Unscriptural teaching is everywhere. But we don't have to bend to the world. The Bible is and always will be relevant—and what you learn from it will have eternal significance.

Discussion Starters:

1. Who are your main teachers? Whom do you listen to most?

2. According to John 7:18, what's the test for a good teacher?

Lifeline:

Help each other identify negative teachers and decide how to respond.

"I HAD THE WORLD"

"But many of the crowd believed in Him; and they were saying, 'When the Christ comes, He will not perform more signs than those which this man has, will He?' The Pharisees heard the crowd muttering these things about Him, and the chief priests and the Pharisees sent officers to seize Him. Therefore Jesus said, 'For a little while longer I am with you, then I go to Him who sent Me.'"

↩ John 7:31-33

One of the richest and most famous athletes who has ever lived is a world champ, millionaire boxer named Muhammad Ali. No doubt, in his prime, Ali was a boxing phenomenon. He even said it himself: "I am the greatest! I am the greatest!"

Just a short 15 years after Ali quit boxing, *Sports Illustrated* did a cover story on him. The writer visited Ali's farm one cold winter day and candidly traced the champ's rise—and fall. Once a legend, Ali had now become a memory. Most of what was left filled the training barn behind Ali's house, which was full of his trophies and life-sized posters—pictures with Ali's arms thrust high overhead in defiant victory. As the writer and the champ toured the old barn, the writer noted that pigeons in the rafters had left droppings streaked across Ali's posters and trophies. One by one, Ali turned them toward the wall in shame and disgust. He walked outside and said softly in self-pity, "I had the world, and it wasn't nothin'."

"I had the world...and it wasn't nothin'."

You can get so much that you don't need God; you can get so famous and successful that you might think you sort of *are* God.

The Pharisees were like that. Those religious bigwigs were so full of pride and arrogance that they didn't recognize the Son of God when He was standing right in front of them. Like Muhammad Ali, they had too much stuff in the way. Their rules and legalism clouded their ability to see Jesus for who He really was.

Don't let other things get in the way of your relationship with the Messiah!

Discussion Starters:

1. Jesus said, "For what will it profit a man to gain the whole world if he forfeits his soul?" (see Matthew 16:26). What does that mean to you?

2. Is there anything in your life that's getting in the way of God? If so, what? What will you do about it?

Lifeline:

Home is the place to remind one another that there's no way to God but through Jesus.

MAN OF PROPHECY

"Others were saying, 'This is the Christ.' Still others were saying, 'Surely the Christ is not going to come from Galilee, is He? Has not the Scripture said that the Christ comes from the descendents of David, and from Bethlehem, the village where David was?'"

↪ John 7:41-42

Josh McDowell is an influential Christian apologist and writer. In his book *Evidence That Demands a Verdict*, Josh pointed out that during the 1,000-year Old Testament writing period before Jesus' birth, several hundred specific prophecies were given that accurately predicted the birth, life, death, and resurrection of the Messiah.[2] Read for yourself:

		Prophesied	**Fulfilled**
1.	Born of a virgin	Isaiah 7:14	Matthew 1:18,24-25
2.	Family line of Jesus	Isaiah 11:1	Luke 3:23-33
3.	House of David	Jeremiah 23:5	Luke 3: 23-33
4.	Born in Bethlehem	Micah 5:2	Matthew 2:1
5.	His pre-existence	Micah 5:2	Colossians 1:17
6.	He shall be called Immanuel	Isaiah 7:14	Matthew 1:23
7.	Preceded by a messenger	Isaiah 40:3	Matthew 3:1-2
8.	Ministry begins in Galilee	Isaiah 9:1	Matthew 4:12-13,17
9.	Sold for 30 pieces of silver	Zechariah 11:12	Matthew 26:15
10.	Hands and feet pierced	Isaiah 53 & Psalm 22:16	Luke 23:33

The odds that any other man could fulfill all these and the other prophetic claims about the Messiah are nearly impossible. The chances of that occurring are about as good as your filling the solar system with golf balls, marking one with a red dot, and then asking a blind golfer to hit the red-dot ball on his first swing.[3]

The evidence is clear: Jesus is Lord and God!

Discussion Starters:

1. What do Jesus' fulfilled prophecies reveal about your faith?

2. How else can we be sure that Jesus is who He claimed to be?

Lifeline:

The Jesus of prophecy lives in His believers and will work through them!

RED-HANDED

"The scribes and the Pharisees brought a woman caught in adultery, and having set her in the center of the court, they said to Him ... 'Now in the Law Moses commanded us to stone such women; what then do You say?' ...But...[He] said to them, 'He who is without sin among you, let him be the first to throw a stone at her.' ...When they heard it, they began to go out one by one, beginning with the older ones, and He was left alone, and the woman, where she was, in the center of the court. Straightening up, Jesus said to her, 'Woman, where are they? Did no one condemn you?' She said, 'No one, Lord.' And Jesus said, 'I do not condemn you, either. Go. From now on sin no more.'"

⏎ John 8:3-5,7,9-11

Pennies were tight in my house as I grew up. We didn't have the money to play video games or buy soda. But God always provided for us—He was good. As a junior high kid, that never seemed to be enough, though.

One Friday night, I wanted to see the high school football game, but my pockets were empty. Those games were big in my hometown. I had to get inside. So I schemed, *I'll just crawl over the fence and get in free.*

Up I went, climbing the chain-link fence. I knew it conveniently led to the top of the grandstands. I'd have no problem getting a seat once I arrived there safely. But when I got two-thirds of the way up, I saw Mr. Ozment, the high school principal, peering down at me through his spectacles. I froze. *I'm gonna be an endangered species,* I realized, gulping.

"Mr. White," Mr. Ozment said sternly, "I want you to report to my office after you get out of school on Monday."

"Yes, sir," I managed to squeak out.

I could already feel the imminent sting of Mr. Ozment's paddle on my bottom. Just anticipating it made me miserable the whole weekend.

But the funny thing about that Monday was that Mr. Ozment *smiled* at me. The paddle was absent. He could tell I was sorry, and he forgave me.

And Christ forgives us so much more! Like the adulteress, we all get caught doing something wrong (by God, even if by no one else). We all mess up. But if we've repented, Christ simply says, "It's already forgiven. Just don't sin anymore."

Discussion Starters:

1. Why did Jesus tell the woman she was forgiven?
2. What does that say about God's love for us?

Lifeline:

Although the Bible commands parents to discipline at times, family members should also give each other the grace Jesus gave the adulteress.

MAKE HIM SMILE

"So Jesus said, 'When you lift up the Son of Man, then you will know that I am He, and I do nothing on My own initiative, but I speak these things as the Father taught Me. And He who sent Me is with Me; He has not left Me alone, for I always do the things that are pleasing to Him.' As He spoke these things, many came to believe in Him."

↪ John 8:28-30

I love to please my daddy. He's 80 years old right now, and I still get thrilled when he notices something I've done. He becomes so excited that I feel special and loved when I meet with his approval. In fact, when I was in college, playing football was worthwhile because Daddy was watching.

We should try to please our earthly fathers, but even more, we ought to win our heavenly Father's favor. It's important. A whole host of people in the Bible pleased God, and they made history. For example:

God flooded the whole sinful world but spared Noah's family because "Noah found favor in the eyes of the Lord" (Genesis 6:8).

God built the entire Jewish nation on David's strength because He was pleased as He saw that David had a heart for God (see 1 Samuel 16).

God the Father built His kingdom for Jesus because He was so pleased and happy with His Son (see Matthew 3).

God loves it when we live a life pleasing to Him!

Julie went to the sophomore party after the game one Friday night. About 11:30 that evening, things got wild. Two football players brought a fifth of Jack Daniels and poured it into the punch. "Everybody" started getting crazy. Julie didn't care that it was "uncool" to leave before midnight. She headed for home. Julie knew Whom to please.

Andy sat crowded in the backseat of Mike's Bronco with all five of the starters on the basketball team. A joint was passed from player to player. "Everyone" took a drag. Andy smelled the smoke and felt the heat as his turn came up. "No thanks, guys. None for me," he said. God smiled.

Every day, you have a choice. Do you want to make God happy? Do you want to have Him look at you and proudly say, "That's My child"? Well, then, make your Daddy grin. It'll be one of your best decisions ever.

Discussion Starters:

1. What other people in the Bible were examples of being God-pleasers?

2. Why did God create people with a choice to please or displease Him?

3. How can you make God happy this week? Why is it so important to gain His approval?

Lifeline:

It takes the encouragement of a caring family to be a God-pleaser.

FREED FROM SLAVERY

"Jesus answered them, 'Truly, truly, I say to you, everyone who commits sin is the slave of sin. The slave does not remain in the house forever; the son does remain forever. So if the Son makes you free, you will be free indeed.'"

◁ John 8:34-36

Harriet was a dear African-American lady who lived in America's historic Civil War days. Born into slavery, at age seven Harriet Tubman was told by her mom that she might as well face the fact that she was a slave, she'd always be a slave, and she'd die a slave.

Harriet didn't buy it. That day, she determined in her heart that she would either be free or die trying to attain liberty. And she reached her goal. By age 40, not only had she crossed the dangerous pathway to freedom by fleeing north, but she had also helped others find dignity, hope, and freedom. Harriet escorted more than 300 slaves from slavery to freedom—or from death to life—on the Underground Railroad.

People called her "Moses."

America is now slave-free, but in some ways we're all enslaved. Sin traps us and restricts us. If we don't have Christ, sin leaves us hopeless. If we do have Christ, it can interfere with our relationship with God.

Be wary of sin. It's sneaky and subtle. No one holds a grudge and intends to end up bitter and hateful at the world. No one "borrows" a few dollars and intends to end up a full-fledged shoplifter. No one starts out with a tiny lie and intends to become outright dishonest. But sin is like that. It starts off seemingly innocent and then leads to a trap of slavery.

Next time you're tempted to cut a few corners, to fudge a bit on the truth, or to indulge in a bad relationship, remember where those things can lead.

Jesus warns, "I love you too much to see you become a slave. Don't give in to the lies. Don't let your foot get caught."

And don't let sin get the better of you.

Discussion Starters:

1. What are some other sins that lead to slavery?

2. How does Satan make sin look so appealing?

3. How can you gain freedom when you find yourself in a sin trap?

4. Why can only Jesus truly set you free?

Lifeline:

Resolve to help one another avoid the trap of sin. Then pray together that God will make you strong enough to resist the sin temptation, and thank Him for ultimately making you free.

LORD, LIAR, OR LUNATIC?

"Jesus answered, 'If I glorify Myself, My glory is nothing; it is My Father who glorifies Me, of whom you say, "He is our God"; and you have not come to know Him, but I know Him; and if I say that I do not know Him, I will be a liar like you, but I do know Him and keep His word. Your father Abraham rejoiced to see My day, and he saw it and was glad.' ...[Then] Jesus said to them, 'Truly, truly, I say to you, before Abraham was born, I am.'"

↝ John 8:54-56,58

What if one of your friends stood up at lunchtime and announced to the rest of the school (or restaurant) that he was the president of the United States? How would people respond?

They would yell, "You're crazy! Sit down."

Or they'd laugh, saying, "You're either kidding or you're lying."

No one would respond, "Well, now that I think about it, you *do* look like the president. Maybe you're right."

Your friend would be a liar or a nutcase if he claimed to be the most powerful political figure in the United States...unless he really was who he claimed to be.

In the same way, Jesus Christ didn't say He was just another prophet. He didn't tell everyone He was simply a good man with some great moral teachings. Jesus claimed to be God in the flesh.

The Jews thought Jesus' claim was blasphemous, so they decided to crucify Him. But I believe Jesus was 100 percent truthful when He told everyone He was God. Jesus knew that statement would lead to His death. Why would He allow Himself to be crucified if He wasn't who He said He was? If He wasn't truly God, Jesus would've confessed at the last minute, "I lied. It's not true! Don't crucify Me!"

But He didn't back down one bit.

As C. S. Lewis pointed out in his work, we all have to decide who Jesus was. Either Jesus was God, He was lying, or He was crazy.

Easter morning and history stand as witnesses that Jesus wasn't a liar or a lunatic. That leaves us with only one choice—He is Lord.

Do you agree?

Discussion Starters:

1. Why do some people try to make Jesus out to be less than who He is? Why is He different from Muhammad, Buddha, or Confucius?

2. What difference does it make in your life that Jesus is Lord?

Lifeline:

How can Jesus be Lord of your household?

BLIND SPOTS

"As He passed by, He saw a man blind from birth.... [So] He spat on the ground, and made clay of the spittle, and applied the clay to his eyes, and said to him, 'Go, wash in the pool of Siloam' (which is translated, Sent). So he went away and washed, and came back seeing."

⟿ John 9:1,6-7

Jerry rips on every kid in school.

Melinda wears clothes that are too tight.

Trevor shows off his muscles.

Doug, a smart businessman, thinks constantly about his computers and his money.

Anna likes her 16-year-old boyfriend more than she loves God.

Stephanie won't listen to her friends' problems, but when she's got a crisis, she expects them to be all ears.

Marvin will do anything to be popular...even dishonor his parents.

Sylvia, a 42-year-old mom, complains constantly about how hard her life is.

Byron, an unemployed father, becomes so preoccupied with finding a job that he virtually ignores his kids.

Adrienne tunes out her best friend when she tries to point out a major red flag in Adrienne's life.

Sports in college made me increasingly self-centered. I had a blind spot in my ego.

Blind spots—places in our lives where we can't see the truth. God knows that we all, in some ways, are spiritually blind. We often don't perceive ourselves clearly. We can't tell when we're in a rut. We overlook the not-so-good things we say and do.

That's why God created accountability—relationships that are close enough and safe enough that our friends can point out blind spots and bad habits that we've chosen not to see.

Make sure you have someone in your life to whom you're accountable. Someone who will pray with and for you. Someone who will point out the blind spots and, with God's help, help you to avoid crashing.

Discussion Starters:

1. How can we get blinded to the truth that's around us?

2. How can Jesus heal our blind spots? How does He use people to help us?

Lifeline:

Jesus can heal physical and spiritual blindness. But He also gives relationships to help us see clearly. Does your family have accountability?

CAN YOU BELIEVE IT?

"Jesus heard that they had put [the blind man] out, and finding him, He said, 'Do you believe in the Son of Man?' He answered, 'Who is He, Lord, that I may believe in Him?' Jesus said to him, 'You have both seen Him, and He is the one who is talking with you.' And he said, 'Lord, I believe.' And he worshiped Him."

⮌ John 9:35-38

Tim was mad! He couldn't believe his parents were moving the family to a new town. His anger got him into fights with his friends. He mouthed off to his parents. Most of all, Tim was mad at God.

Seeing that my friend was in trouble, I confronted him in love. "Tim, why are you striking out at everyone?" I asked.

Tim mumbled with hot tears in his eyes, "My dad's moving me across the country from my friends. I don't trust God. Actually, I don't even like Him now. I just don't believe in anything anymore. What's Christianity anyway except a bunch of rules?"

After talking with him for a while about how he could hold on to his faith again, I took off my watch and handed it to him. Tim looked up with a "whatever" look in his eye.

"Whose watch is this, Tim?" I asked.

"Yours," he said gruffly.

"But *you're* holding it."

"It's still yours," Tim said, getting bored with my example.

"Well, I want you to have it. It's a gift."

"It is? Your watch? For me?" He was pleased and puzzled.

"Whose is it now, Tim?" I said with a grin.

"Uh, it's mine, I guess. Yeah, it's mine."

"When did it become yours? When I handed it to you or when you accepted the gift into your heart?"

Tim smiled softly. He, like the blind man Jesus healed, finally understood belief. And it helped him hold on to his faith.

Belief and faith come when you accept God's gift of life into your heart. Don't try to fight it or give the gift up. It's yours—because God loves you that much.

Discussion Starters:

1. Why did the blind man instantly worship Jesus once he believed?

2. What does it mean to believe in Jesus?

3. What happens when a person puts his or her faith in God?

Lifeline:

How can you help one another when struggling with unbelief?

MORE THAN ENOUGH

"So Jesus said to them again, 'Truly, truly, I say to you, I am the door of the sheep. All who came before Me are thieves and robbers, but the sheep did not hear them. I am the door; if anyone enters through Me, he will be saved, and will go in and out and find pasture. The thief comes only to steal and kill and destroy; I came that they might have life, and have it abundantly.'"

↪ John 10:7-10, emphasis added

The original *Webster's Dictionary* was written by a devoted Christian man who, like many of Western society's great early scholars, knew the Bible backward and forward. Webster defined the word *abundant* as "more than enough."

More than enough. Think about it. Jesus came to give abundant life, abundant peace, and abundant joy. Can beer, popularity, sports, money, a car, or a girlfriend do that? How much beauty is more than enough? How much pleasure is more than enough? How much fame and success are more than enough? How much money is more than enough?

When Jesus healed the hemorrhaging woman, she didn't need to go visit more doctors. She was completely well!

When Jesus fed the 5,000, they didn't leave the conference and head for McDonald's. They were full, and there were even baskets of food left over!

When Jesus gave the Samaritan woman His living water, she didn't go buy a Big Gulp at 7-Eleven. She was satisfied.

When will we stop trying to get high on this world's stuff? Ten thousand kids come to our Christian camps every year, and they get high on God! I see kids tapping into Christ's abundance all over this country, attending Bible studies, listening to Christian music on the stereo, enjoying quiet times before bed, participating in youth groups with a purpose, and having parents who encourage their kids to make honest, godly choices. All those things bring fulfillment to their lives because God is in them.

Life with God is abundant. Don't try living any other way.

Discussion Starters:

1. What's the difference between living and abundant living?
2. Why do real believers have more fun?
3. Why did God invent fun and happiness and pleasure, and how did He intend for us to have it?

Lifeline:

Ask one another, how abundant is your life today? How can you, as a family, help each other to make it better?

TWICE MINE

"Jesus answered them, 'I told you, and you do not believe; the works that I do in My Father's name, these testify of Me. But you do not believe because you are not of My sheep. My sheep hear My voice, and I know them, and they follow Me; and I give eternal life to them, and they will never perish; and no one will snatch them out of My hand. My Father, who has given them to Me, is greater than all; and no one is able to snatch them out of the Father's hand.'"

⌁ John 10:25-29

Joey was only 12 years old, but he was especially handy with a pocketknife and a block of wood. Because he was quite poor, his few precious toys were all handmade.

For three months, he poured his spare time into carving a beautiful little boat...a miniature replica of the Pinta that brought Columbus across the Atlantic Ocean. Joey took his boat to a nearby creek after a rain shower to test his prize. As the boat took off in the current, Joey's expression of satisfaction and accomplishment quickly turned to panic as the water rushed off with his one-of-a-kind masterpiece. He ran and ran to catch up with it, but the shore was too muddy and the waters were too swift to save the boat. In tears, he wandered back home.

Two months later, Joey was walking by a hobby shop when he saw his boat for sale in the window. Someone had found it! He rubbed his eyes in disbelief. The price tag was $10, but it might as well have been $100. He rushed home, emptied his entire piggy bank, scraped the $10 in change into a paper bag, and hurried back to town.

He bought his boat back and walked proudly out of the store. With tears in his eyes, he looked down at the boat and said, "Little boat, I made you, and you ran away. But I bought you back. So now you're twice mine."

Do you ever wonder if God loves you? Well, He does care for His sheep (that's what the Bible calls God's children). He looks after them, holds them, and, as Joey did, will fight to bring them back if they drift.

Next time you get carried away on the waves of life, remember that your Father in heaven is closer than you realize. He loves you—and He won't let *anything* separate you from Him (see Romans 8:38-39).

Discussion Starters:

1. How are we like Joey's little boat?
2. What did God do to buy us back?
3. How does it make you feel to be God's beloved child?

Lifeline:

Let's remember our God who gave us His Son so we could be twice His!

MY FATHER IN ME

"'If I do not do the works of My Father, do not believe Me; but if I do them, though you do not believe Me, believe the works, so that you may know and understand that the Father is in Me, and I in the Father.'"

John 10:37-38

Yesterday had to be one of the most "sheer fun" days of my life. I flew across the Tennessee pasture on a red-hot four-wheeler behind Paul Overstreet, one of country music's greatest songwriters and recording artists. Paul loves Jesus Christ. He writes and sings to help families love the Lord and serve each other. One of my favorite songs of Paul's says:

> I'm seeing my Father in me, I guess that's how it's meant to be
> And I find I'm more like Him each day
> I notice I walk the way He walks.
> I'm seeing I talk the way He talks.
> I'm starting to see my Father in me.

Jesus had all of His Father in Him. People could tell that Jesus was completely God because His actions were totally consistent with God's will. Jesus never wavered in producing a godly lifestyle.

Our responsibility as Christians is to follow God at home, work, and church, making sure our lifestyles are in line with the Lord. It's important for two reasons: First, we're supposed to become more like Christ as we grow in relationship with Him. Second, we're called to be witnesses to unbelievers, and they will be watching our words and actions.

If imitation is the sincerest form of flattery, pay Jesus a compliment—mold your life after His.

Discussion Starters:

1. How could people tell that Jesus was, indeed, God in the flesh?
2. Parents, how are your kids becoming more like Christ? Kids, in what ways do you see Jesus in your parents?
3. Practically speaking, in what ways can you more closely model your life after Christ at school? At home? At work?

Lifeline:

People can best see God when they see His love in Christians.

THE HUMAN MAZE

"Jesus answered, 'Are there not twelve hours in the day? If anyone walks in the day, he does not stumble, because he sees the light of this world. But if anyone walks in the night, he stumbles, because the light is not in him.'"

↪ John 11:9-10

Last week, my son Brady drew a maze on a sheet of paper for me to try to solve. There were so many detours and dead ends that I never did get to the finish.

In our tourist town, there's a human maze. It's designed for people to race one another to the finish line. You have only five minutes to run through the giant hallways and walls and discover four carefully hidden stations. At those stations, you get the marks "M" "A" "Z" "E" on a card. If you make it in time, you get a free T-shirt.

I went through that maze once. After I lost the race to my son, a curious thing occurred to me. I climbed the stairs to an observation deck where I could see the pathways and walls clearly from above. It was simple to memorize the path to victory. Anyone could win after a careful view from the top.

If we could see the outcome of our actions or what the future holds, we'd be less likely to run into sin. I'm sure Wendy would agree. On a dare, she once stole her biology teacher's master test and passed it out to her friends. She was caught and immediately expelled from school. Now she's in a different school, struggling to make friends and to get rid of her bad reputation.

Wendy couldn't have known what was going to result from her dare. But she could have consulted a Guide—Jesus. He knows the future (see Psalm 139), and He works all things out for our good (see Romans 8:28). If we call on Him, He will help us make godly decisions. His Spirit will direct us through our lives (see Psalm 48:14).

Jesus will be your light and your leader if you call on Him. He knows what's best for you. After all, He's got the view from above.

Discussion Starters:

1. What does it mean to walk in the light?
2. How is life like a maze?
3. What "walls" and "dead ends" do we often run into as we're growing up?
4. How can we get the view from above—God's perspective?

Lifeline:

Discuss how your family can help each other keep a godly perspective.

JESUS WEPT

"Therefore, when Mary came where Jesus was, she saw Him, and fell at His feet, saying to Him, 'Lord, if You had been here, my brother would not have died.' When Jesus therefore saw her weeping, and the Jews who came with her also weeping, He was deeply moved in spirit and was troubled, and said, 'Where have you laid him?' They said to Him, 'Lord, come and see.' Jesus wept. So the Jews were saying, 'See how He loved him!'"

↩ John 11:32-36

Have you ever wondered where tears come from? Have you cried so long that you wondered if your tear ducts would dry up? Physical hurt from life's bumps and bruises brings a certain kind of tears. But real tears come from heart pain—when you're emotionally upset. That usually happens when friends move, relationships break up, loved ones pass away, and people disappoint you.

In the original Greek language in which the New Testament was written, the apostle John said that Jesus sobbed, boo-hoo'd. He actually groaned with pain when Lazarus died. *Why?* we might wonder. *Didn't He know that He'd bring Lazarus back to life again?*

I think Jesus wept because He loves His people so much that although He knows all our pain will eventually be over forever, He feels every hurt we have. He cares deeply and knows your pain when your boyfriend breaks up with you. He grieves when someone calls you names or spreads rumors about you. He empathizes when you lose your job or when your dog runs away.

Only a deeply caring, loving, sensitive God would weep real tears for His children.

What was the source of Jesus' tears? Love.

Discussion Starters:

1. What do Jesus' tears say about God's love for you?
2. When was the last time you cried over someone else's pain? What did those tears mean?
3. Who needs your empathy right now?

Lifeline:

Empathy means feeling someone else's pain and caring deeply for him or her. Sometimes at home it's easy to overlook your family members' hurt. How can your family become more compassionate?

SECURITY

"Therefore the chief priests and the Pharisees convened a council, and were saying, 'What are we doing? For this man is performing many signs. If we let Him go on like this, all men will believe in Him, and the Romans will come and take away both our place and our nation.'"

⇜ John 11:47-48

Fear of losing our security—wherever we place it—can tempt us to do wrong things. I admire people who face up to that fear and take a stand for what's right.

Yesterday, a grateful mom came and told me about her daughter, Janis, who was running for junior class president. Janis was well liked in her public high school and prepared an excellent campaign. At the completion of her "make it or break it" 20-minute speech, which she gave in front of the entire student body, the panel of judges asked her, "Janis, who is your hero?"

Janis responded quickly, "My hero is undoubtedly Jesus Christ, who died for my sins." She didn't care that the truth could make her unpopular.

I know some businessmen who are so secure in their faith that they're able to make choices that cost them, both professionally and financially. My friend Michael Jones recently refused to negotiate a $100,000 real estate deal because it was unethical. And Dr. Cristman passes up thousands of dollars each year because he won't do abortions. His pro-life stance has hurt his reputation, but he doesn't care. He knows his standing with Christ is more important.

Jill also knows about finding security in God. Last week at a youth group party, she told me how tough junior high social life is.

"I couldn't believe it," Jill said. "This guy brought some stuff to this party that went way against my morals. Almost everyone told him he was cool. But I didn't think so. I called my mom, and she came to get me. No one thought I was cool, but I know that Jesus thinks I am."

It's tough to stand up for what you know is right. But if you find your security in Jesus and not in what others think, you'll be standing on eternally solid ground.

Discussion Starters:

1. How did Jesus shake the Jewish leaders' security?

2. How does being a Christian put your temporary security at risk?

3. Why is it often difficult to find our security in Jesus?

Lifeline:

Encourage each other to build your security in Christ.

PARADES

"On the next day the large crowd who had come to the feast, when they heard that Jesus was coming to Jerusalem, took the branches of the palm trees and went out to meet Him, and began to shout, 'Hosanna! Blessed is He who comes in the name of the Lord, even the King of Israel.' Jesus, finding a young donkey, sat on it; as it is written, 'Fear not, daughter of Zion; behold, your King is coming, seated on a donkey's colt.'"

⌒ John 12:12-15

Kids of all ages used to wait in line for days to buy a ticket to an Elvis Presley concert. Tens of thousands would scream 'til they were breathless when the Beatles or the Jackson Five played at a show.

What would we do if Jesus came to town?

Rock stars travel in personal jets.

Jesus rode on a donkey.

Rock stars make so much money that they could walk into their concerts on carpets of gold.

Jesus entered on simple palm leaves.

Music stars are raised up on concert stages, which are arrayed with hundreds of lights and lasers.

Jesus was raised up on a Roman cross.

Your favorite rock stars will be forgotten almost before they play their last chorus.

Jesus' words will be remembered forever.

Christ's coming changed the world. Do *you* want to make a difference in your lifetime? Well, you sure can't do it through money, popularity, achievement, or power. Those things will mean nothing in God's eternal perspective …unless you use them—your gifts, finances, and talents—to glorify Jesus. Want to make an impact on the people around you? Talk about Christ. He's the Alpha and the Omega, the beginning and the end.

And His name will be life-or-death significant in the long run.

Discussion Starters:

1. Why did the crowd say on Palm Sunday, "Blessed is He who comes in the name of the Lord"?

2. Why didn't Jesus demand royal treatment?

3. Why do money, talent, and fame mean nothing in God's perspective?

Lifeline:

How can your family make an impact for Jesus?

THE PACK

"'Now My soul has become troubled; and what shall I say, "Father, save Me from this hour"? But for this purpose I came to this hour. Father, glorify Your name.' Then a voice came out of heaven: 'I have both glorified it, and will glorify it again.'"

⟿ John 12:27-28

Jim Ryun has a great talent and an even more terrific heart. When he was in ninth grade, Jim wanted to run track, but he was too slow, so he got cut from the team. The setback didn't make him angry, though. It just made him eager to train even harder. He ran hours and hours every day. When asked if he was in pain, Jim would say, "Yes, but I've learned to run with the pain." Jim was the first high school runner to break the four-minute mile. He held the world record in the mile for 15 years.

But he never won the Olympics.

I watched him run for the U.S. track team at the Munich Olympics in Germany. There, a tragic event occurred. As Jim rounded the curve on the last lap of the race, he got caught—and trapped—in a pack of runners. I could see the pain etched on his face as he tripped and fell. Although he was the best in the world, Jim finished last. But his spirit and smile never dimmed. He continues to be one of the greatest men I've ever known, someone I and thousands of others admire.

Jim demonstrates the grace of Jesus Christ, and it is evident to those around him.

Jesus showed even more dignity on His way to the cross. Like Jim, He had a tough obstacle in His path. He was troubled, too (see verse 27). But Jesus knew that even the hardest things in life can glorify God. He was able to endure His pain on the cross because God had a purpose in it.

God has a purpose for your pain, too. Maybe that seems unthinkable. Maybe you feel hopeless. Maybe you're trapped in the pack of peer pressure, disappointment, or brokenness. But God will help you through it, and He can be glorified through your suffering.

He did it in Jim Ryun's life. But if you really want proof, look at how God's love broke through Jesus' pain.

Discussion Starters:

1. How was God glorified through Jesus' suffering?

2. What difficulty are you facing? How can God work in your situation?

Lifeline:

Pray that God would enable your family to see His purpose through hard times.

ARE YOU A JUDGE OF CHARACTER?

" 'If anyone hears My sayings and does not keep them, I do not judge him; for I did not come to judge the world, but to save the world.' "

⌒ John 12:47

"Pssst. Hey, did you hear what that Jesus guy said in the synagogue yesterday?" one Pharisee whispered to another.

"I know. What a joke! He didn't come to *judge* the world? That's what religion is all about. We're supposed to watch for all those bad people out there and then tell God about them," the other Pharisee said confidently.

"It's a good thing God has us to keep everyone else in line," the first Pharisee agreed. "What would He do without us to—?"

"Hey," the second Pharisee interrupted, "look at Joseph with that woman over there. Isn't he supposed to be in the synagogue, praying? We'd better go talk to him...."

And they walked off, thankful to be doing "God's work."

The Pharisees' biggest downfall was their judgmental attitude. They were so determined to set other people straight that they couldn't see their own crookedness.

The funny thing is, Jesus said He didn't come to earth (the first time) to judge His people. He came to save the world instead.

So why do we as Christians often feel it's our responsibility to criticize everyone around us? We're not much different from the Pharisees of Jesus' time when we condemn others. But it's easy to think:

Marc goes to those bonfire parties. How can he say he's a Christian?

Or, *I saw Suzie holding a beer. She's really gone downhill.*

Even, *Joanna's never prepared for Bible study. She has a weak faith.*

Maybe those things are true about Marc, Suzie, and Joanna. But our job as believers is to love others, not judge them. Sure, we should be concerned when those we love are sinning, but judging them isn't going to do us—or them—any good. God will deal with those people in His time.

Be thankful that Jesus didn't come to judge the world. After all, nobody's perfect, including us.

Discussion Starters:

1. What did Jesus mean by saying He wasn't going to judge the world?

2. What are the dangers of being judgmental?

3. How can we love others without condoning their sins?

Lifeline:

Together, thank God for His continual forgiveness. Then ask Him to help you love others and avoid being judgmental.

WASHING FEET

"Jesus, knowing that the Father had given all things into His hands, and that He had come forth from God and was going back to God, got up from supper, and laid aside His garments; and taking a towel, He girded Himself. Then He poured water into the basin, and began to wash the disciples' feet and to wipe them with the towel with which He was girded."

↝ John 13:3-5

The dishes get dirty three times a day. Who's going to wash them? The front porch is filled with leaves every time the wind blows. Who's going to sweep it?

The dog wets the rug. Who will clean it?

The baby needs a bottle. Who's gonna feed her?

Dad had a hard day at the office. Mom's back is killing her. Larry just lost the student council elections. Angie missed becoming a cheerleader by one vote. Who will encourage them?

Opportunities for foot washing are all around the house. These are great times to show your love for Jesus.

No one should brush off Jesus' commandment to follow His example of service (see John 13:15).

Jesus is Lord, and He still washed His disciples' feet, which was the lowliest chore He could've done back then. He even initiated the whole thing. He *wanted* to do it. Wow!

It's so easy to let your parents serve, or your wife serve, or to make your kid brother serve while you lord your authority (while sitting on a La-Z-Boy) over them. But until you serve others, you'll never know how fulfilling it is to "wash feet" and express your care to those you love. Foot washers hold homes together. They bring love to relationships and meaning to Christianity. Do you really want to imitate Christ and follow His commandment? Wash other people's feet; serve them.

And, for good measure, start with the person who has the dirtiest feet.

Discussion Starters:

1. Why did Jesus decide to wash the disciples' feet? Why were they so surprised?
2. Why is it hard to be a "foot washer"?
3. What are some practical ways to "wash feet" in your home? At your school? Your job?

Lifeline:

Have each family member decide to concentrate on serving three people for the next week. Then report back on your results. How did you feel? How did those people respond? Why is it so important to wash feet?

THE BROKEN FINGER

"When Jesus had said this, He became troubled in spirit, and testified and said, 'Truly, truly, I say to you, that one of you will betray Me.' ...There was reclining on Jesus' bosom one of His disciples, whom Jesus loved. So Simon Peter gestured to him, and said to him, 'Tell us who it is of whom He is speaking.' He, leaning back thus on Jesus' bosom, said to Him, 'Lord, who is it?' Jesus then answered, 'That is the one for whom I shall dip the morsel and give it to him.' So when He had dipped the morsel, He took and gave it to Judas, the son of Simon Iscariot."

⌐ John 13:21,23-26

Have you heard the joke about the man who went to the doctor? Well, the guy was in pain, so the doctor asked him, "Where do you hurt?"

The man, gritting his teeth, replied, "Doc, I hurt everywhere."

"Show me where," the doctor said with concern.

The man placed his right forefinger on his knee and said, "Doc, every time I touch my knee, I hurt bad." Then he touched his forehead. "Every time I touch my head, I hurt bad." Then he pressed his finger to his chest. "Every time I touch my chest, I hurt bad." Then he touched his nose. "Every time I touch my nose, I hurt bad."

The doctor took the man's hand and said, "Buddy, let me examine your finger." One close look was all it took. The doctor exclaimed, "You crazy boy, you've got a broken finger. No wonder it hurts!"

Well, maybe the joke wasn't *that* funny, but it does illustrate a profound truth. Sin is like having a broken finger. When you let sin run your life, everything you touch hurts! If you make money, you become greedy. If you make a friend, the relationship turns sour. If you succeed, you become arrogant. You wonder why you're struggling until someone points out your "broken finger"—the sin in your heart.

Judas was exactly like that. He spent years listening to Jesus talk, watched His miracles, and saw prophecies fulfilled, yet he was willing to betray Jesus for 30 pieces of silver. Judas had a "broken finger," and after he handed his Lord over he died of a broken heart (see Matthew 27).

We all are broken and sinful. But we can decide either to allow sin to taint us or go to the great Physician—Jesus—and let Him heal us.

What will you choose to do?

Discussion Starters:

1. What was the root of Judas' sin?

2. What are some ways we betray Jesus? How is betrayal a sin?

Lifeline:

Make a family pact that you will be loyal to Jesus every day, in every way.

WHOSE WAY?

"Jesus said to him, 'I am the way, and the truth, and the life; no one comes to the Father but through Me.'"

↪ John 14:6

America has over 1,800 active religious cults (at the time of this writing), and they all have a lot in common. Each one has a self-righteous leader who claims to be the only way to God. Every cult makes Jesus less than He truly was and elevates its leader until he or she is like a god. They all claim to have a special word from God, and to verify their unique message they add to or replace Scripture with their own personal beliefs, which are supposedly obtained from "divine revelations."

Listed below are some popular cults. Read what the cult leaders have said about faith and how their words conflict with Christianity:

- Joseph Smith (founder of Mormonism) said, "All Christian denominations are wrong, and their creeds are an abomination in God's sight."[4] Mormon church father Joseph Fielding Smith said, "There is no salvation without accepting Joseph Smith."[5]

- Shirley MacLaine (part of the New Age movement) said, "I was one with the water.... I am God, I am God."[6]

- Mary Baker Eddy was the founder of Christian Science. Her "Bible," *Science and Health*, reads, "The material blood of Jesus was no more efficacious to cleanse from sin when it was shed upon 'the accursed tree,' than it was when it was flowing in His veins as He went daily about His Father's business."[7]

- The *Watchtower* (of the Jehovah's Witnesses) teaches that Jesus was not God incarnate and that the doctrine of the Trinity is false.[8]

These cults are all tragically mistaken. Jesus stated simply and firmly, "I am the [only] way, the [only] truth, the [only] life; no one comes to the Father but through Me" (John 14:6).

Jesus is the true God, and you can find salvation only in Him. Don't let any cult tell you otherwise.

Discussion Starters:

1. Why do people follow cult leaders?
2. What's wrong with cults and other world religions? How are they different from Christianity?

Lifeline:

Some cult members are more devoted to their faith than Christians are to Christ. Is your family following Christ and His Word closely enough?

IN GOD WE TRUST

"'I will not leave you as orphans; I will come to you.... But the Helper, the Holy Spirit, whom the Father will send in My name, He will teach you all things, and bring to your remembrance all that I said to you.'"

↪ John 14:18,26

I had just spoken to a terrific group of high school athletes in Kansas City when the point guard of the girls' basketball team came up to me, wanting to talk. Melinda, a dynamic athlete, spoke softly as tears pooled in her beautiful brown eyes.

"Last summer," she began, "I was going to come to your camp for the whole month of July. I was so excited, it was practically all I dreamed about for nine months. Then—" her voice broke off "—four days before Kamp started, I got mono. I was so sick, I had to be put in the hospital. I almost died. I felt so alone and betrayed. I kept asking God why He took Kamp away from me."

She stopped and wiped her eyes. "But one day, my friend gave me a cross. Over and over again, I kept looking at that cross and thinking about all Jesus had done for me. I knew He said He'd never leave me, and His promise pulled me through." She continued, saying, "I got better—miraculously—and in a couple of weeks, I left the hospital. I drove to Kamp at the end of the term to see my friends, and the neatest thing happened. A girl I'd never met walked up to me and told me she got to go to Kamp in my place. Just seeing her so happy about it made me feel a lot better."

Melinda grinned and added, "You know what happened? She became a Christian at Kamp! If I hadn't gotten sick, she never would've been able to come. But because I had mono, she came to know God. Now I understand what Jesus meant when He said He'd never leave us. He worked everything out and brought the Holy Spirit to comfort me. God is good!"

Amen.

Discussion Starters:

1. Jesus knew we'd be put to the test as Christians, so He gave us the Holy Spirit to live in our hearts. How does the Holy Spirit comfort believers when troubles come?

2. What is the Holy Spirit's role in your life as a believer?

3. How did the Holy Spirit help Melinda? How can He encourage you?

Lifeline:

When you accepted Christ, the Holy Spirit came into your heart. Make your heart a good home for the Spirit by getting rid of your worries and doubts. Trust the Lord when He says He won't leave you.

FRIENDS WITH GOD

"'This is My commandment, that you love one another, just as I have loved you. Greater love has no one than this, that one lay down his life for his friends. You are My friends if you do what I command you. No longer do I call you slaves, for the slave does not know what his master is doing; but I have called you friends, for all things that I have heard from My Father I have made known to you.'"

⮑ John 15:12-15

Have you ever truly had a best friend? One who never let you down? One who was always there when you needed him or her? One who brought the best out in you? One who never talked behind your back?

Greg saw the power of friendship as a soldier fighting in Vietnam. During one battle, he and three other guys were in a foxhole, into which the enemy threw a hand grenade. Instantly, one of the other soldiers dove on the grenade and took the explosion so his friends would live. The soldier died instantly, but his commitment to friendship will live forever.

God's friendship with us is even more powerful.

It's easy to see God as Lord, as a taskmaster, and as the almighty Ruler. But it's often hard to see Him as your best friend, too. You probably wonder, *Why would a powerful God want to be friends with little ol' me?*

Why? Because He loves you.

God's the best friend you've got. He knows all your hopes, secrets, and needs. He's a gift-giver, a comforter, and a helper. Jesus is completely unselfish. In fact, He literally died for you.

The word *friend* originally comes from the Bible. It's translated as "loving kindness." It means the amount of love you have for someone isn't based on what he has done for you, but on what *you've* done for him!

Have you kept up your end of the friendship with God? Jesus wants you to talk with Him, to spend time with Him, and to share your gifts with Him. You wouldn't expect to stay friends with someone from school if you only talked with the person once a month—and you can't expect to be great friends with God if you only call on Him when you feel guilty or in an emergency. ("Lord, save me from this math test!")

Are you cultivating your friendship with God?

Discussion Starters:

1. Is Jesus your best friend? How can you be a better friend to Jesus?
2. What has Jesus done for you? How much does He love you?

Lifeline:

Do you give your friendship with Jesus as much attention as you give your human friendships? Write Him a letter as you would to a good friend.

THE COUNSELOR

"'When the Helper comes, whom I will send to you from the Father, that is the Spirit of truth who proceeds from the Father, He will testify about Me.'"

↞ John 15:26

Clink. Rattle. Clink. The dishes in the Kanakuk kitchen passed from hand to hand as dinner was prepared for the hungry campers. Cassandra, one of the college-aged cooks, sighed as she grabbed her spatula and leaned over to look into the oven. As I chatted with the other kitchen staff, I noticed a tiny tear run down Cassandra's cheek.

"Hey, Cassandra," I called to her, "can we talk for a minute?"

She nodded her head hesitantly, and we sat down at a table in the corner. After we had talked for an hour and she had cried enough to finish a box of tissues, Cassandra told me she'd been abused as a small child.

"I feel hopeless, like I can't escape my problems," she admitted.

"Cassandra," I said gently, "God knows that you have needs and problems. He loves you so much—unconditionally—that He gave you His Word (the Bible) and a counselor (the Holy Spirit) to live in your heart. The Spirit will help you work through these issues."

After our talk, Cassandra realized she had a problem-solver living in her heart. She began to memorize God's Word so she'd feed her mind with her "Counselor's" thoughts. She prayed constantly that God would fill her heart with her Counselor's love. She trusted Him continuously to fill her soul with her Counselor's assurance.

A week went by, and I saw her smile. A month went by, and I saw her happy heart. A year went by, and I saw her dance. The Lord was working in Cassandra.

Cassandra's not the only one with a built-in Counselor. The Holy Spirit comes into your heart the moment you accept Christ as Savior. He comes from the Father to testify about the Son. The Spirit is your Helper and your Teacher, and His purpose is to be with you and enable you to become more like Christ. Give your problems to the Holy Spirit.

There's nothing He can't handle.

Discussion Starters:

1. What are some other names for the Holy Spirit?

2. How can His ability as a counselor help you today?

3. Why did God give us His Spirit?

Lifeline:

How can your family recognize the power of the Holy Spirit in your prayers, and especially in your daily lives?

THAT VOICE INSIDE YOU

"'And [the Helper], when He comes, will convict the world concerning sin and righteousness and judgment; concerning sin, because they do not believe in Me; and concerning righteousness, because I go to the Father and you no longer see Me; and concerning judgment, because the ruler of this world has been judged.'"

⟿ John 16:8-11

Mary is a Christian psychologist who specializes in helping people get rid of their bad habits, relieve their stress, and put their lives back on track. Early last fall, a young lady named Rachel entered her office. Her eyes were dark and disturbed. After just one look, Mary could tell she was dealing with someone deep into a life of misery and sin.

As Rachel sat down, Mary asked what was wrong.

Immediately, Rachel told her that she was involved in an affair with a married man and felt really guilty about it. Rachel threw up her hands, saying, "I'm just completely miserable!"

Mary asked her, "Do you want me to help you change your ways?"

Rachel crossed her arms and quickly replied, "No, I don't want to change—I just want you to weaken my conscience."

Unfortunately, Rachel didn't realize that your conscience is actually helpful. It protects your heart just as the nerves in your hand protect your skin by making you pull away from a hot flame.

Your conscience keeps you from jumping into spiritual bonfires.

Your conscience is actually the Spirit of God. If you're a believer, the Spirit will guide you into the things that are right and will lead you away from sinful mistakes. The Holy Spirit will put the red sirens on when you say or do something displeasing to God. (That's how conviction works.) On the flip side, the Spirit will also let you know if you're becoming a righteous young man or woman of God.

The Holy Spirit is important. Who else could really let us know whether we're pleasing God?

When your conscience speaks, you'd better listen! God's still, small Voice knows best.

Discussion Starters:

1. How does the Holy Spirit speak to us?

2. How does the Bible speak to our conscience?

3. What happens when we ignore God's Voice inside?

4. How does the Holy Spirit glorify Jesus?

Lifeline:

As you keep God's Word alive at home, you'll keep your conscience sharp.

DO YOU SUFFER FROM PRAYER PROCRASTINATION?

"'In that day you will not question Me about anything. Truly, truly, I say to you, if you ask the Father for anything in My name, He will give it to you. Until now you have asked for nothing in My name; ask and you will receive, so that your joy may be made full.'"

↪ John 16:23-24

Some people will try anything to avoid doing their chores. And it seems some Christians will do anything to avoid praying.

Prayer procrastination. Everyone does it. We reason, *I'm too tired to pray right now. I'll do it when I'm fresh, when I have something interesting to say to God.* We put it off, thinking, *I'll pray after I finish this assignment,* or, *I need to run some errands, get advice from my best friend, and clean my room first.*

Why do we put off praying when it's so powerful?

I think it's because we forget how effective prayer really is. We forget that God is listening and that He promised to answer us.

Jesus said that if we pray in His name, He will hear our prayers. Every prayer we send toward heaven is answered—not always in the way we'd like, but always in God's timing (which, as we know, is best). There is no call-waiting in heaven. God will not "click over" to someone else while we're pouring our hearts out to Him.

Simply worrying about getting a job isn't going to help make you employable, but prayer can. Trying to do too many things will only tire you out unless you enlist God's help. Merely wishing for a new friend won't go as far as praying about finding a Christian buddy.

Why does prayer work? Because God cares about every detail of your life. He wants to provide for all your needs (see Matthew 7). But He desires for you to *rely on Him* for those things. He commands you not to be stressed, fearful, or anxious. God wants you to pray instead.

Jesus said prayers are best when they're honest, from the heart, simple, and not done for show (see Matthew 6). All you've got to do is ask in humility and faith. The rest is up to God.

Discussion Starters:

1. Since God can accomplish everything He wants to anyway, why did He give us the gift of prayer?

2. Why is prayer such an important part of our lives as Christians?

3. Who or what do you pray for the most? Why?

Lifeline:

Committed prayer will bring your family closer together, allowing you to grow in Christ. Don't put off prayer. Make sure it has top priority.

ONE NATION UNDER GOD

"'I glorified You on the earth, having accomplished the work which You have given Me to do. Now, Father, glorify Me together with Yourself, with the glory which I had with You before the world was. I have manifested Your name to the men whom You gave Me out of the world; they were Yours and You gave them to Me, and they have kept Your word.'"

⟿ John 17:4-6

Have we kept our word of commitment to God? If you look at the United States, it sure doesn't appear that those of us who live here have.

Did you know the phrase "One nation under God" is being thrown out of the pledge of allegiance in many public places, including schools?

Or that the Boy Scouts are under legal fire for saying "I will do my duty to God and my country"?

Have you heard that it's illegal in some cities to put up a manger scene on government grounds? Courts say it's a violation of the First Amendment. But the politics are pretty twisted. According to the same courts, the First Amendment also makes it illegal to deny government funding to a national art program that paints pornographic pictures of Jesus and mocks His work on the cross.

The laws that govern America are being twisted from their original God-fearing meaning to an anti-God bias that makes it more difficult every day for Christians to live for and worship God.

This shouldn't come as any surprise, though. Jesus told us we would be persecuted by a hostile world because of His name (see Matthew 24).

He also promised to guide us through it.

How can we live in a world that disrespects the One we love and honor? We can persevere, trusting that God is stronger than this world and that He will give us the ability to stand firm. We can give Him the honor and glory He deserves, regardless of what others are doing around us.

When it seems that everything in society is crumbling, your faith should only get stronger. After all, as the prophet Isaiah said, "If you do not stand firm in your faith, you will not stand at all" (Isaiah 7:9, NIV).

Discussion Starters:

1. How is your country turning its back on God?

2. What does today's scripture say about reverencing God?

Lifeline:

Focus on keeping your word to God and, as a family, standing up for Him.

FAMILY TIES

" 'For their sakes I sanctify Myself, that they themselves also may be sanctified in truth. I do not ask on behalf of these alone, but for those also who believe in Me through their word; that they may all be one; even as You, Father, are in Me and I in You, that they also may be in Us, so that the world may believe that You sent Me. The glory which You have given Me I have given to them, that they may be one, just as We are one; I in them and You in Me, that they may be perfected in unity, so that the world may know that You sent Me, and loved them, even as You have loved Me.' "

⤚ John 17:19-23

Unity. What does it mean to your family?

To Grant, family love and unity were of life-or-death importance. During the Vietnam War, Grant and his son, Mickey, both military men, watched battlefield reports carefully from their home base as thousands of American soldiers lost their lives in the fierce battles overseas. Not far into the war, Grant was called to do a 12-month duty on the worst battlefront. Miraculously, he returned home without injury. A few months later, when Mickey was called to Vietnam to fight, Grant asked the commanding officer if he could take his son's place on the battlefield so Mickey could stay home. The substitution was approved, and Grant returned to battle. Grant was so bonded to his son that he risked death so Mickey might be safe.

That's the kind of unity Jesus was talking about—love, devotion, and selfless acts of courage done in His name. Is your family that unified?

Jesus also wants His divine family to be bonded together. If you're a Christian, you have countless brothers and sisters in Christ, and you are all called to be one body. That means you don't laugh when John in the pew next to you raises his hands and sings off-tune on Sunday mornings. You also don't let petty arguments or cliques drive your youth group apart. And you build your brothers and sisters up by praying for them, encouraging them, and sometimes even confronting them in love.

As much as you need unity within your family at home, you also need it in the church around the world. You've got millions of brothers and sisters in Christ. Make your Father proud—be unified.

Discussion Starters:

1. How can our family and church body be one as God the Father and Son are one? How does God unify us?

2. Why does our love for each other reveal Christ in us?

Lifeline:

They'll know we're His disciples if we love one another.

HOLY

"Judas then, having received the Roman cohort and officers from the chief priests and the Pharisees, came there with lanterns and torches and weapons. So Jesus, knowing all the things that were coming upon Him, went forth and said to them, 'Whom do you seek?' They answered Him, 'Jesus the Nazarene.' He said to them, 'I am He.' And Judas also, who was betraying Him, was standing with them. So when He said to them, 'I am He,' they drew back and fell to the ground."

⟿ John 18:3-6

Jesus' bold statement struck those who had come to arrest Him with a sense of awe. It seems as if they got a glimpse of His power as the Son of God—power and glory that ought to get more respect today than they usually do.

Long before copy machines, during a wonderful era of early Jewish tradition, a scribe would make copies of holy Scripture by taking his feather pen (quill) and carefully, accurately, perfectly hand-copying God's Word from one scroll to another. When the scribe would get to the word God, he would stop, pray, undress, take a bath, put on clean clothes, get a new quill, and then go back to his work and write "God."

It's quite a bit different today. Now we defy God's fourth commandment —"Don't take the Lord's name in vain"—by trampling God's name as if it's dirt. We degrade Him in our conversations, on TV, in movies, and in books.

"Oh, my God!" "My God!" "Jesus Christ!" people exclaim when they're mad, upset, or just want words to fill in the blanks of day-to-day conversation.

It's no longer necessary to bathe and change clothes before we say or write God's name, but Jesus made it clear that God is holy and awesome. He should be revered and respected. Do your language and attitude reveal that you honor the living God?

Discussion Starters:

1. What did Jesus mean when He said, "I am He"?
2. What did God mean when He said, "You shall not take My name in vain" (see Exodus 20:7)?
3. In what ways is God holy? Why is His holiness so powerful?

Lifeline:

As we've discussed, each day Christians are surrounded by others who take God's name in vain. How should your family respond to those who don't give God the respect and honor He deserves?

SPREAD THE GOOD NEWS!

"Now Simon Peter was standing and warming himself. So they said to him, 'You are not also one of His disciples, are you?' He denied it, and said, 'I am not.' One of the slaves of the high priest, being a relative of the one whose ear Peter cut off, said, 'Did I not see you in the garden with Him?' Peter then denied it again, and immediately a rooster crowed."

↪ John 18:25-27

Amanda didn't know *what* to do. After a long, lonely semester, Stacey, a popular girl in the ninth grade, had started talking to her. Stacey sat behind Amanda in fifth-period history and, lately, she'd been passing notes to Amanda during class. Ordinarily, Amanda would've been thrilled with the other girl's attention. She knew that if she became friends with Stacey, she'd be "in" with the popular group. But strangely, all of Stacey's notes had focused on questions about God and church.

Stacey doesn't seem like the kind of person who'd go to church, Amanda thought, confused. *She must be making fun of me. If she thinks I'm a nerdy Christian, I'll never make friends in this school.*

So after the third note, Amanda stopped beating around the bush and instead lied. "I don't know what you're talking about, Stacey. I don't go to church. It's boring," she wrote back. Amanda took a deep breath, leaned back, and slipped the note under Stacey's elbow.

When the bell rang, Stacey got up, brushed past Amanda's desk, and hurried out the door. No smiles, no extra notes—nothing.

The following Sunday morning, Amanda found out why she'd been snubbed. As she stood talking with her youth pastor, Amanda felt a tap on her shoulder.

"Hi, Amanda," Stacey said. She was clutching a new Bible.

Amanda smiled meekly, feeling about as low as pond scum.

Selfishness and insecurity—that's why Amanda denied Jesus, and Peter denied his Lord for the same reasons. Next time you've got an opportunity to talk about Christ, don't think of yourself. Don't look around to see who's watching. Be bold. Be courageous. Spread the awesome news!

Someone else's eternal life could hinge on what you say.

Discussion Starters:

1. What keeps you from witnessing to others about Jesus?

2. How can you be bolder in talking about Christ? More prepared?

Lifeline:

Some people are afraid to tell others about Jesus because they don't feel they know enough about Christianity. How can your family learn more?

TAKE IT THERE, PUT IT THERE, AND LEAVE IT THERE

"Pilate came out again and said to them, 'Behold, I am bringing Him out to you so that you may know that I find no guilt in Him.' Jesus then came out, wearing the crown of thorns and the purple robe. Pilate said to them, 'Behold, the Man!' So when the chief priests and the officers saw Him, they cried out saying, 'Crucify, crucify!' Pilate said to them, 'Take Him yourselves and crucify Him, for I find no guilt in Him.'"

↪ John 19:4-6

I looked across the sea of multicolored faces and whistled. It was our summer camp for forgotten kids, and our staff had gathered 300 urban teenagers from projects, gangs, and city streets to hear the gospel. As I attempted to explain the miracle of the cross, I could see the question marks in their eyes. To them, this Jesus man seemed too good to be true.

With a large ax and a 15-foot elm tree, I hacked out the form of a huge cross. The kids were silent, watching and thinking.

I finished hacking at the cross. "You've all heard a lot about how Jesus died to forgive your sins," I said. "Well, I challenge you to take Him up on His offer of forgiveness. Without looking at your neighbor, write your sins on a paper and, one by one, come nail your sins to the cross."

The atmosphere grew somber and pensive as each kid made his way forward and pounded his sins into the cross.

The cross was already filled with paper when Dustin stopped. I could see he was scared and confused. One of the youth workers noticed, too. He put his arm around Dustin's shoulder and simply said, "What's wrong?"

Dustin mumbled, "I dunno." He shuffled his feet in the dirt.

The youth worker pointed to Dustin's sin-filled paper, showed him the hammer and nail, then motioned to the cross and said, "Just take it there, put it there, and leave it there."

"That's it?" Dustin asked.

"That's all there is to it. Take it there, put it there, and leave it there."

Jesus is the only person who truly never sinned, yet He was willing to die to save us from our burdens. Once you've confessed to Him, your sins are gone. Has He pronounced you not guilty?

Discussion Starters:

1. Why is Jesus the only One who is able to forgive our sins?
2. What happens when we repent and ask forgiveness?

Lifeline:

As a family, give your sins to Jesus by secretly writing them down and then throwing them into the fireplace or trash can.

DON'T FORGET THE CROSS

"They took Jesus, therefore, and He went out, bearing His own cross, to the place called the Place of a Skull, which is called in Hebrew, Golgotha. There they crucified Him, and with Him two other men, one on either side, and Jesus in between."

↪ John 19:17-18

Albert, an elderly friend of mine, has worked closely with Billy Graham, helping him and a large team of committed evangelists put on thousands of crusades across America. One summer evening in New York, during one of Dr. Graham's early crusades, the fiery evangelist left the event disheartened, believing the crusade was weak and ineffective. He walked to a bench and slumped, holding his head in his hands.

Dr. Graham tells my friend that in his moment of disappointment, he got a "word" from God. Just as Graham was about to walk back inside the building, an old German man spotted Dr. Graham and, seeing him upset and disillusioned, firmly but lovingly confronted the young evangelist.

"Dr. Graham," the old man said gruffly, "you forgot the cross tonight. Don't forget the cross, Billy! Don't forget the cross."

These words rang in Graham's ears—he knew God had planted that message for him to hear. The old man's advice has since guided Billy Graham and his staff through years of crusades. Graham has led more people to faith in Christ than any person alive. What's his secret?

Dr. Graham reaches the lost when he talks about the cross.

Jesus' death on the cross is what makes the Christian faith powerful and meaningful—it saved you (and all believers) from your sins. The cross isn't just another piece of jewelry. It's not simply another symbol. It's the centerpiece of your faith, the hope of your life, and your ticket to heaven. Does your life reflect the significance of what Jesus did for you on the cross?

Discussion Starters:

1. Why was Jesus' crucifixion so powerful?
2. What happens when you forget Jesus' death on the cross?
3. What does the cross mean to you? Why?

Lifeline:

Christ loved you enough to endure the cross. Make sure you're modeling His sacrificial love in your family!

WHEN ALL IS SAID AND DONE

"Therefore when Jesus had received the sour wine, He said, 'It is finished!' And He bowed His head and gave up His spirit."

⏎ John 19:30

During President Bush's term as president of the United States, I toured the White House with his receptionist, Kathy Wills. Kathy took me to the historic Oval Office where the president did his daily work. In a pencil holder on top of his desk stood a simple 2" x 4" American flag glued to a small stick (the kind you buy at Wal-Mart for 49 cents).

"Why is it in such a prominent place in his office?" I asked, intrigued about why, out of all the beautiful gifts the president no doubt possessed, he had decided to place such a cheap flag on his expensive desk.

Kathy explained that as the president was visiting some injured soldiers in a military hospital, a badly wounded paratrooper had called him over to his bedside. The president had greeted the soldier, and the man had given him the flag. President Bush had smiled and thanked him.

Then the soldier had shaken the president's hand, looked him in the eye, and said from the bottom of his dedicated heart, "Mr. President, my only regret is that I cannot fight again."

Of all the famous and invaluable historical relics in the Oval Office, that tiny flag meant more to the president than anything else because it portrayed perseverence, dedication, and love of America.

Jesus finished His fight with the same integrity. He lived an exemplary life. He loved, taught, turned the other cheek, remained devoted to His Father, and died selflessly. He had no regrets at the end. Jesus didn't say, "Wait, I need to patch things up with Peter" while they dragged Him off to be crucified. He didn't exclaim, "You think I'*m* a sinner? Wait 'til *you* die. Then we'll see who goes where!"

Christ simply looked upward, where His Father was watching from heaven. It gave Him the strength to finish His life honorably and sinlessly. Jesus' death was brutal, but even then, He still glorified God.

You, too, will have obstacles and suffering in life. How will you live? Will you have no regrets when all is said and done?

Discussion Starters:

1. Why was Jesus able to die with no regrets?

2. How can we be as dedicated to God as the soldier was to his country?

3. How do you think God wants you to live your life? What qualities does He want you to cultivate so you will eventually have no regrets?

Lifeline:

What kind of "flag" will your family give God when life is over?

MUCH LOVE, LONG WALK

"So the soldiers came, and broke the legs of the first man and of the other who was crucified with Him; but coming to Jesus, when they saw that He was already dead, they did not break His legs. But one of the soldiers pierced His side with a spear, and immediately blood and water came out."

↩ John 19:32-34

Abigail was a kind missionary lady who gave her life to teach African kids how to read, write, and understand Jesus Christ. In a secluded country along the African coast, she spent a lot of time tutoring a nine-year-old orphan boy, Eman. As the boy grew in his skills, he also grew to appreciate and love his teacher who had given him the gift of knowledge.

One Christmas (Abigail had taught the children about Jesus' birth), Eman worried about what to give his teacher. Without any money, what could he do? Then he smiled. He remembered reading about a rare seashell that could be found on a secluded beach three walking days from his hut. So a week before Christmas, Eman began his long walk of love.

Early on Christmas morning, the teacher heard a knock on her door. As she opened it, she saw the giant grin lighting up the boy's face. He opened his hand and presented his valuable and unusual gift.

"Oh, this is so beautiful! Where did you get it?" Abigail asked.

"Three days walk down beach."

"Why? Why did you go get it for me?"

"Much love," Eman said and smiled again.

"I know, but you walked so far!" Abigail exclaimed in amazement.

And Eman humbly replied, "Much love...long walk."

Eman's devotion and love for his teacher reminds me of our Lord's unconditional love for His children. The day of His crucifixion (and even the days leading up to it) was excruciating. The humiliation and pain Christ went through are unimaginable to us. The ordeal seemed to linger forever, too. Even after Jesus was dead, the soldiers still stabbed Him in the side.

And He endured it all out of love for us.

I'll bet that if we asked Jesus, "Lord, why did You go through all that suffering for me?" He would answer much the same way Eman did.

"Much love...long day."

Discussion Starters:

1. What does sacrifice have to do with love?

2. What do you think was the longest part of Jesus' day of pain? Why?

Lifeline:

How can we, like Eman, sacrifice to thank Jesus for His incredible love?

HE'S NOT FINISHED YET

"Now on the first day of the week Mary Magdalene came early to the tomb, while it was still dark, and saw the stone already taken away from the tomb. So she ran and came to Simon Peter and to the other disciple whom Jesus loved, and said to them, 'They have taken away the Lord out of the tomb, and we do not know where they have laid Him.' ...For as yet they did not understand the Scripture, that He must rise again from the dead. So the disciples went away again to their own homes. But Mary was standing outside the tomb weeping; and so, as she wept, she stooped and looked into the tomb."

⤳ John 20:1-2,9-11

Dashed dreams. Everyone struggles with disappointment, even the most successful people. But losing a battle doesn't have to mean losing the fight. For example, did you know Abraham Lincoln lost at least six elections before he became one of the most famous presidents in U.S. history? Or that Michael Jordan was cut from his ninth-grade basketball team because he wasn't good enough? Even Joe Montana was knocked from the game "permanently" (so they said) before he led the 49ers to four Super Bowl championships.

And Jesus was buried as a dead man before He rose from the grave. No one thought He had a chance of rising on the third day. The stone was too heavy, the entrance too guarded. Jesus was dead, and His disciples all decided they'd just have to deal with it.

They were going to the tomb to mourn.

They got even more discouraged when they arrived. Someone had taken Jesus! It was another slap in the face.

Little did they understand what God was doing. The disciples didn't realize Jesus had risen and that His ascent to heaven had fulfilled the Scriptures. The fact that Jesus wasn't there even further backed up His claim to be the Son of God.

The disciples didn't get it. They thought their beloved Lord was gone forever. But Christ was already working in ways they couldn't see.

God is more powerful than your disappointments. He knows your dreams, and He won't leave you hanging.

I think the disciples would tell you that.

Discussion Starters:

1. Why do you think God allowed the disciples to mourn His death?

2. What did Jesus promise the disciples about His death?

Lifeline:

Describe a time when God worked through your disappointments.

WINGS

"Then He said to Thomas, 'Reach here with your finger, and see My hands; and reach here your hand and put it into My side; and do not be unbelieving, but believing.' Thomas answered and said to Him, 'My Lord and my God!' Jesus said to him, 'Because you have seen Me, have you believed? Blessed are they who did not see, and yet believed.'"

↪ John 20:27-29

Have you ever stood at the airport and watched the planes take off? Do you know how those big metal birds lift themselves off the ground? Well, when an airplane shoots down a runway, the wind rushing over the top of the wing creates a vacuum under it. The air that rushes up to fill the vacuum under the wing pushes the wing upward and gives the plane the lift it needs to get off the ground. If you didn't have that rushing air, you couldn't fly the friendly skies.

There's a good parallel here with our faith. Thomas had "wings." He knew Jesus intimately and should have had a faith that soared. He didn't have to run or do a bunch of work to activate his wings, but he needed to trust that Jesus would provide the wind and the lift.

Thomas wanted evidence. Like a baby bird, he stayed perched on the nest of familiarity. He was afraid to take that step of faith into the unknown. He wanted proof from Jesus before he'd exercise his wings.

You've got wings, too. The more you swiftly activate the wings—your faith—the higher you'll go. Jesus promised that. He knows you haven't seen Him, and He'll bless you for stepping out in faith.

How can you make your faith soar? By trusting God with your needs, hopes, and plans. By reading God's Word carefully and doing what it says, believing that God knows better than the world. By praying to God sincerely, with total dependence on Him.

Christians shouldn't be doubters.

Ask yourself some questions. Do you constantly worry about your life? Do you doubt God will come through in a crisis? Are you too self-reliant? Must you always see proof? Is it hard for you to release things?

The Lord knows it's tough to have faith. But you don't have to stay on the spiritual runway. If you'll trust Him, He will enable you to "mount up with wings like eagles" (Isaiah 40:31).

Discussion Starters:

1. Why did Thomas need to touch Jesus to believe?

2. How can you put faith in Jesus if you've never seen Him?

3. Why do you have to put your wings in motion before you can fly?

Lifeline:

Read Isaiah 40:28-31. How do Isaiah's words encourage your family?

JUST DO IT—JESUS' WAY

"After these things Jesus manifested Himself again to the disciples at the Sea of Tiberias, and He manifested Himself in this way.... Simon Peter said [to the disciples], 'I am going fishing.' They said to him, 'We will also come with you.' They went out and got into the boat; and that night they caught nothing. But when the day was now breaking, Jesus stood on the beach; yet the disciples did not know that it was Jesus. So Jesus said to them, 'Children, you do not have any fish, do you?' They answered Him, 'No.' And He said to them, 'Cast the net on the right-hand side of the boat and you will find a catch.' So they cast, and then they were not able to haul it in because of the great number of fish."

⏪ John 21:1,3-6

There weren't any grocery stores back in biblical times. So when the disciples went fishing, they didn't go for fun—they went out of necessity.

All night they stood in that boat, casting their nets and waiting. Well, Jesus wasn't going to let them starve. Miraculously, He appeared just at the right time to help. The disciples obediently cast their nets on the right side of the boat and caught enough fish to feed the entire community.

Notice that Jesus told them to cast on the *right* side? That's the side He'll call His children to sit on when they enter heaven (see Matthew 25). When Jesus commands us to do things a certain way, there's always a reason. And since the disciples fished in God's way, they were rewarded.

Few of us fish for a living nowadays, but we do decide on which side of the boat to "cast our nets" in life. The left side is the world's way of fishing, or living. Drop your net there and you'll join the crowd in gossiping, cheating, lying, drinking, watching questionable movies, and taking advantage of others. Most people have fished on the left side of the boat. Often it feels good over there, but the net always comes up empty in the long run. You can't be truly successful fishing the way the world does.

Just as Jesus called the disciples to fish in His way, so He commands us to live in His way. We're still to live our lives on the right side of the boat—on His side. It might seem awkward. It might look as if everyone else is fishing on the left. You might feel as though you're not reaping any rewards. But although your catch might not always be in material possessions, it'll be eternally abundant.

Discussion Starters:

1. What are the benefits of fishing on God's side of the boat?

2. When is it tempting for you to fish on the world's side? Why?

Lifeline:

Together, make a list of what your family has gained from doing things God's way.

DESIRE

"So when they had finished breakfast, Jesus said to Simon Peter, 'Simon, son of John, do you love Me more than these?' He said to Him, 'Yes, Lord; You know that I love You.' He said to him, 'Tend My lambs.' He said to him again a second time, 'Simon, son of John, do you love Me?' He said to Him, 'Yes, Lord; You know that I love You.' He said to him, 'Shepherd My sheep.' He said to him the third time, 'Simon, son of John, do you love Me?' Peter was grieved because He said to him the third time, 'Do you love Me?' And he said to Him, 'Lord, You know all things; You know that I love You.' Jesus said to him, 'Tend My sheep.'"

↪ John 21:15-17

A poor, young boy in India sought out a great Indian sage (wise man) to ask him a pressing question. When the boy found the sage, he said to him, "Sir, how might I find the kingdom of God?"

The sage looked carefully into the boy's eyes and said, "You don't want it bad enough."

The boy departed, greatly disappointed. But the next day he returned and asked, "Sir, how might I find the kingdom of God?"

Again the sage said, "Boy, you don't want it bad enough."

The third day, the boy repeated his question persistently.

So the sage replied, "Meet me at the river tomorrow."

The next day, the boy arrived at the river, ready for his answer. The sage walked into the water with the boy until they were waist deep. Then the man abruptly dunked the boy under the water and held him there until he ran out of breath. The boy jerked his head up, gasping for breath.

The old sage said to him, "Boy, when you were under the water, what did you want more than anything?"

"Oxygen, sir, oxygen. I wanted air!"

"Well, boy," the sage said, "when you desire the kingdom of God as much as you desired that breath, you'll find it!"

With his equally challenging words to Peter, Jesus asked His disciple to demonstrate his love for God by caring for His people. It's easy to say "I love God," but to show it to others takes great commitment and desire.

Discussion Starters:

1. How can great desire enable you to love God by loving others more?

2. What did Jesus mean when He said to Peter, "Tend My lambs"?

3. Why must we love others if we truly love Christ?

Lifeline:

Love begins at home. If it doesn't happen there, it can't truly happen anywhere.

The book of Acts was written by Luke, primarily as a historical account of the early church. It begins by documenting the risen Savior and His last discourse with His disciples and continues by focusing on the powerful work of the Holy Spirit. Luke emphasized the work of the early believers and their heroic quest to make Christ known to all the world.

This book is an encouragement for all of Christ's followers to utilize the power of the Holy Spirit who lives within us. If we are sensitive to God's Spirit, we will live pure and purposeful lives that seek to bring others into a relationship with Jesus Christ.

WAITING

"Gathering them together, He commanded them not to leave Jerusalem, but to wait for what the Father had promised, 'Which,' He said, 'you heard of from Me; for John baptized with water, but you will be baptized with the Holy Spirit not many days from now.' So when they had come together, they were asking Him, saying, 'Lord, is it at this time You are restoring the kingdom to Israel?' He said to them, 'It is not for you to know times or epochs which the Father has fixed by His own authority; but you will receive power when the Holy Spirit has come upon you; and you shall be My witnesses.'"

↬ Acts 1:4-8

Waiting. I'm the world's worst sport when it comes to being patient! Red lights, grocery store lines, drive-thrus, and—I have to admit—God's promises can all get me frustrated if they don't fit into my schedule.

The disciples were weary and impatient from Israel's long years of political unrest. And since Jesus had been crucified, they were understandably worried about what would happen to them. *Who will be the next to hang on the Roman cross?* they wondered. They wanted an end to it all and knew that if Jesus set up His kingdom, their fears would be gone.

"C'mon, Jesus, set up Your kingdom. Let us rule with You," they said.

"Wait," was His disappointing reply. "God promises He'll be with you. That's all you need to know. I told you I'll be back, and I told you My Spirit would come to live inside you. Now wait. Believe and wait."

Like the disciples, we, too, know a lot about waiting for God. Growing up requires lots of believing and waiting, doesn't it?

"Sex is for marriage only," God says. "Wait. It's best that way."

"I want you to be happy, but leave the drugs and alcohol alone. I'll bring you all the joy you need. Wait on Me."

"I know you need direction in your life, and you want the answers right now. But I'll guide you. Wait and listen for My voice."

It's tough to be patient. But God will bless us when we wait. The disciples were patient, and God sent His Spirit. Together, they changed the world.

You can, too—if you wait for God's hand on your life.

Discussion Starters:

1. How can God enable you to wait on Him?
2. What other biblical figures had patience and waited on the Lord? How did God reward them?

Lifeline:

Ask the Holy Spirit to help your family *wait* for God's best in your lives.

THE ASCENSION

"And after He had said these things, He was lifted up while they were looking on, and a cloud received Him out of their sight. And as they were gazing intently into the sky while He was going, behold, two men in white clothing stood beside them. They also said, 'Men of Galilee, why do you stand looking into the sky? This Jesus, who has been taken up from you into heaven, will come in just the same way as you have watched Him go into heaven.'"

↪ Acts 1:9-11

"If you kill me, I'll be even stronger," Obi-Wan Kenobi told Darth Vader in the first movie of the *Star Wars* trilogy. Kenobi knew "the force" would only become more powerful if he died.

Now, I don't believe in the forces the movie portrayed, and it's a sad comparison in magnitude and reality, but in a way, Jesus said the same thing to His disciples as they fretted over His impending death.

"When I go, I'll still be with you. You'll be able to do even bigger things than I ever did," Jesus reassured them.

When Jesus left that day, He didn't leave orphans behind. He left men who would receive His Holy Spirit and be stronger than ever, able to perform miracles and healings through Jesus' power. In fact, the disciples were able to lead even more people to faith in Christ *after* Jesus left because people could see God's hand working through His followers.

Jesus also got busy helping the disciples after He ascended to heaven. Three significant things occurred when Jesus went home, and they still affect you and I to this day: First, Christ began to build a home for His children. Second, He began to pray for us regularly. And finally, He released His Spirit to live in our hearts.

The disciples "gazed into the sky" as He departed. Wouldn't you?How often do you see Jesus fly back to heaven? But the apostles didn't look for long. Quickly, they went out to fulfill the Great Commission and spread the gospel to the world, teaching people about the power and purpose of Christ.

The book of Acts tells all about it.

Discussion Starters:

1. Why did Jesus leave earth? How did His departure strengthen us?

2. What difference does it make in your life that Jesus is building a home for you, praying for you, and allowing His Spirit to live inside you?

3. How can you utilize Christ's power more effectively in your life?

Lifeline:

Live each day in the power of His presence.

A MISTAKEN CASE OF THE WOBBLES

"And they were all filled with the Holy Spirit and began to speak with other tongues, as the Spirit was giving them utterance. Now there were Jews living in Jerusalem, devout men from every nation under heaven. And when this sound occurred, the crowd came together, and were bewildered because each one of them was hearing them speak in his own language.... And they all continued in amazement and great perplexity, saying to one another, 'What does this mean?' But others were mocking and saying, 'They are full of sweet wine.'"

↪ Acts 2:4-6,12-13

Phil, a college student, loved Jesus, Carol, and a good laugh. One night in October, Phil took Carol out for a date. They arrived at the Beta Theta Pi house, where the fraternity was putting on its annual skit night. Sitting on the lawn were at least 100 students crammed knee to knee, watching the frat boys ham it up for their peers. Everyone was having a blast.

Except Phil. He'd been squeezed into the center of the crowd, sitting cross-legged for much too long. He and Carol decided to leave early. They stood up, brushed the backside of their jeans, and prepared to go.

Then it happened. Phil fell straight into the lap of a muscle-bound Theta. But even worse, Phil couldn't get up. He rolled off the Theta and ended up whacking a sorority girl in the face as he tried to stand.

"What are you—drunk?" the Theta shouted.

The crowd joined in with the accusations. They didn't know Phil's foot had fallen asleep. And they'd never understood that Phil's joyful attitude came from Christ—not alcohol. So they decided he'd been drinking.

The disciples were also misunderstood. The crowd at the Pentecost couldn't grasp the power of the Holy Spirit. When the disciples were given the gift of speaking in tongues, they, too, were mistaken for being drunk.

If you're a Christian, a lot of people will misunderstand you. Having the gifts of the Spirit or the joy of God won't make sense to others. They won't comprehend that as a child of God, the Lord lives in you.

When that happens, don't worry. As He did with Peter, the Holy Spirit will give you the words to say to those who don't believe.

Discussion Starters:

1. How did Peter refute the accusation that the disciples were drunk (see verses 14-22)?
2. Besides speaking in tongues, what are the other gifts of the Spirit (see 1 Corinthians 12)?

Lifeline:

Will you let God's Spirit rule your life, even if it makes you look different?

DRY-CLEANED FOR JESUS

"Peter said to them, 'Repent, and each of you be baptized in the name of Jesus Christ for the forgiveness of your sins; and you will receive the gift of the Holy Spirit. For the promise is for you and your children and for all who are far off, as many as the Lord our God will call to Himself.' ...So then, those who had received his word were baptized; and that day there were added about three thousand souls."

↩ Acts 2:38-39,41

Sprinkle. Dunk. Dedicate. Immerse. Only the young. Just the old.

It seems there are as many disagreements over baptism as there are books in the Bible. Why do Christians argue over this beautiful act of obedience?

After all, baptism doesn't make us clean, or good, or right, or better friends with God. It merely tells the world that Jesus Christ did our laundry on the cross, and now we're thankful to be wearing cleaner clothes.

Nevertheless, that doesn't mean baptism is optional. In fact, it was so central in Christ's mind that He had it done to Himself. Jesus commands us to follow the millions of believers who've been baptized in oceans, rivers, ponds, pools, and churches since the days of Peter, James, and John.

Why do it? It's important to profess your faith. When you get baptized, you make the statement that Jesus is your Lord and Savior and you want to live in obedience to Him. Baptism also shows that you've let Jesus wash your soul, and you want the world to know about it.

So whether you want to be dry-cleaned, starched, or spin-dried, the important thing is that you repent and get baptized.

If Jesus obediently did it, so should you.

Discussion Starters:

1. If someone asked you to explain baptism, what would you say?

2. The commands "repent" and "be baptized" are often linked. Why?

3. The Greeks used the word *baptizo* to signify the dyeing of a garment. What insight does this give you into baptism?

4. Have you been baptized? If so, describe the experience. Why did you do it? How did it strengthen your faith?

Lifeline:

There may be someone in your family who still hasn't been baptized. Pray about doing it. Set a date with your pastor. Then have your whole family join in celebrating the event.

TAKING NOTES

"And a man who had been lame from his mother's womb was being carried along, whom they used to set down every day at the gate of the temple which is called Beautiful, in order to beg alms of those who were entering the temple. When he saw Peter and John about to go into the temple, he began asking to receive alms. But Peter, along with John, fixed his gaze on him and said, 'Look at us!' ...But Peter said, 'I do not possess silver and gold, but what I do have I give to you: In the name of Jesus Christ the Nazarene—walk!' And seizing him by the right hand, he raised him up; and immediately his feet and his ankles were strengthened."

↪ Acts 3:2-4,6-7

A root canal...a disloyal friend...losing a job...Pain is an inevitable part of life. And there are few things more painful than hearing a sermon on charitable giving. We fidget, sweat, and squirm under the pastor's gaze. No matter how much we try to avoid eye contact, the minister still seems to stare straight into our hearts and wallets.

Now, the preacher enjoys the experience even less than we do. Nevertheless, he knows that—like the lame man in Acts 3:5—the needy are looking to the church, expecting help from us. And like Peter and John, we have two options. We can try to meet their needs, or we can keep walking.

If we do pass them by, we're not exactly being obedient to Jesus' command to "feed His sheep." As Christians, we're called to reach out to others less fortunate by giving our time, money, and love. When we help others, we're revealing Jesus and His power.

You may not have gold or silver, but you do have a powerful Savior. And everyone, especially the poor and hungry, deserves to hear about Him and what He's done for us. People need to know the saving grace of Jesus.

As Peter and John did, we're to give of ourselves and allow others the chance to hear the gospel. When we do, the world around us will be taking notes on Christian charity. What notes are they taking on you?

Discussion Starters:

1. Peter and John were going to the temple to pray. How can prayer be an act of service? How do we give to others through prayer?

2. How did Peter and John use their charitable act to point to the incredible charity of the crucifixion?

Lifeline:

Make your monthly financial giving a family experience. Pray together for the ministries you help before you mail the checks. And discuss with your kids the importance of giving from their money, too.

DRIVERS' EDUCATION

"'And now, brethren, I know that you [crucified Jesus] in ignorance, just as your rulers did also. But the things which God announced beforehand by the mouth of all the prophets, that His Christ should suffer, He has thus fulfilled.'"

↫ Acts 3:17-18

"Ignorance is no excuse." Every day, that statement is proved true all over the highways and streets of this world.

> Driver: "Sixty-eight! Gee, officer, I thought I was only doing 55."
> Police officer: "But son, this is a 25 mph school zone."
> Driver: "I didn't know *that*."
> Police officer: "Did you see the sign?"
> Driver: "No."
> Police officer: "Did you see the swing set?"
> Driver: "Er...no."
> Police officer: "The slide? The teeter totters? The bright yellow buses? Did you see any of those?"
> Driver: "Well...not exactly."
> Police officer (quite angrily):"So...what *did* you see, son?"
> Driver: "I saw the building—just before I hit it!"

I'll say it again. Ignorance is no excuse for irresponsibility. And just as it's irresponsible to drive recklessly, it's even more so for Christians not to educate the people around them who claim to be ignorant of God. If we don't talk with them about the Lord, every day they'll speed a little closer to the brick-hard realities of hell.

The apostles Peter and John didn't just stand by, watching humanity collide with destiny. They warned the people about the consequences of their wicked ways. They told them how to avoid disaster.

Peter and John made sure everyone knew about Jesus.

You have the same responsibility as Peter and John did. How are you educating your fellow travelers?

Discussion Starters:

1. What's the difference between being ignorant of Christ and outright denying Him? Give some examples.
2. Who do you know that claims to be ignorant of Christ? How can you educate him or her?

Lifeline:

Role-play presenting the gospel to one another. Anticipate questions and objections, and help one another form a clear plan of evangelism. Then pray for the people to whom you'll be witnessing.

THE EDUCATED FOOL

"Then Peter, filled with the Holy Spirit, said to them, 'Rulers and elders of the people, if we are on trial today for a benefit done to a sick man, as to how this man has been made well, let it be known ... that by the name of Jesus Christ ... this man stands here before you in good health.... And there is salvation in no one else; for there is no other name under heaven that has been given among men by which we must be saved.' Now as they observed the confidence of Peter and John and understood that they were uneducated and untrained men, they were amazed and began to recognize them as having been with Jesus. And seeing the man who had been healed standing with them, they had nothing to say in reply."

⌐ Acts 4:8-10,12-14

There are many smart people in this world. Look at John, who lives in my town. This pastor holds theological degrees from prestigious colleges and sits on synod committees that shape the thinking of his entire denomination. In a lot of ways, John is a great guy. But although he's respected by many, John's an educated fool. Every Sunday, he puts on his robe, pounds his pulpit, and demonstrates the little respect he has for God's Word. He twists and alters Scripture to maintain his popularity with his congregation and to fit his own faith. His faith is intellectual—not heartfelt.

Chuck was also an educated fool. He was president of his fraternity in the late '70s and even a member of the student council and the Blue Key organization. Chuck was handsome, athletic, popular, and smart. He almost had a double major in German and marketing. But he wasn't smart about everything. In the spring of '79, he drank himself to death at a rush party.

Peter and John, on the other hand, never had a lick of schooling. In fact, their educational shortcomings were glaring. They were simple men with simple solutions. No degrees. No robes. No impressive titles. But the Pharisees and learned scholars looked at them and marveled. Why? Because Peter and John were so confident and eloquent, and there was no mistaking that they had been Jesus' disciples.

You don't need to be a scholar to talk confidently and accurately—as the disciples did—about Jesus. Christ will give you all the knowledge you need to witness. You'll never be a fool if you hang with Him!

Discussion Starters:

1. How could the Pharisees tell that Peter and John had been "with Jesus"?

2. Peter's sermon was short. Why was it so powerful?

3. Which Christians do you admire for their deep knowledge of God? Why?

Lifeline:

Does your family know Christ as Peter and John did?

IN TROUBLE WITH THE LAW

"[And the leaders began] saying, 'What shall we do with these men? For the fact that a noteworthy miracle has taken place through them is apparent to all who live in Jerusalem, and we cannot deny it. But so that it will not spread any further among the people, let us warn them to speak no longer to any man in this name.' And when they had summoned them, they commanded them not to speak or teach at all in the name of Jesus. But Peter and John answered and said to them, 'Whether it is right in the sight of God to give heed to you rather than to God, you be the judge; for we cannot stop speaking about what we have seen and heard.'"

↩ Acts 4:16-20

Kevin felt terrible. This counselor friend of mine had been arrested for a felony. "Can you imagine explaining to your rebellious teenage clients that you're leaving the office to go post bond?" Kevin asked me after the incident. "The kids loved it. They teased me for weeks about being one of 'them.'"

Kevin's arrest was related to a check he'd canceled—a $256 check.

"I was furious with the car dealership," Kevin explained. "I mean, I took my vehicle in to have the brakes worked on, and when I got it back, the engine needed overhauling. So I refused to pay."

Fortunately, the sheriff didn't make Kevin post the $2,000 bond or spend any time in jail. He only had to pay the bill. But Kevin was still mad.

The next day, though, he was sheepish. The night Kevin was supposed to be behind bars, the jail burned down, injuring numerous prisoners and even killing one. When Kevin heard the news, his anger disappeared. He realized that if he'd been in jail, he might have died, too.

Kevin shouldn't have disobeyed the law in his case. But it was a different story with Peter and John. They knew it wasn't unlawful to talk about Jesus, and they intended to continue witnessing—no matter what.

What's the difference between Kevin's incident and the disciples'? For one thing, Kevin listened to his anger, while Peter and John listened to God. We're to follow our authorities, but God's leadership always comes first.

Discussion Starters:

1. Is there ever an appropriate time for disobedience? Give an example.

2. In today's society, where does God's law clash with man's law?

3. What might be the result of defying man's law while following God's?

Lifeline:

Just as the disciples did, pray that God will give your family the confidence to keep putting His laws first.

ALL LIES ARE BIG

"But a man named Ananias, with his wife Sapphira, sold a piece of property, and kept back some of the price for himself, with his wife's full knowledge, and bringing a portion of it, he laid it at the apostles' feet. But Peter said, 'Ananias, why has Satan filled your heart to lie to the Holy Spirit and to keep back some of the price of the land? ...You have not lied to men but to God.' And as he heard these words, Ananias fell down and breathed his last; and great fear came over all who heard of it... [and the same happened to Sapphira, his wife]."

↩ Acts 5:1-5

Have you ever wondered why we use the words "falling in love" to describe such a blissful state? "Falling in love" sounds so painful.

Kent fell hard when he was 14. Like all the boys in his eighth grade class, Kent thought Sharon was a goddess. Unfortunately, Sharon had her eye on Andy, which made Kent wonder what Andy had that he *didn't*.

Soon Kent figured it out. Andy had a broken leg!

Girls must fall for guys who are injured! Kent deduced. So he quickly settled on the least painful way to injure himself.

"I'm getting my tonsils out this weekend," he told Sharon on Friday.

"Oh! That sounds awful!" Sharon said with more sympathy than she'd ever shown him. "I hope it doesn't hurt too bad."

Of course, Kent soon realized that his lie had put him in a terrible mess. So that December night, Kent stripped down to his T-shirt, went out into the backyard, and screamed until he was hoarse. At any rate, by Monday, Kent definitely sounded as if he'd had his tonsils removed.

Now, I'd love to tell you Kent got the girl. But he didn't. Andy won Sharon's affection. Kent got a wonderful case of pneumonia.

As Kent discovered, lying will always backfire on you. If the person you lied to doesn't discover your fib, God always will. You can't pull *any* wool over God's eyes; even a half-lie will be found out. And if Ananias and Sapphira were still alive, they'd tell you the same thing.

Discussion Starters:

1. How was Ananias and Sapphira's lie only a "half-lie"?

2. What were the consequences of their lie? How did others respond?

3. When is it tempting for you to lie? Why? How can you avoid lying?

Lifeline:

Promise one another to be honest at all times in your household. Then decide together what the consequences will be for dishonesty. (Parents should ensure those consequences are administered immediately and effectively.)

SUFFERING SHAME FOR HIS NAME

"But the high priest rose up, along with all his associates (that is the sect of the Sadducees), and they were filled with jealousy. They laid hands on the apostles and put them in a public jail.... [And after they'd escaped,] Peter and the apostles answered [the priest and Council], 'We must obey God rather than men.' ...But when they heard this, they were cut to the quick and intended to kill them.... [Instead] they took [Gamaliel's] advice; and after calling the apostles in, they flogged them and ordered them not to speak in the name of Jesus, and then released them. So they went on their way from the presence of the Council, rejoicing that they had been considered worthy to suffer shame for His name."

⇜ Acts 5:17-18,29,33,40-41

Persecution didn't just take place in biblical times. In fact, today 2.5 billion people are denied freedom of religion, and 1 million are imprisoned because of their faith. More Christians have been persecuted for their beliefs in the twentieth century than in any other century.[1]

Ha Sieng, of Vietnam, is an evangelical Christian preacher who endured a life-threatening beating when police arrested him for preaching the gospel in 1996. Sieng had been repeatedly warned by the police to stop evangelizing the Koho people, a poor tribe that lives in the central highlands of Vietnam. But Sieng adamantly refused to quit preaching and wouldn't hand over any Bibles or spiritual books to the authorities. For that, he was whacked with a heavy iron rod for seven straight days. On the last day, his body couldn't bear the pain any longer, and he passed out.

The police sent him home, and soon after, he fell into a coma. Sieng became delirious, and hospital authorities told his wife that Sieng might never regain consciousness or be his normal self again.

Miraculously, he left the hospital a few weeks later, completely well. Despite the terrible suffering Sieng endured, he still continues his work undaunted. He claims that neither laws nor persecution will stop him from telling people about Jesus Christ. And to date, about one-third of the 150,000 Koho people have become Christians as a result of Sieng's work.

Many of them believed because of Sieng's strength in suffering.[2]

Discussion Starters:

1. Why is it important to rejoice when we suffer for God?

2. Have you ever suffered for your beliefs? If so, when?

Lifeline:

People are often persecuted today for speaking the truth. Make a pact that your family will always follow God's Word, no matter what.

BEHIND THE SCENES

"Now at this time while the disciples were increasing in number, a complaint arose on the part of the Hellenistic Jews against the native Hebrews, because their widows were being overlooked in the daily serving of food. So the twelve summoned the congregation of the disciples and said, 'It is not desirable for us to neglect the word of God in order to serve tables. Therefore, brethren, select from among you seven men of good reputation, full of the Spirit and of wisdom, whom we may put in charge of this task. But we will devote ourselves to prayer and to the ministry of the word.'"

⟿ Acts 6:1-4

My life is a little crazy. There's no need to pretend it's not. But in the midst of all my busyness, I'm thankful for those people who make my work possible. Here's my tribute to the "behind-the-sceners" in my life:

> For every sermon I preach, I have a wife who prays.
> For every book I submit, I have a secretary who sweats.
> For every recruiting trip I go on, I have a staff who holds the fort.
> For every teen I touch, I have a kid at home who touches me.
> For every "good thing" I do, I have a God who bears my sins.

Travis also knows the value of support people. When he kicked the winning field goal in the playoffs, he put the spotlight on his teammates.

In the locker room, a gleeful reporter raced up to Travis and said, "Travis, that was a fantastic kick! How does it feel to win the big game?"

Travis, being a humble Christian athlete, replied, "Talk to the center who made a perfect snap, the quarterback who held the ball perfectly, and the line who blocked the other team. They won the game."

Every job is important. Often it's not the up-front people who make things happen, it's the people who work behind the scenes. The disciples knew that, too. They needed others to handle the details of their ministry. Preaching, traveling, and witnessing for Christ took up most of their time, so they found deacons to help—support people who'd keep things running.

No one can do it all. That's why God created us to have such different gifts—so we'd be unified as one body, dependent on one another to carry out His ministry.

Discussion Starters:

1. What were the criteria by which the deacons were selected?
2. What did their service free the 12 apostles to do? What was the result?
3. In general, what does this say about the body of Christ?

Lifeline:

Every family has silent servers. Take the time now to praise them.

EVERY BUSBOY HAS HIS DAY

"And Stephen [one of the deacons], full of grace and power, was performing great wonders and signs among the people.... But they were unable to cope with the wisdom and the Spirit with which he was speaking.... And they stirred up the people, the elders and the scribes, and they came up to him and dragged him away and brought him before the Council.... And fixing their gaze on him, all who were sitting in the Council saw his face like the face of an angel."

⮑ Acts 6:8,10,12,15

One summer, I ate in the same restaurant, at the same table, by the same window, every day. I always ordered chocolate pie for dessert. I always read the paper with my pie. And I always said hello to Frank, the redheaded busboy who cleared my table.

Frank and I got to be friends. So of course I missed him when one day I noticed he was no longer working at the restaurant.

"Oh, Frank's still here," my waitress said when I asked about him. "That's him back there in the kitchen. He's a prep cook now. The hours are a little earlier. The pay's a little better. You understand."

I understood perfectly. The boy was moving up in the world.

Ten years have passed, and Frank has long since left his cook position. After three other kitchen jobs, a stint behind the cash register, and a year and a half of management, the boy has become a man—and part owner of one of America's fastest-growing restaurant chains.

At one point, Stephen was also a strong, silent, behind-the-scenes server. As one of the support deacons, his main responsibilities were far from the limelight. But when God planted him in the Council to testify about Jesus, he amazed and angered people with his grace, knowledge, and eloquence. The crowd was shocked to see that Stephen, the "blue-collar deacon," had the face of an angel.

Work hard where God has placed you, and do your best to follow His will. In the meantime, remember this: Every busboy—every silent server—has his or her day. Serve well, and God will bless you.

By His Spirit, He will make you great.

Discussion Starters:

1. Quiet servants still have an obligation to speak up for Christ. When it was Stephen's turn to speak, what inner qualities aided him?

2. Where do you think Stephen acquired his incredible wisdom?

3. What is your definition of godly "greatness"? How can you attain it?

Lifeline:

Pray for grace and power as you serve in God's world today.

GOOD NEWS ... BAD NEWS

"And he said, 'Hear me, brethren and fathers! The God of glory appeared to our father Abraham when he was in Mesopotamia, before he lived in Haran.... But as the time of the promise was approaching which God had assured to Abraham, the people increased and multiplied in Egypt.... Which one of the prophets did your fathers not persecute? They killed those who had previously announced the coming of the Righteous One, whose betrayers and murderers you have now become.'"

↪ Acts 7:2,17,52

Life is full of instances in which good news and bad news go together. My hometown of Branson, Missouri, is like that right now. The good news is that we've got a booming economy. We've got a smorgasbord of superstars to satisfy our hunger for entertainment. We've got Silver Dollar City, a family theme park. We've got lunker rainbow trout. We've got hills, trees, and miles of liquid glass to waterski upon.

The bad news is that we finally have crime.

Amazingly, 75 percent of Branson's shoplifters are female tourists over 75, who have no use at all for the dime-store trinkets they're taking.

Can you believe it?

What has become of a world where grandmas sip their soda pops at the Andy Williams Christmas Show and giggle about the 17 porcelain panda bears they stole in the gift shop—which are now responsible for those conspicuous bulges in their shoulder bags?

Stephen, in his speech to the Sanhedrin in Acts 7, likewise gave the people both good news and bad. The good news was that God had been faithful to His promises to Israel, ultimately sending them a Savior. The bad news was that they had rejected Him.

That's bad news with eternal consequences.

Discussion Starters:

1. The Bible demonstrates how God was faithful to the Israelites even when they rejected Him. What does that reveal about His character?

2. How has God's faithfulness to His promises touched your life?

3. What measure of faithfulness have you shown God? How have you been unfaithful to Him?

Lifeline:

Discuss how your family can be more faithful to God.

"HEY, TAXI!"

"'You men who are stiff-necked and uncircumcised in heart and ears are always resisting the Holy Spirit; you are doing just as your fathers did. Which one of the prophets did your fathers not persecute? They killed those who had previously announced the coming of the Righteous One, whose betrayers and murderers you have now become; you who received the law as ordained by angels, and yet did not keep it.'"

↪ Acts 7:51-53

I was standing outside the airport recently and heard a man calling a cab. "Hey, taxi!" he shouted as the yellow car pulled forward. The taxi stopped, the man got in, and quickly he drove off in the rain.

But his two words, *Hey, taxi!* remained with me. They reminded me of a painful time in my childhood. See, I was born with ears the size of Africa, just like my dad, who took after *his* dad, who took after *his* dad. Our ears go back centuries, to the time when real men carried clubs.

It's hard for me to hear the word *taxi* without cringing. When I was in sixth grade, Tommy Kite said my ears made me look like a taxi going down the street with its doors open. Tommy was twice my size, so I never said anything back, and eventually, most of the sting went away. But since that day, I've always grown my hair fairly long—especially on the sides. My ears are still a big part of my inheritance I'd love to hide.

In some ways, we're all an extension of our families. I inherited my dad's big ears. My son got my skill in football. And the religious people Stephen spoke to had inherited their parents' rebellious, godless, hypocritical natures. Unfortunately, they were still so blind that they couldn't accept the truth of who they'd become. So they stoned Stephen for being honest (see Acts 7:54-60).

The reality is, we've all inherited a little doubt, deceitfulness, and dishonor. But we have a choice. We can break from the problems of the past and follow God as others before us should have done, or we can continue old patterns and walk in the footsteps of our not-so-good Israelite ancestors. What heritage will your family leave behind?

Discussion Starters:

1. We inherit both good and bad attributes from our parents. In what ways are you like your stiff-necked, hard-hearted Israelite ancestors?

2. As Stephen pointed out earlier in his speech, the Israelites built golden calves. What "idols" do you focus on in your life?

Lifeline:

Ask God to help you break from the negative parts of your past.

THE STRONG HAND OF LOVE

"Now Saul, still breathing threats and murder against the disciples of the Lord, went to the high priest.... As he was traveling, it happened that he was approaching Damascus, and suddenly a light from heaven flashed around him; and he fell to the ground and heard a voice saying to him, 'Saul, Saul, why are you persecuting Me? ...But get up and enter the city, and it will be told you what you must do.' ...Now there was a disciple at Damascus named Ananias; and the Lord said to him in a vision, 'Ananias.' And he said, 'Here I am, Lord.' And the Lord said to him, 'Get up and go to the street called Straight, and inquire at the house of Judas for a man from Tarsus named Saul, for he is praying.' ...But Ananias answered, 'Lord, I have heard from many about this man, how much harm he did to Your saints at Jerusalem.' ...But the Lord said to him, 'Go, for he is a chosen instrument of Mine, to bear My name.'"

⟿ Acts 9:1,3-4,6,10-11,13,15

Curt was the last person I expected to make friends with Jesus.

He was a notorious troublemaker, drug dealer, and thief. Curt was the largest coke dealer in his junior high until he got busted and was sent to a treatment center. There he thumbed his nose at people's efforts to help him, continuing to smuggle drugs whenever he went home for visitation. Curt used everybody. He cared only about himself.

Finally, maddened by Curt's behavior, a powerful Christian man literally threw Curt through a glass door to get him to listen. The man's scare tactic worked. Curt turned his life around. And today Curt loves and serves Jesus Christ with a greater commitment than most men I know.

No one thought Saul would give his life to Christ, either. But God had other plans. The Lord had to be harsh to get Saul's attention, so He blinded him. Once Saul wised up, he became a devoted, lifelong follower of Jesus.

No one is hopeless. Not the biggest partyer, the worst drug dealer, the scariest robber, or the meanest atheist. God can use any one of them. Just look at what He did in Saul's life.

Saul started out persecuting Christians and ended up writing 1 Corinthians 13—the famous love chapter in the Bible.

Discussion Starters:

1. Why did God have to be so harsh with Saul?
2. Notice that He started by asking Saul a question. Why are questions often so effective in situations like this?
3. How do you think Saul convinced the skeptics that he'd really changed?

Lifeline:

Pray regularly for the most hostile and hardened unbeliever you know.

PASSING DOWN THE TIE

"Now in Joppa there was a disciple named Tabitha (which translated in Greek is called Dorcas); this woman was abounding with deeds of kindness and charity which she continually did. And it happened at that time that she fell sick and died; and when they had washed her body, they laid it in an upper room.... So Peter arose and went with them. When he arrived, they brought him into the upper room; and all the widows stood beside him weeping and showing all the tunics and garments that Dorcas used to make while she was with them. But Peter sent them all out and knelt down and prayed, and turning to the body, he said, 'Tabitha, arise.' And she opened her eyes, and when she saw Peter, she sat up."

↩ Acts 9:36-37,39-40

Our actions should always point back to God's glory and goodness. Peter's did. When he raised Tabitha from the dead through the power of God, Peter was imitating the ministry of his Lord, Jesus Christ. Peter's decision to model Jesus reminds me of an incident that took place not so long ago.

In the back of the van, Grayson was in tears.

"What's wrong?" my son Cooper asked as we sped toward the kids' Christian school, 20 miles away.

"I forgot my tie! I f-f-f-forgot my tie!" blubbered Grayson.

Cooper immediately knew why the boy was so upset. You see, at Riverview Baptist School, Tuesdays are chapel days. And forgetting to wear a tie spells "D-E-M-E-R-I-T." To a boy as sensitive as Grayson, getting a demerit is as bad as getting the death penalty. Cooper considered the consequences, then slowly removed his own tie.

"Here, Grayson," said Cooper. "You can wear mine."

Grayson's face lit up.

It was moving to witness Cooper's act of compassion. But the best part about the incident was that four years earlier, my elder son, Brady White, had done the same thing for Cooper. (Way to go, guys!)

There are countless opportunities to imitate Christ's ministry of compassion. How can you model God's love to those around you?

Discussion Starters:

1. Why did Peter send the crowds outside before he raised Tabitha?

2. How well are you imitating Christ these days? Explain.

Lifeline:

Think of a Christian brother or sister who has been kind to you in the past. Imitate that kindness as soon as you have the opportunity.

CHANGE

"But [Peter] became hungry and was desiring to eat; but while they were making prepara-
tions, he fell into a trance; and he saw the sky opened up, and an object like a great sheet
coming down, lowered by four corners to the ground, and there were in it all kinds of four-
footed animals and crawling creatures of the earth and birds of the air. A voice came to him,
'Get up, Peter, kill and eat!' But Peter said, 'By no means, Lord, for I have never eaten
anything unholy and unclean.' Again a voice came to him a second time, 'What God has
cleansed, no longer consider unholy.' ...And [later Peter] said to them, 'You yourselves know
how unlawful it is for a man who is a Jew to associate with a foreigner or to visit him; and
yet God has shown me that I should not call any man unholy or unclean.' "

⌒ Acts 10:10-15, 28

We quickly take things for granted, don't we? When the car dies, we become
helpless without our wheels. After the electricity goes out, we wonder how
we'll wake up in the morning without the alarm. And when a blizzard hits, we
complain if the roads aren't plowed right away.

The funny thing is, cars, electricity, and snowplows are all relatively
recent inventions. One hundred years ago, most folks wouldn't have
expected to have those things at their beck and call. But a lot has changed
between then and now—because change is a huge part of life.

With all the traveling I do, I'm thankful that we stopped riding horses
and started driving cars. There's too much I want to do for God. I could never
reach thousands of kids for Christ if I had to travel in a buggy.

God thought change was important, too. The Lord turned society upside
down when He gave Peter a vision and told him that, from now on, all meat
was acceptable to eat. God was teaching Peter a lesson about food *and*
people. No longer would only the Jewish people be favored by God. Now the
gospel was available for everyone.

If God hadn't made that change, you probably wouldn't be reading
about Him right now. Aren't you glad the Lord decided it was time for a
major adjustment?

Discussion Starters:

1. Why was God's message to Peter so significant?

2. How did Peter feel about the vision? Why was he apprehensive at first?

3. How did this event affect biblical society?

Lifeline:

Thank God today that Jesus changed the world by cleansing *all* people who
will believe in Him.

JUST A MAN!

"When Peter entered, Cornelius met him, and fell at his feet and worshiped him. But Peter raised him up, saying, 'Stand up; I too am just a man.'"

 Acts 10:25-26

I'm always impressed with humility—especially when I see it in people who have reason to brag.

The late U.S. Senator Stuart Symington used to breeze through Kamp— and I do mean *breeze*. He brought a freshness and love of life. He never put on any stuffy airs or acted important. Stuart just blended in to the point that when you went looking for him, he was difficult to locate.

You'd never find him signing autographs for the campers. He'd never be seen giving impressive speeches. Not Stuart. We usually found him in the kitchen, with his sleeves rolled up and his forearms plunged into a sink full of suds. This politician, who could probably afford 10 maids, would be cleaning pots and pans!

He wasn't campaigning for votes because he wasn't running for anything. Stuart was simply a man who loved God and people, plain and simple. Senator Stuart Symington modeled the humility and grace of Jesus, his Lord and Savior.

Maybe in the world's eyes, you have a reason to flaunt your feathers. Maybe you're the most popular kid in school, a talented musician, or a young Einstein. If you've been given gifts or popularity, thank God for those blessings, and be humble. You can't manufacture your gifts. The Lord is responsible for every one of them (see James 1:17).

That's why when Cornelius fell to the floor, Peter said, "Get up!" Peter knew he was just a man. Any strength or power he had was from God.

All glory should go to God. He's the only One who deserves to be exalted. Next time you're complimented, don't pat yourself on the back. Humbly give God the praise.

Discussion Starters:

1. How do you think Peter felt when Cornelius began to worship him?
2. What does Cornelius's reaction reveal about the culture in which he lived?
3. What's the difference between having low self-esteem and being humble?

Lifeline:

Have each family member name someone they know who is humble and Christlike. What qualities does he or she have that make him or her that way? How can you learn to be more humble, too?

IT'S BIG NEWS

"But Peter began speaking and proceeded to explain to them in orderly sequence, saying, 'I was in the city of Joppa praying; and in a trance I saw a vision, an object coming down like a great sheet lowered by four corners from the sky; and it came right down to me, and when I had fixed my gaze on it and was observing it I saw the four-footed animals of the earth and the wild beasts and the crawling creatures and the birds of the air. I also heard a voice saying to me, "Get up, Peter; kill and eat."'"

⤿ Acts 11:4-7

God is imaginative. He finds all sorts of ways to speak to us—through friends, books, sermons, the Bible, and even, as Peter found, in dreams. My friend Whit would tell you that, too. This author spent two years writing a novel, and a week before its publication date, he had a dream.

"I've got big news!" his editor said over the phone in Whit's dream.

Whit smiled and rolled over in bed. I *must be a Pulitzer Prize candidate. Why else would he call?* Whit thought.

"We're not going to publish your novel," came the voice.

At that, Whit woke up and told his wife the story. They both laughed, reassuring themselves it was only a dream.

But the next day, Whit's editor did call. "I've got big news for you," he said. "Your book is canned."

Whit could've been mad. But he trusted God. Just six months after his novel was canceled, the largest Christian publisher in the nation printed it.

Sometimes dreams are big news, indeed! Peter's dream/vision sure was. God intentionally spoke to him in that vision and, as we discussed before, He changed society through it. What if Peter hadn't listened to God's voice? What if he'd just decided his mind was playing tricks on him? Fortunately, Peter knew God well enough to recognize that it was the Lord talking—he wasn't just going crazy.

God will often communicate to us in creative ways. Be prepared. Study Him and His methods. Otherwise, you'll never know when He's sending you a message. And when God talks, it's *always* big news.

Discussion Starters:

1. How did the people respond to Peter's dream (see Acts 11:18)?

2. How can we tell if God is speaking to us through our dreams?

3. In what ways does God speak to you about important things?

Lifeline:

Describe another time in Scripture where God spoke to someone through a dream. What was He trying to say? How did the person respond?

WHAT'S IN A NAME?

"And when he had found him, he brought him to Antioch. And for an entire year they met with the church and taught considerable numbers; and the disciples were first called Christians in Antioch."

⤙ Acts 11:26

Behind every name, there's an interesting story.

Take, for instance, teddy bears. In 1903, Morris Michtom, a 32-year-old Russian immigrant from Brooklyn, made the first teddy bear in honor of Theodore Roosevelt, who mercifully spared a bear cub while on a hunting trip. Ever since, the toy has been a symbol of love and tenderness.

The hot dog was once called the dachshund sausage. But in 1906, when New York syndicated cartoonist Tad Dorgan set out to capture the lovable sandwich in art, he balked at the spelling of *dachshund*. Instead, he wrote the words "Get your hot dogs!" at the bottom of his cartoon. Soon, all other names for the food vanished.

The S.O.S. pad was invented in 1917 by cookware peddler Edwin Cox, who handed out the scrubbers as free gifts to get his foot in the door with prospective customers. The gifts went over well, since most women had been frustrated about having food stick to their pans. Cox, who manufactured the pads in his own kitchen, asked his wife to help him name the product. "S.O.S!" Mrs. Cox suggested, "as in 'save our saucepans!'" The name stuck.[3]

Names carry great significance, especially for followers of Christ. If you call yourself a Christian, you should be prepared to live as Christ did—with His grace, kindness, mercy, holiness, and love.

The word *Christian* isn't a title; it describes a lifestyle. If you say you're a disciple of Christ, live in a way that makes Jesus proud.

Otherwise, don't call yourself a Christian at all.

Discussion Starters:

1. What does the name *Christian* mean?

2. Why did it take a while for the disciples to be called Christians?

3. What characteristics come to mind when you hear the word *Christian*?

4. Is it difficult for you to tell friends you're a Christian? Why or why not? How do they respond when you say you're a follower of Christ?

Lifeline:

Would the people in your school or workplace know you're a Christian just by watching your actions? Are you living in a way that would make Jesus proud that you bear His name? Explain your answers.

RELEASE ME

"And behold, an angel of the Lord suddenly appeared and a light shone in the cell; and he struck Peter's side and woke him up, saying, 'Get up quickly.' And his chains fell off his hands. And the angel said to him, 'Gird yourself and put on your sandals.' And he did so. And he said to him, 'Wrap your cloak around you and follow me.' And he went out and continued to follow, and he did not know that what was being done by the angel was real, but thought he was seeing a vision. When they had passed the first and second guard, they came to the iron gate that leads into the city, which opened for them by itself; and they went out and went along one street, and immediately the angel departed from him."

⤳ Acts 12:7-10

A few years ago, I heard an incredible story of one man's struggle to survive. While hunting alone in the woods, he got his leg caught beneath an enormous tree. No one was around to help. He knew that if he stayed pinned under the tree, he'd die. So in order to escape, the man cut his leg off with a dull pocketknife! Then he bandaged it with a tourniquet and hobbled back to civilization.

The man had been trapped. He had only one chance to save himself and only a few minutes to think about it.

Peter was trapped, too. He'd been jailed for preaching God's Word. The situation wasn't good. Christians were being persecuted everywhere. Herod wanted to nail Peter, so he assigned four squads of soldiers to guard him (see Acts 12:4). But God was working harder than Herod. At the last minute, God sent an angel to lead Peter out of prison.

Just when Peter thought he would become another victim of Herod's, he was saved by God's mighty hand.

Life can have a way of trapping us, too. Peer pressure, depression, family conflict, and illness can make you feel weighed down by the world. But God will always come to your aid. Sometimes, as in the hunter's case, He'll give you the courage to make an important decision. Often, as in Peter's instance, He'll send someone to intercede and help you. No situation or temptation is too great for God. You're never helpless with Him around.

Discussion Starters:

1. Why do you think God allowed Peter to be jailed if He was already planning to release him?

2. When do you feel trapped? How does God help you in those times?

Lifeline:

Read 1 Corinthians 10:13. How does that encourage each of you?

WHAT WERE YOU THINKING?

"When [Peter] knocked at the door of the gate, a servant-girl named Rhoda came to answer. When she recognized Peter's voice, because of her joy she did not open the gate, but ran in and announced that Peter was standing in front of the gate. They said to her, 'You are out of your mind!' But she kept insisting that it was so. They kept saying, 'It is his angel.' But Peter continued knocking; and when they had opened the door, they saw him and were amazed.... Now when day came, there was no small disturbance among the soldiers as to what could have become of Peter. When Herod had searched for him and had not found him, he examined the guards and ordered that they be led away to execution."

↪ Acts 12:13-16,18-19

One winter, Seth was skiing in Colorado, tackling an expert slope. When he was just 30 yards from the end of the run, Seth saw a familiar brunette standing in the lift line. Actually, he saw only a tuft of brown hair sticking out from under a ski cap. But Seth was so overjoyed that he overlooked the fact that the skier was hidden beneath layers of thermal clothing. He was sure it was Valerie, the prettiest girl at his university.

"Valerie!" Seth shouted, elated to bump into her so far from home. Unfortunately, he didn't check his speed, and he *did* bump into her—or rather, *him*. When Seth looked up, he realized he'd mistaken a 40-year-old man for the cutest girl on campus. Seth's ego was shattered.

As Seth found, joy can make you impulsive. The servant girl who heard Peter at the door got so excited that she forgot about Peter, leaving him out in the cold—right where Herod's men could have found him. She wasn't thinking clearly, and her jubilation actually endangered Peter's life.

Emotions are great! God created them. But they need to be tempered with sound judgment. When you let your feelings run wild, it becomes easier to say yes to sex and no to God, to be self-absorbed and forget your friends' needs, and to dismiss your promises to the Lord.

In the heat of the moment, call on God. Ask Him to help you make a sound decision. It's important. Your feelings will come and go, but what comes from them—the results of your decisions—will stay with you forever.

Discussion Starters:

1. Why are impulsive acts (like the servant girl's) sometimes dangerous?

2. How can you let God take control of your feelings?

Lifeline:

Does anyone in your family have an important decision to make? If so, pray together that God would enable him or her to use godly discretion.

PRAY FAST!

"Now there were at Antioch, in the church that was there, prophets and teachers: Barnabas, and Simeon who was called Niger, and Lucius of Cyrene, and Manaen who had been brought up with Herod the tetrarch, and Saul. While they were ministering to the Lord and fasting, the Holy Spirit said, 'Set apart for Me Barnabas and Saul for the work to which I have called them.' Then, when they had fasted and prayed and laid their hands on them, they sent them away."

↪ Acts 13:1-3

Wouldn't it be great if our relationship with the Lord was so intimate that we always heard His instructions clearly and obeyed Him?

We'd know exactly where to go to college. What job to take. Which friends to hang with. What extracurricular activities we should be doing.

Of course, no Christian has a perfect pipeline to God. But the Bible does prescribe some things for us to do that will open the channels of communication with Him—in particular, prayer and fasting.

Now, most of us confuse prayer and fasting with praying fast so we can get on with the meal. We say, "God is great, God is good. Lord, we thank You for this food.... Let's eat!"

But that's not how the Bible portrays the disciplines of prayer and fasting at all. There are times when we must empty our stomachs in order to receive spiritual food from heaven.

Paul and Barnabas knew that. They'd been fasting and praying with the prophets and teachers in Antioch when the Holy Spirit spoke to them.

"I've prepared Paul and Barnabas to do My work. I want them to go preach the gospel," the Spirit said.

It was clear. God had spoken, and the church leaders understood what He wanted. So right away, they sent Paul and Barnabas on a worldwide (well, almost) missionary journey.

Those first-century Christians weren't any different from you. They didn't have a perfect relationship with God, either—but they knew that when they prayed and fasted, the Holy Spirit would give them direction.

And God will do the same for you.

Discussion Starters:

1. Paul and Barnabas were sent out after they'd spent a lot of time praying and fasting. How did doing this help the disciples to discern the Holy Spirit's guidance?

2. How does praying and fasting enable us to make better decisions?

3. Describe a time when Jesus fasted and prayed. What big decision was He about to make?

Lifeline:

Next time your family is facing a big decision, choose a day to fast and pray. Then use the time you'd normally eat to consult God about the matter. The following day, break the fast and share your insights with each other.

WHOM DO YOU FEAR?

"[Paul said to the people], 'Brethren, sons of Abraham's family, and those among you who fear God, to us the message of this salvation has been sent.'"

↜ Acts 13:26, emphasis added

Parachuting, bungee jumping, cliff diving, and hang gliding may sound really exciting to you. I'm so afraid of heights, though, that I'd rather fight a rattlesnake than do any of those things.

What scares you? Spiders? Car accidents? Earthquakes? Big dogs? What about God?

I'm not afraid of God any more than I'm afraid of the picturesque Table Rock Lake that we play on at our sports camps. We jet ski, sail, kayak, windsurf, and do a zillion other fun sports on that lake. But let me tell you, we deeply respect Table Rock. Why? A few years ago, Ricky, a 19-year-old dear friend of mine, drowned in that lake. One minute he was playing sports, and the next minute he was gone. Ricky didn't respect that the lake had the potential to take his life. He went out by himself at night—when he shouldn't have—and was caught in some of the lake's thick reeds.

It's a poor comparison, but I respect God in the same way I respect that lake. God is my Father, my almighty Lord and Savior. There's no comparison to what I can do and what God can accomplish through His enormous power. But His power and holiness don't make me afraid of Him—those qualities cause me to respect Him immensely.

God doesn't want you to tremble when you pray or be afraid to spend time with Him. But He does want you to honor Him and His ways. One way to do that is to turn your back on evil (see Proverbs 8:13). Evil is anything that defies God and His Word. So because I love and fear God, I choose—every day—to walk away from evil of any kind: evil movies, TV, music, and magazines; evil thoughts, motives, and lies.

God will bless your socks off when you fear Him. When you respect the living God, He'll give you abundant life (see Proverbs 14:27).

Discussion Starters:

1. Why must we respect God if we claim to fear Him? How do respect for and fear of God go hand in hand?

2. Why do only those who fear God understand the gospel message?

3. Why does Proverbs say that when you fear the Lord, you'll hate evil?

Lifeline:

Discuss God's different characteristics. What makes you respect, honor, and fear Him? How can your family encourage a healthy fear of the Lord?

THE TRUNK

"When the crowds saw [that Paul had healed a man], they raised their voice, saying in the Lycaonian language, 'The gods have become like men and have come down to us.' And they began calling Barnabas, Zeus, and Paul, Hermes, because he was the chief speaker.... But when the apostles Barnabas and Paul heard of it, they tore their robes and rushed out into the crowd, crying out and saying, 'Men, why are you doing these things? We are also men of the same nature as you, and preach the gospel to you that you should turn from these vain things to a living God, who made the heaven and the earth and the sea and all that is in them.'"

↪ Acts 14:11-12,14-15

William Alfred Cunningham left the military at precisely the same rank he entered it—private first class. Figuring there was little use for a high-speed radio operator in the civilian world, he re-enrolled in college. He was 26, shy, and poor. All his possessions fit in his father's old trunk.

At first, the trunk drew little attention from Bill's younger fraternity brothers. Then one day, a pledge noticed the white-stenciled letters.

Captain William Edward Cunningham, the pledge read. *Bill's an officer!* he decided. In no time, the rumor spread through the Kappa Sigma house. The guys invented entire histories about "quiet Captain Bill" who, it should be said, didn't go out of his way to end the rumors.

Bill never told his fraternity brothers the truth. Instead, he turned the trunk around to face the wall so no one would notice the smaller inscription: World War I. He also never told anyone his middle name.

In spite of all the popularity Bill received from it, the trunk became a heavy burden. William Alfred knew he'd stolen his father's glory.

Stolen honor. Paul and Barnabas had a chance to take their heavenly Father's glory for themselves, too. But they were strong enough to let people know the truth. They loved God so much that they wanted Him to get all the credit. The last thing they wanted was to be lifted up as gods.

People probably don't think you're a god, but they might build you up as an amazing tennis player, a star actress, or an incredible painter. Whatever your talents, though, they didn't come from you—God provided them. Do you take the praise, or do you give God the kudos He deserves?

Discussion Starters:

1. How did Paul and Barnabas respond to the rumors that they were gods?

2. Why were they so upset that the people wanted to worship them?

Lifeline:

How can your family more regularly give God the glory for His blessings?

HOME BASE

"After they had preached the gospel to that city and had made many disciples, they returned to Lystra and to Iconium and to Antioch.... When they had spoken the word in Perga, they went down to Attalia. From there they sailed to Antioch, from which they had been commended to the grace of God for the work that they had accomplished. When they had arrived and gathered the church together, they began to report all things that God had done with them and how He had opened a door of faith to the Gentiles. And they spent a long time with the disciples."

⮌ Acts 14:21,25-28

Dorothy was right about one thing—there's no place like home!

About 25 years ago, I left my boyhood home in Texas. But last week, I did something I've wanted to do for a long time. I went to Texas and took a nostalgic four-mile run up and down the streets where I grew up.

I jogged by my elementary school and reminisced about Mrs. Manning, my dear first grade teacher, who once cracked my knuckles with a yardstick. (I deserved it.) I passed my junior high girlfriend's house, remembering when she dropped me for my best friend. (So much for that!) As I got closer to home, my heart quickened. In my mind, I could see the yard I mowed, the pond where I caught crawdads, and the dog pen I built.

When I reached my boyhood home, I became overwhelmed with memories. I could picture Mom in the kitchen, loving us with her good Texas hospitality. I saw Dad out on the old baseball field behind the house, teaching me to play catch. At least a dozen memories flooded me.

That jog back home was one of the greatest adventures of my life. Our house wasn't perfect. But it was and always will be home base to me.

Paul and Barnabas also knew the value of home. After their journeys, they returned to Antioch. For them, it was a place where they could rest, catch up with the disciples they loved, and report to the church on their ministry. Their travels were grueling. They needed the support of home.

Be sure your family makes its home an encouraging environment. The world can be tough. Allow God to turn your home into a retreat.

Discussion Starters:

1. Why was it so important for Paul and Barnabas to return to Antioch?
2. What did they do when they arrived back home?

Lifeline:

Paul and Barnabas spent a lot of time with the disciples at their home base in Antioch. Make one night this week a family night at home. Play a game. Talk. Pray. Tell jokes. Discuss a video. Enjoy some quality time together.

A WEIGHTY MATTER

"Some men came down from Judea and began teaching the brethren, 'Unless you are circumcised according to the custom of Moses, you cannot be saved.' ...After there had been much debate, Peter stood up and said to them, ... 'Why do you put God to the test by placing upon the neck of the disciples a yoke which neither our fathers nor we have been able to bear? But we believe that we are saved through the grace of the Lord Jesus, in the same way as they also are.... Therefore it is my judgment that we do not trouble those who are turning to God from among the Gentiles, but that we write to them that they abstain from things contaminated by idols and from fornication and from what is strangled and from blood.'"

↬ Acts 15:1,7,10-11,19-20

Brad's mom often warned him not to lift weights alone. But Brad always said, "Aw, Mom, I can take care of myself." Then he'd smile and point to his biceps. "Look at these guns! I'm invincible!"

One day, when Brad was home alone, he went for a personal weight-lifting record. He didn't have the proper equipment, so he balanced the weights on two stacks of encyclopedias. Lying on the floor between A and Z, Brad bench pressed 250 pounds 10 *times*! But when he lowered the weights, the books fell over, and the bar pinned his throat to the floor.

Brad was too tired to move it off, so he inched along the floor, rolling the bar as he moved toward a phone on a corner table. He reached the table, yanked the phone's cord, and the phone crashed down on his head. He groaned, then dialed his neighbor. But Brad's mother got home first. She lugged the weights off her son, wrapped his head in a towel, and drove to the hospital, chuckling inside at her "invincible" son with the weird turban.

Strapped and weighted down. For years, the Pharisees made religion out to be a burden. The apostles didn't want Christianity to be a weighty matter, though. They knew Jesus had saved people by grace, not by burdensome works. So they made careful decisions about what Christians should be required to do, and they focused on the core issues of the faith.

Next time you feel trapped by rule-based religion, remember that Jesus' message was plain and simple. What you do for God is important, but what He did for you on the cross matters more. Following burdensome rules won't help you get to heaven—but having a deep faith in Jesus will.

Discussion Starters:

1. How do you think the disciples decided what was important?

2. How are we saved by grace? How should works fit in with our faith?

Lifeline:

Read 1 John 5:3. Why isn't it a burden to keep God's commandments?

THE POWER OF THE PEN

"Then it seemed good to the apostles and the elders, with the whole church, to choose men from among them to send to Antioch with Paul and Barnabas—Judas called Barsabbas, and Silas, leading men among the brethren, and they sent this letter by them.... So when they were sent away, they went down to Antioch; and having gathered the congregation together, they delivered the letter. When they had read it, they rejoiced because of its encouragement."

⮑ Acts 15:22-23,30-31

Letter writing is a lost art. It's back there somewhere with records and rotary phones. Perhaps that's why I save most of my mail.

I have mountains of correspondence from teens. I read them from time to time—it keeps me connected to my friends. Some letters make me laugh. Others make me cry. All of them find lodging in my heart.

I have notes from former camp counselors—occasionally scrawled on the backs of business cards. Most write that the summers they spent at Kamp were some of the greatest times in their lives.

It always hurts to read the sad letters. But they motivate me to write these people back—to "visit" as many of them as possible, even though they now live far from me. I always think, *Maybe they'll save my words of encouragement. Then one day when they're feeling low, they'll pull my letter from the back of some dark drawer, and the two of us will chat.*

Many of the New Testament books were originally letters, written by an apostle to churches far away. Some congregations needed encouragement. Some needed to be warned about cults and idols. Some needed more teaching and instruction. Probably every church read and reread those letters—just as we pore over them now.

Can you imagine what our Christian lives would be like if it weren't for Paul, Timothy, John, and the other apostles who took the time to impart biblical wisdom to their brothers and sisters in Christ?

Few deeds take so little time, with such great results, as letter writing. Take the time today to write to someone. The apostles' notes ended up in the Bible. Don't underestimate what God could do with your words of encouragement.

Discussion Starters:

1. What seems to be the purpose of the letter in this passage?

2. Have you ever received an encouraging letter? If so, how were you helped by it?

3. Have you ever sent an encouraging letter? What did it say? Did it achieve its purpose? If so, how?

Lifeline:

Encourage one person today by writing him or her a letter.

BAD THINGS AND GOOD PEOPLE

"When [the chief magistrates] had struck [Paul and Silas] with many blows, they threw them into prison, commanding the jailer to guard them securely.... But about midnight Paul and Silas were praying and singing hymns of praise to God, and the prisoners were listening to them; and suddenly there came a great earthquake...and immediately all the doors were opened and everyone's chains were unfastened. When the jailer...saw the prison doors opened, he drew his sword and was about to kill himself, supposing that the prisoners had escaped. But Paul cried out with a loud voice, saying, 'Do not harm yourself, for we are all here!' ...And after he brought [Paul and Silas] out, he said, 'Sirs, what must I do to be saved?' They said, 'Believe in the Lord Jesus, and you shall be saved, you and your household.'"

⇝ Acts 16:23,25-28,30-31

I was married my junior year in college and faithfully loved my wife for 14 months. I was a college football player, and the life was fun and glamorous. But when I graduated and began working, my wife fell in love with my best friend and left me. After a few months, they were married.

I cried for months—I was heartbroken, without hope. But by God's grace, I never got bitter or blamed either of them. I still respect them both and realize now that I could have been a much better husband and friend.

You know what? I survived! And after I'd healed, God led me to Debbie-Jo, my lifetime bride and the mother of our four kids, whom I *adore*. Every year I love Debbie-Jo more than I first did 25 years ago.

God hates divorce. It's totally wrong. God wants men and women to marry for life. But God is merciful and gracious, able to work through any circumstance and bring good from it (see Romans 8:28). He did in my case.

Bad things *do* happen to good people. Paul and Silas didn't have it easy. They were beaten, mocked, and jailed for preaching the gospel. But although Satan might have worked to get them behind bars, God had the last word. That night in prison, the jailer and his household accepted Christ.

God doesn't cause the messes in our lives, but He uses them to draw us closer to Him. He worked through my difficulty and Paul and Silas's crisis, and He'll bring good from your problems, too. Do you believe that?

Discussion Starters:

1. Name three good things that came from Paul and Silas's imprisonment.
2. What do you think was the purpose of the earthquake?
3. How do we grow closer to God through tough times?

Lifeline:

Describe a time when God used a crisis to bless you and others as well.

WHEN REASON FAILS

"Now when they had traveled through Amphipolis and Apollonia, they came to Thessalonica, where there was a synagogue of the Jews. And according to Paul's custom, he went to them, and for three Sabbaths reasoned with them from the Scriptures, explaining and giving evidence that the Christ had to suffer and rise again from the dead, and saying, 'This Jesus whom I am proclaiming to you is the Christ.'"

↪ Acts 17:1-3

I like to debate with evolutionists. I try to reason with them about the pitfalls and problems the evolutionary theory poses. To the scientist who believes Piltdown Man was the bridge between ape and Adam, I'll say, "That's impossible. Fifty years after its discovery, Piltdown Man was proved to be the clever combination of an ape jawbone and a modern human skull, planted as a fossil to fool the experts." To the scientist who believes Nebraska Man was the missing link, I'll remark, "Hold your horses. We can't base our beliefs about the existence of humanity on a single pig's tooth found in a Nebraska cornfield."

Unfortunately, my reasoning with the scientific elite usually has little effect on them. They go on believing in pig teeth and monkey mandibles because that's what they want to believe.

I could talk to these staunch evolutionists until I was blue in the face, but I've realized that even reason has its limits. Paul discovered this when he tried to reason with the Jews at Thessalonica. Sure, he may have persuaded some of them to join the faith. But the rest of the Jews mobbed Paul and even tried to hurt his friends. Nevertheless (as the book of Acts reveals), Paul continued his custom of reasoning with the Jews and kept trying to convince them to follow Christ. And as his letters to various churches reveal, Paul never ceased to pray for them.

You, too, might have friends who don't support your faith. What should you do when they won't listen to you or they mock your beliefs? As Paul did, keep preaching the gospel and praying for your friends.

Don't give up. You never know what God can do in a person's life!

Discussion Starters:

1. Note that in Thessalonica, Berea, and Athens, Paul always preached to the Jews first. Why do you think he did that?

2. As Paul experienced rejection, what did he do in the next town?

3. When has reasoning with someone for Christ failed for you?

Lifeline:

Do you know any unbelieving people—Jews or Gentiles? If so, pray consistently that the Father would direct them to the Son.

DAUGHTER OF AN UNKNOWN GOD

"So Paul stood in the midst of the Areopagus and said, 'Men of Athens, I observe that you are very religious in all respects. For while I was passing through and examining the objects of your worship, I also found an altar with this inscription, "TO AN UNKNOWN GOD." Therefore what you worship in ignorance, this I proclaim to you. The God who made the world and all things in it, since He is Lord of heaven and earth, does not dwell in temples made with hands; nor is He served by human hands, as though He needed anything, since He Himself gives to all people life and breath and all things.... For in Him we live and move and exist, as even some of your own poets have said, "For we also are His children."'"

↜ Acts 17:22-25,28

I'll bet the men and women of Athens were confused the day Paul delivered his sermon on Mars Hill. Those people were used to having objects of worship. They preferred their gods cold, hard, and tangible. But Paul was undeterred. He pointed to their altar of the Unknown God and suggested He could be known. Then Paul said the God he was talking about didn't dwell in temples made with human hands (verse 24).

"A god who has no home? Where does He live?" the people must have asked.

Well, let me tell you where I think He lives. God dwells in people like Jeannie. This woman could be dancing on any stage in the world. Instead, Jeannie has chosen motherhood. Occasionally, she still performs in town, and when she does, the audience holds its breath. Jeannie's ballet interpretation of the crucifixion moves people from head to toe.

If the Athenians could've seen Jeannie dance, they probably would've stuck her up on that empty, unnamed altar and called her a goddess. Now, you and I know Jeannie isn't a goddess, but she is an offspring of the Unknown God, who dwells in her heart and enables her to minister to people through dance.

God lives in your heart, too, and not just on Sundays or at summer camp. He's *always* there. Does your life reflect God's presence in you?

Discussion Starters:

1. Why is it so amazing that God dwells in His children?

2. How can God dwell in all believers all the time?

3. If our hearts are Christ's home, what's your heart like? Does it resemble a messy bedroom? A cold, orderly living room? A cozy den? Explain your answer.

Lifeline:

Discuss ways you all can make your hearts more accommodating for Christ.

HOLY DIRT

"And [Paul] found [in Corinth] a Jew named Aquila, a native of Pontus, having recently come from Italy with his wife Priscilla, because Claudius had commanded all the Jews to leave Rome. He came to them, and because he was of the same trade, he stayed with them and they were working, for by trade they were tent-makers. And he was reasoning in the synagogue every Sabbath and trying to persuade Jews and Greeks. But when Silas and Timothy came down from Macedonia, Paul began devoting himself completely to the word, solemnly testifying to the Jews that Jesus was the Christ."

↫ Acts 18:2-5

Over the years, there has been such a separation of the spiritual and secular that it would take a rocket to launch a Bible across the chasm—especially when it comes to what we do, our occupations.

Maybe you're a student, a business professional, or a parent. Maybe you spend your days going to class, or you're top dog in the office, or you home-school your kids.

But whatever our jobs, shouldn't we all be pastors first? In other words, shouldn't we be messengers of Christ who also happen to work for a living?

Isn't the Christian who hauls trash a minister of sorts? Or how about the truck driver, attorney, or homemaker who loves Jesus? Isn't it his or her business to work heartily for the Lord as well? My favorite pastors are those who wear their jeans to the office occasionally and spend their lunch hours at the playground with their kids. I also like those ministers who pour concrete with the construction guys in the church parking lot, pray for their fellow students, or cook meals for families who need help.

Paul was a tentmaker when he first arrived in Corinth. He stayed with Priscilla and Aquila because they made tents, too. But Paul's *lifestyle* showed that he was an apostle. His true job was ministry.

All Christians are, in some ways, ministers. The world is our church—humanity, our congregation. Whatever your occupation, make sure you live as Christ's evangelist. There are a million ways to touch the people around you. Don't just leave it up to your pastor to fulfill the Great Commission.

Discussion Starters:

1. How do you think Paul ministered to people while making tents?
2. When Silas and Timothy arrived, Paul was free to devote himself to preaching. How do you think he was supported?

Lifeline:

How can you be a pastor in your neighborhood, school, or workplace?

HAIRCUTS

"Paul, having remained many days longer, took leave of the brethren and put out to sea for Syria, and with him were Priscilla and Aquila. In Cenchrea he had his hair cut, for he was keeping a vow."

           ↫ Acts 18:18

Haircuts—routine mutilations of a living organism—often go unnoticed. They do! Of course, getting a haircut isn't as extreme as having your leg chopped off or getting your forehead tattooed, but if you ask me, people should pay more attention to them.

For example, take Paul's haircut in Acts 18:18. I'll bet you were reading along so fast, you hardly saw it. You probably said to yourself, Aw, *it's just a haircut. Let's move on to the next verse.*

But it wasn't *just a haircut* for Paul. It was a significant event, which marked the end of an 18-month promise—called a Nazarite vow. In general, it simply meant that during his ministry in Corinth, Paul had vowed to God that he'd remain spiritually and physically pure. And as a symbol of that vow, he pledged not to cut his hair. Consequently, he had a natural reminder of his agreement with God every time the wind blew a lock of hair in his face.

In the apostle Paul's days, Corinth was a wicked place to take up residence. You could find a way to indulge every desire and temptation. For a Christian, it practically required a vow to be able to live in Corinth and remain pure. So that's what Paul did—made a vow to God.

But did you know people still make vows today? Recently, I heard that thousands of teens pledged to remain virgins until marriage and signed documents as testimonies to the fact. Next year, they'll go to Washington to display these documents as a testimony to the world that *abstinence is cool!* The peace and joy of their honeymoons will bear witness to the unspeakable value of that vow.

And hopefully, that's a vow that won't go unnoticed.

Discussion Starters:

1. Is your high school or workplace similar to Corinth? If so, how?

2. What vows might God be leading you to make for the next year?

3. How might your vow help you to live a more godly life in that atmosphere?

Lifeline:

Because none of us is perfectly like Christ, we'll all blow our vows from time to time. Read Numbers 6:1-21 for insight about what to do when you've blown it.

HANKIES AND HOODWINKERS

"God was performing extraordinary miracles by the hands of Paul.... But also some of the Jewish exorcists, who went from place to place, attempted to name over those who had the evil spirits the name of the Lord Jesus, saying, 'I adjure you by Jesus whom Paul preaches.' ... And the evil spirit answered and said to them, 'I recognize Jesus, and I know about Paul, but who are you?' And the man, in whom was the evil spirit, leaped on them and subdued all of them and overpowered them, so that they fled out of that house naked and wounded. This became known to all, both Jews and Greeks, who lived in Ephesus; and fear fell upon them all and the name of the Lord Jesus was being magnified."

                                               ⌐ Acts 19:11,13,15-17

I was in the lobby of a college dorm one Sunday morning and overheard some students talking as they watched a religious show on TV.

"Here's another one of those hokey handkerchief guys. Could someone please change the channel!" a young man said as the televangelist prayed over a piece of cloth, promising to send it to some viewer for a donation of $100 or more.

I shook my head and walked away. But I couldn't blame the young man. He was right. Too many people in this world have tried to reproduce the work of the Spirit without first letting the Spirit work *in them*.

Satan laughs at such vain attempts. In fact (as you probably noticed in verse 16), he waits for just the right moment—then he pounces on the unsuspecting hoodwinker, and the gig is finished. No more fame, money, or reputation. Without the work of the Holy Spirit, many ministries—like the Jewish exorcists—are stripped naked and made into a joke.

You should respond to supernatural power as the Ephesian Christians did in verse 17. They realized that only the power of the Holy Spirit can subdue evil, and it made them honor God even more.

God's miracles are a far cry from the world of fluffy preaching. He sovereignly chooses to perform miracles in His timing, with His discretion, and solely for the purpose of glorifying His name and deepening His relationship with us. There's nothing hocus-pocus about His power.

Discussion Starters:

1. What was the purpose of such miracles in Paul's day?

2. What was the difference in motive between Paul and the exorcists?

3. What miracles have you seen God work in your own life?

Lifeline:

Pray for Christians involved in healing ministries. A lot of good can result from the ministries, but the people involved need guidance and protection.

SHORT ON GUTS

"'You see and hear that not only in Ephesus, but in almost all of Asia, this Paul has persuaded and turned away a considerable number of people, saying that gods made with hands are no gods at all.' ...The city was filled with the confusion, and they rushed with one accord into the theater, dragging along Gaius and Aristarchus, Paul's traveling companions from Macedonia. And when Paul wanted to go into the assembly, the disciples would not let him. Also some of the Asiarchs who were friends of his sent to him and repeatedly urged him not to venture into the theater."

↩ Acts 19:26,29-31

The Ephesians were in an uproar. Paul had just told them their god, Artemis, wasn't worth worshiping, and they were steaming mad. The people flocked to the theater, chanting and yelling, all on account of Paul. You'd think Paul would have ducked and covered. But he wanted to go into the assembly—so much so that the disciples had to restrain the guy.

Paul had heroic courage. But unfortunately, his kind of bravery isn't common today. I only have to read the movie listings or scan the TV to see that we've got a lot of "heroes" but only a few brave people in our society.

Think about it....

It takes courage to work through a troubled relationship. But most Hollywood stars jump from marriage to marriage the way monkeys swing from tree to tree.

It takes guts to rely on your personality instead of alcohol. But many famous people are in and out of substance abuse hospitals, unable to live without the crutch of drugs and alcohol.

It takes bravery to stand up for your beliefs when they go against the norm. But most TV stars will only endorse socially acceptable things. Most public people nowadays lack true grit. Whatever happened to *real* heroes? Why aren't more people like Paul, who was willing to rush into the thick of things because he knew it was right?

The apostle Paul was an authentic hero. There may be a dearth of courage in Hollywood, but there's no shortage of guts in the Bible.

Discussion Starters:

1. What do you think Paul wanted to accomplish by entering the assembly?

2. Why did Paul's companions try to keep him outside?

3. What's your definition of courage? Do your heros exhibit bravery? Why or why not?

Lifeline:

Pray today for those people you hold in high esteem.

FALLING ASLEEP

"On the first day of the week, when we were gathered together to break bread, Paul began talking to them, intending to leave the next day, and he prolonged his message until midnight. There were many lamps in the upper room where we were gathered together. And there was a young man named Eutychus sitting on the window sill, sinking into a deep sleep; and as Paul kept on talking, he was overcome by sleep and fell down from the third floor and was picked up dead. But Paul went down and fell upon him, and after embracing him, he said, 'Do not be troubled, for his life is in him.' ...They took away the boy alive, and were greatly comforted."

↪ Acts 20:7-10,12

I've already talked about the ridiculous way we describe "falling in love." Ever notice that we talk the same way about "falling asleep"?

Once, I watched a man fall asleep on national TV. He was sitting barely five feet behind First Lady Hillary Clinton as she addressed the Senate subcommittee on health care. The man's eyelids fluttered. His head bobbed. Then he woke up quickly, trying desperately to stay alert. He turned toward Mrs. Clinton's voice, struggling to make sense of her words. But his head bobbed again. I shouted for my wife to come watch, and she ran in from the kitchen. The man's chin inched slowly toward his chest.

"Uh-oh. He's history," I said.

"Going...going...gone," said my wife, Debbie-Jo.

For a moment, the camera lingered on the sleeping man. In that moment, I was almost certain I saw a slight smile on his face, and I wondered if he was dreaming of the new job he'd start tomorrow morning—sweeping peanut shells on Pennsylvania Avenue.

Sometimes falling asleep can be dangerous. The young man who fell asleep listening to Paul almost died from snoozing in church. His situation was extreme, but how many times have you dozed off in church? How often do you take mental vacations while the pastor's talking?

It's easy to take for granted the privilege of hearing God's Word. It's easy to tune out sermons. But *God isn't boring.*

How can you make His Word come alive in your heart?

Discussion Starters:

1. Why is it sometimes so hard to concentrate on God's Word?
2. What keeps you from focusing on God? What can you do about it?

Lifeline:

Discuss ways your family can make time with God more interesting and fulfilling, and talk about how you all can learn more in church.

GOD BLESS TEARS

"And when they had come to him, he said to them, 'You yourselves know, from the first day that I set foot in Asia, how I was with you the whole time, serving the Lord with all humility and with tears and with trials which came upon me through the plots of the Jews.' ...And they began to weep aloud and embraced Paul, and repeatedly kissed him, grieving especially over the word which he had spoken, that they would not see his face again. And they were accompanying him to the ship."

ᗡ Acts 20:18-19,37-38

Whenever I see an unusual word more than once in a passage, I take note of it. This passage describes grown people crying. And Paul stated that he served "with tears," indicating that he probably cried many more times as well.

Apparently Paul cried freely. And because he did, his audience heard the Word of God seasoned with emotion. They were able to see God's hand on Paul's heart, and it inspired his Ephesus congregation to be more open with their feelings as well.

Our faith should touch our emotions. We should cry tears of joy when our friends meet Jesus and weep with sorrow when people reject Him. I don't know where society got the idea that people—especially men—who show emotion are weak. Our Lord was emotional, and He modeled the perfect life. Jesus sobbed in the Garden of Gethsemane. He wept over His dear friend Lazarus's death. And He cried out to God twice when He was being crucified on the cross.

Most men (and some women) struggle with being open about their feelings. If you're a stoic, I challenge you to learn from Christ's (and Paul's) example. It is possible to be both strong and emotional. Expressing your feelings at the appropriate times will strengthen your relationships—with people and with God.

Let the One who's Lord over your life be Lord over your heart.

Discussion Starters:

1. How do you think Paul's tears strengthened the Ephesians?

2. How can revealing your emotions strengthen your relationships?

3. Does your family encourage everyone to be open with his or her feelings? Explain.

4. When are tears inappropriate?

Lifeline:

Read Ecclesiastes 3:1-8. As Solomon noted, there's a time for everything. How do you know when it's appropriate to talk about your feelings?

HOLD THE LINE

"And coming to us [the disciples], [Agabus] took Paul's belt and bound his own feet and hands, and said, 'This is what the Holy Spirit says: "In this way the Jews at Jerusalem will bind the man who owns this belt and deliver him into the hands of the Gentiles." ' ...[So] we as well as the local residents began begging him not to go up to Jerusalem. Then Paul answered, 'What are you doing, weeping and breaking my heart? For I am ready not only to be bound, but even to die at Jerusalem for the name of the Lord Jesus.' And since he would not be persuaded, we fell silent, remarking, 'The will of the Lord be done!' "

↩ Acts 21:11-14

In my opinion, God gets blamed too often for our dumb moves. We pray, and we think we heard Him correctly. So we rush into action, never once imagining that our ears were full of wax and we hadn't heard Him at all. Oh, the things we do in the name of God's will!

Intelligent men propose marriage to women, claiming that God has told them she's "the one." They're astounded when the women say, "Well, He hasn't told me that yet."

Pro-lifers murder abortionists because they think it's God's will.

Cult leaders everywhere lead their members to steal, lie, and sometimes even commit suicide—based on a "word" they've gotten from God. I'm certain those cult leaders need to swab their ears with Q-tips.

With all the confusion over God's voice, how do you and I know if we've *really* heard Him? Well, we do what Paul did (see Acts 21).

We pray (verse 5).

We listen (verses 4,12).

We consider the advice of other Christians (verses 4,11-12).

We study Scripture.

But most importantly, we *wait* (verses 4,10). When all else fails, and we can't figure out God's will when we need to make tough decisions, we should "hold the line" until we can hear His voice clearly.

Then, like Paul, we must go forth boldly to do God's will—regardless of what He has in store for us.

Discussion Starters:

1. Why do you think Paul's friends urged him not to go to Jerusalem?

2. Was Paul being stubborn not to heed their advice? Why or why not?

3. Is it possible that Paul's friends advised him according to their own emotions rather than God's will? Have you ever done that? If so, when?

Lifeline:

Describe a time you were certain of God's will for you in a particular area.

WE STAND ACCUSED

"When the seven days were almost over, the Jews from Asia, upon seeing him in the temple, began to stir up all the crowd and laid hands on him, crying out, 'Men of Israel, come to our aid! This is the man who preaches to all men everywhere against our people and the Law and this place; and besides he has even brought Greeks into the temple and has defiled this holy place.' ...Then all the city was provoked, and the people rushed together; and taking hold of Paul, they dragged him out of the temple, and immediately the doors were shut."

↪ Acts 21:27-28,30

If you were brought before a court of law and were tried for being a Christian, would there be enough evidence to convict you?

I'm a longtime fan of that saying, for, in the span of a sentence, it forces me to put my life on the witness stand.

The apostles lived a dangerous testimony. The early church was accused of all sorts of heinous crimes. Christians were called "cannibals" for their practice of communion, "politically disloyal" for their refusal to burn incense to Caesar, "anti-family" for the divisions that naturally occurred when one family member left the Jewish faith to follow Christ, "sexually perverted" for the love feasts they held (which were nothing more than sincerely motivated potluck suppers), and, ironically, "atheists" because they had no visible idols.

My friends, history repeats itself. Are you prepared to call yourself a Christian in an age when accusations are being made once more? Need I remind you that if you hesitate even the tiniest bit over issues of homosexuality, abortion, pornography, or radical feminism, you risk being labeled a "narrow-minded bigot" and a "hate monger"?

I don't want to create a martyr complex. But I do believe when we say we're Christians, we—like our ancestors—will be unjustly accused by our culture. So I urge you—wear the name bravely or don't wear it at all.

Discussion Starters:

1. Of what things was Paul falsely accused?

2. How did Paul respond to those accusations?

3. In Paul's day, the Jews were most offended by the Christian message. In our culture today, who is most offended by Christ?

4. Are you prepared to offend others because of your beliefs? Explain.

Lifeline:

What does it mean to be politically correct? How does political correctness sometimes conflict with biblical correctness? Decide as a family where you stand on today's important issues.

IT'S *HISTORY*

" 'I am a Jew, born in Tarsus of Cilicia, but brought up in this city, educated under Gamaliel, strictly according to the law of our fathers, being zealous for God just as you all are today. And I persecuted this Way to the death, binding and putting both men and women into prisons... [but on the road to Damascus] I fell to the ground and heard a voice saying to me, "Saul, Saul, why are you persecuting Me?" And I answered, "Who are You, Lord?" And He said to me, "I am Jesus the Nazarene, whom you are persecuting." ...And I said, "What shall I do, Lord?" And the Lord said to me, "Get up and go on into Damascus, and there you will be told of all that has been appointed for you to do." ' "

↪ Acts 22:3-4,7-8,10

Do you have a testimony? A story of renewal, telling how your life was transformed?

A girl named Helen did. Born deaf and blind, Helen was unruly and selfish as a young child. But Anne, her teacher, changed all that. Anne was kind and patient, but she made Helen let go of her self-pity, and she worked to teach Helen how to talk. Anne succeeded. By age 10, Helen knew the alphabet and could read and write in Braille. When she turned 16, she spoke well enough to attend preparatory school. Eventually, Helen even attended college. She graduated with honors and went on to become one of the most influential people of the twentieth century. By the time she died at the age of 88, Helen Keller had lectured for the cause of the blind on five major continents, written eight books about her life, and become the subject of numerous motion pictures and plays.

Helen's life was physically transformed, but Paul's life was *spiritually* changed. His testimony was powerful. As he told the Jews, he started out persecuting Christians and ended up risking his life for the gospel.

Your story may not be as exciting as Paul's. You may not have wandered far from God. But He has worked in your life, and you can tell others about it. Your story is part of History and is therefore worthy of being told again and again. Tell your testimony as often as you can.

Discussion Starters:

1. A Christian's testimony explains how Christ saved him or her. In your own words, summarize Paul's testimony in this passage.

2. Why is a testimony an effective means of evangelism?

3. Have you ever told your testimony to someone? Why or why not?

Lifeline:

Take a step of faith and tell your testimony to a friend. Then relay the results to your family.

AN AMERICAN FISHTALE

"But when they stretched him out with thongs, Paul said to the centurion who was standing by, 'Is it lawful for you to scourge a man who is a Roman and uncondemned?' ...The commander came and said to him, 'Tell me, are you a Roman?' And he said, 'Yes.' The commander answered, 'I acquired this citizenship with a large sum of money.' And Paul said, 'But I was actually born a citizen.' Therefore those who were about to examine him immediately let go of him; and the commander also was afraid when he found out that he was a Roman, and because he had put him in chains."

⤳ Acts 22:25,27-29

We've talked a bit about living in a godless society. And it's true—America (and Western culture generally) is becoming that way. But overall, few would deny that the United States is still a pretty good country.

I was thinking about my blessings one day in Quetico Park as I sat on the border between Canada and the United States, staring at my fishing line.

I'd been casting from my canoe toward King's Point, on Canada's side, for about half an hour with no luck. Suddenly, I turned to glimpse the largest tail I'd ever seen, waving "bye-bye." I felt as if the fish were saying, "You don't have to leave the country to find good fishing." I whirled around, cast my line on the American side, and...bingo! Mr. Hogbody Fish was on my line.

My, how that proud bass fought! He must have broken water at least a dozen times—once with such gusto that he cleared the bow of my canoe with ease. He was smart. But in the end, I was smarter. Finally, I held his tired body in my hands and grinned at what I saw. There, imbedded in his bony jaw, were two lures. One was mine. The other obviously belonged to an unsuccessful fisherman. When I turned the rusted lure over I read, "Made in the U.S.A."

Today, that lure hangs on my wall. It's there to remind me of the great bounty that still exists in the United States.

Being an American citizen is a bit like it was to be born a Roman in New Testament times—a privilege and blessing. Paul knew that. His Roman citizenship got him out of a sticky situation or two. His birth made him such an elite that when the centurion and commander realized they were dealing with a Roman citizen, they got scared and quickly let Paul go.

If you're a citizen of the United States (or any other democratic, prosperous nation), you've been incredibly blessed. You have privileges third world people couldn't even imagine having. Today, thank God for the gift of living where you do.

Discussion Starters:

1. How did Paul's appeal to his citizenship help him?

2. How do you benefit from your own citizenship?

3. Why is it wrong to be disloyal to your country?

Lifeline:

As a family, list the blessings your country provides for you.

DIVIDE AND CONQUER

"But perceiving that one group were Sadducees and the other Pharisees, Paul began crying out in the Council, 'Brethren, I am a Pharisee, a son of Pharisees; I am on trial for the hope and resurrection of the dead!' As he said this, there occurred a dissension between the Pharisees and Sadducees, and the assembly was divided. For the Sadducees say that there is no resurrection, nor an angel, nor a spirit, but the Pharisees acknowledge them all. And there occurred a great uproar; and some of the scribes of the Pharisaic party [said],...'We find nothing wrong with this man; suppose a spirit or an angel has spoken to him?'"

↩ Acts 23:6-9

Pete was barely three when he launched his first campaign against the citadel of parental authority.

"That will be quite enough, young man!" said Pete's mother when she caught him slurping milk from his bowl at the breakfast table.

Pete peered at his mother. "Daddy does it," he declared confidently.

Pete's mother glared across the table at her sheepish husband. "Yes, he does," she said, "but that doesn't mean it's okay for his children to do it."

"Daddy said I could," added Pete.

"Now, wait," Pete's father said. "Surely, you don't believe that I..."

But it was too late. The division had been made, and the conquering had begun. From that statement forward, it wouldn't have mattered if Pete dumped cereal onto the dog and poured his milk on the floor. His parents had forgotten the real issue. And so, while his parents took up the new battle, Pete declared victory with a slurp and a grin.

Paul did the same thing when he stood in front of the Council. He was well aware of the animosity between the Pharisees and Sadducees, and he used it to his advantage.

"Hey," he said, "I'm one of you Pharisees. I was born and raised that way. How can my teaching be wrong?"

In one breath, Paul gained the loyalty of the Pharisees, angered the Sadducees, and further divided the Council. He threw them into such an uproar that they forgot the real issue—and Paul was let off the hook.

Discussion Starters:

1. Describe the dividing and conquering that took place in this passage.

2. When is it okay for a Christian to act shrewdly?

3. Was Christ ever shrewd? Give examples. (See John 8:1-11 and Luke 20:20-26.)

Lifeline:

Describe a time when you used clever discernment (shrewdness).

227

THE BROTHERHOOD OF THE HIVE

"And he said, 'The Jews have agreed to ask you to bring Paul down tomorrow to the Council, as though they were going to inquire somewhat more thoroughly about him. So do not listen to them, for more than forty of them are lying in wait for him who have bound themselves under a curse not to eat or drink until they slay him; and now they are ready and waiting for the promise from you.' ...[So the commander] called to him two of the centurions and said, 'Get two hundred soldiers ready by the third hour of the night to proceed to Caesarea, with seventy horsemen and two hundred spearmen.' ...So the soldiers, in accordance with their orders, took Paul and brought him by night to Antipatris."

→ Acts 23:20-21,23,31

I once saw a beehive...at closer range than I'd planned.

The brothers of that hive had hardly seemed to notice me when I crawled in at one end of the long, rectangular juniper bush. After all, how much interest *should* a bee have in a second grader playing hide-and-go-seek? But they showed a surprising fascination with me when I exited that bush by the opposite end—right through their living room.

"Look out!" my friend Gary screamed. "Keep running! They're after you!"

Sure enough, a glance over my shoulder revealed a black line of winged things buzzing after me. For a microsecond, I imagined the bee at the head of the line was the one I'd offended...and the rest were merely avenging him. Then they attacked.

That night, with my head bandaged tightly and my swollen lips throbbing, I had a vision that has stuck with me for a lifetime. Thirty years later, I put it into poetry:

> If brother bee backs brother bee,
> how much more wilt Thou
> back me!

Discussion Starters:

1. To what lengths did the commander go to protect Paul, a citizen of Rome? What does that reveal about the value of being a Roman citizen?

2. What are some of the benefits of having a heavenly citizenship? What scriptures describe those benefits (see, for example, Ephesians 1)?

Lifeline:

Discuss your rights as a citizen of heaven. Then thank God in prayer for those rights.

PESTS

"'For we have found this man a real pest and a fellow who stirs up dissension among all the Jews throughout the world, and a ringleader of the sect of the Nazarenes.'"

↪ Acts 24:5

"Why mosquitoes?" That's one question I'm going to ask God when I get to heaven.

On a recent camping trip, I spent an hour slaving over a dehydrated lemon pie. The meal was finished. The frying pan was cooling on a flat, mossy rock. And through the trees, my friends and I watched the sun drop. Everything was beautiful and peaceful.

But at the first waning of the breeze, the mosquitoes came in hordes. Like great, black packs of hungry dogs, they circled me, filling my ears, my nose, my eyes, jabbing me with their sharp snouts. I tried to shoo them off and dropped the pie. Needless to say, we spent the rest of the evening in our tents, with no dessert.

"Why did You create mosquitoes?" I'm going to ask God the moment I set foot inside heaven's gates. "What right did those blood-dependent creatures have to spoil so many get-togethers back on earth?"

But now that I think of it, I know what His answer will be.

"Joe," He'll say, turning the question around without batting an eye, "what right did a blood-dependent creature like *you* have to spoil so many get-togethers back on earth?"

We all have the ability to be as pesky as mosquitoes. In fact, even Paul was called a pest. He was constantly around where the Jews didn't want him. He stirred things up. He repeatedly, painfully reminded the people of the truth. To many, Paul was someone they didn't want around.

Being called a pest is not usually considered a compliment. But I'll bet Paul smiled and considered that label evidence that he'd done his job of witnessing to the Jews.

Sometimes even mosquites can teach us a thing or two about God.

Discussion Starters:

1. Why do you think Tertullus called Paul a pest?

2. The Greek rendering of the word *pest* can mean "plague." In what ways was Paul an annoying plague to the Jews?

3. The word *pest* is usually negative in connotation. But is there a *positive* way that you can be a pest to the nonbelieving world?

Lifeline:

What aspects of being a pest are necessary for effective ministry?

LIFE VERSUS DEATH

" 'Or else let these men themselves tell what misdeed they found when I stood before the Council, other than for this one statement which I shouted out while standing among them, "For the resurrection of the dead I am on trial before you today." '"

↩ Acts 24:20-21

Isn't it amazing how often life itself is put on trial?

Take abortion. The 1973 landmark decision Roe v. Wade made abortion legal, and life lost a valuable battle. Now life's losing its value again as doctors argue the "right" to assist patients in suicide.

But these trials are nothing new.

Paul himself stood testifying for the cause of life—eternal life, that is. Clearly stating his charges, he said, "For the *resurrection* of the dead I am on trial before you today" (verse 21, emphasis added).

You would think such words would bring a cheer that could raise the courtroom roof. "Hurrah for resurrection!" "Hip! Hip! for life!"

Instead, Felix, Paul's judge, ignored Paul's profound statement about life and put his trial on hold.

Felix didn't want to deal with the powerful truth—that what Paul said about the resurrection was exciting. He didn't want to admit that Paul didn't deserve to stand trial for defending eternal life.

Next time the sanctity of life is on the witness stand and you are tempted to ignore its value, consider what would happen if everyone on earth lived by the advice of life's chief prosecutors.

If every child was aborted, our population would soon disappear.

If assisted suicide became the norm, many human beings would perish.

And if we didn't have the hope of the resurrection, we would look forward only to death.

Every day, life is put on trial. How will you defend its value?

Discussion Starters:

1. Which segment of Paul's audience was most offended by the topic of the resurrection? Why were they so offended?

2. Why are people still offended by Christianity today?

3. Why is Jesus Christ's resurrection central to the Christian faith?

4. How does life get put on trial every day? Why should you defend it? How can you make the case for the value of earthly and eternal life?

Lifeline:

What would you say to someone who asked you to prove the resurrection beyond reasonable doubt? (Check out Josh McDowell's *Evidence That Demands a Verdict*. I recommend that every teen read it before college.)

I CAN'T WAIT TO GET PATIENCE

"But after two years had passed, Felix was succeeded by Porcius Festus; and wishing to do the Jews a favor, Felix left Paul imprisoned.... After Paul arrived, the Jews who had come down from Jerusalem stood around him, bringing many and serious charges against him which they could not prove.... But Festus, wishing to do the Jews a favor...said, 'Are you willing to go up to Jerusalem and stand trial before me on these charges?' But Paul said, 'I am standing before Caesar's tribunal, where I ought to be tried. I have done no wrong to the Jews, as you also very well know. If, then, I am a wrongdoer and have committed anything worthy of death, I do not refuse to die; but if none of those things is true of which these men accuse me, no one can hand me over to them. I appeal to Caesar.'"

↪ Acts 24:27;25:7,9-11

"I prayed for patience, and I got pregnant with Savannah," one woman said in my Sunday school class. Indeed, it seems God often answers our prayers for patience by giving us a child. Now, you'd think parents could learn a ton of patience from having just one kid. But in reality, the first kid doesn't teach his parents actual patience. Junior only introduces the *opportunity* for parents to learn patience. When the opportunity arises—like at 3:30 A.M. when Junior is singing opera in his crib—his parents once again pray the "P" prayer, and *poof!* along comes another kid. This continues until the parents finally get wise and quit asking for patience.

These wizened adults are the ones you see strolling calmly through the mall with 13 wild things hanging from their ankles and elbows. You wonder how they can be so patient. But they're not being patient at all.

They've merely learned to keep their mouths shut.

The apostle Paul never mentioned anything about having kids, but he certainly had his patience tested. He awaited trial for two years before he could even appear before Governor Festus. But for all the grief Paul went through, he still testified with respect and patience.

Are you able to keep your cool in the same way?

Discussion Starters:

1. How did Paul demonstrate patience when he addressed the Romans?

2. What might have happened if he'd spoken impatiently?

3. What things most test your patience? How can you learn to stay calm?

Lifeline:

As I mentioned above, kids often try their parents' patience. In what ways do parents frustrate kids? How can your family learn to be more patient with one another?

RUMORS

"'I answered them that it is not the custom of the Romans to hand over any man before the accused meets his accusers face to face and has an opportunity to make his defense against the charges.'"

→ Acts 25:16

The Roman Empire was pretty rotten. But I've always been impressed by its practice of allowing people to face their accusers and defend themselves. I only wish Becky could've done that. Confronting her peers might have spared her a lot of pain—and saved her life as well.

Becky was beautiful. Her honey-blonde hair, creamy skin, and green eyes made Becky the secret object of every boy's dreams at my junior high. Unfortunately, she was also painfully shy. She never talked long with anyone and always ate lunch by herself. Our classmates decided that anyone who was beautiful and quiet must be stuck-up. So instead of drawing her out, they snubbed her.

Becky became the brunt of jokes and rumors—many of them started, no doubt, by the awkward, less-than-pretty girls who envied her.

"She's easy," kids whispered in the halls at Hoover Junior High.

"Yeah, and she thinks she's better than everyone," jealous girls said when they saw her in gym, standing by herself.

Often I could see Becky was right on the verge of confronting her classmates about their untrue (and unfair) accusations. Then her eyes would fill with tears and she'd shyly back down.

One morning, Becky didn't show up for class. Once again, rumors circulated. "She hung herself," our classmates said softly.

But their whispers turned to gasps when they found out it was true.

I think about Becky from time to time, and I'm embarrassed to admit I failed to help her. I wish I would have done something to dispel the rumors. I wish she would've had the strength to face her accusers.

There's no such thing as a harmless rumor. False accusations are painful and destructive. If you know someone who's being wrongfully accused, take a stand. Help the person.

You never know the difference you could make in someone's life.

Discussion Starters:

1. Why was it so important for Paul to defend himself?

2. Why did Paul's accusers start rumors about him?

3. Why else do people start rumors? How can you help stop a rumor?

Lifeline:

Do you know someone who is being unfairly accused? If so, how can you help him or her?

CARL'S WORLD

" 'In regard to all the things of which I am accused by the Jews, I consider myself fortunate, King Agrippa, that I am about to make my defense before you today; especially because you are an expert in all customs and questions among the Jews; therefore I beg you to listen to me patiently.' "

↜ Acts 26:2-3, emphasis added

In the summer of '79, Carl came to Kanakuk, one-winged and full of life. Our staff had hired him that winter, having no idea the shape he'd be in six months later. He walked through the gates with his right arm bound tight against his chest in a sling, wearing a smile as wide as Kansas. Immediately, the misfits were attracted to him. And before long, Carl had a following of every uncoordinated, frail child in Kamp.

"How'd ya hurt yer arm?" they'd ask, their eyes fixed on their hero.

"Shark bit it," he'd say casually.

"Really?" they'd gasp.

"Nah. I hurt it lifting weights," he'd say.

With his hurt arm, he couldn't lead any of the sports activities. So Carl would herd them into our tiny leather room, where all day he'd put up with pounding mallets and hordes of kids clamoring for his attention.

Someone once asked him if he was going insane being trapped in the leather room all day. Carl said, "No way! Look at all the friends I've made!"

Carl was a great basketball player. He'd probably been looking forward to playing sports with the kids all summer. It could have been bitterly disappointing for him to end up in the craft room, but Carl made the most of his circumstances. In fact, he saw his condition as a blessing.

Paul was like that, too. He'd been persecuted, jailed, mocked, and finally, after years, put on trial. But the first thing he said to Agrippa was, "I'm a lucky man to be testifying in front of you."

Your attitude can be your most valuable asset or your biggest hindrance. In life, you *will* have trials. But what makes the difference is how you deal with those difficulties.

God's hand is always at work, especially during dark times. Choose to look for the good. With God in your life, things will ultimately work out.

Discussion Starters:

1. Why did Paul claim to be fortunate? Could you have said the same?

2. How can you develop a positive attitude during tough times?

Lifeline:

Discuss one trial your family is facing. How might God be working through this difficulty? How can you be more positive about it?

THE COMPASS

"Since neither sun nor stars appeared for many days, and no small storm was assailing us, from then on all hope of our being saved was gradually abandoned.... [But Paul said,] 'Yet now I urge you to keep up your courage, for there will be no loss of life among you, but only of the ship. For this very night an angel of the God to whom I belong and whom I serve stood before me, saying, "Do not be afraid, Paul; you must stand before Caesar; and behold, God has granted you all those who are sailing with you." Therefore, keep up your courage, men, for I believe God that it will turn out exactly as I have been told.'"

↩ Acts 27:20,22-25

On Table Rock Lake, near Kamp, lies an island. Groups of boys and girls from Kamp often go there for weekends of sailing and bluff jumping. They come back with deep tans and grand stories.

One foggy night, I left the island to retrieve a boy's asthma medicine, which had been left behind at Kanakuk. My partner, Ken, and I climbed in our boat, and for nearly an hour we puttered through a thick, troublesome fog. Finally, we realized we were lost.

"Man, I'm so disoriented, I wouldn't know if we were about to crash into shore!" Ken said, shuddering. Immediately the same creeping feeling of disorientation washed over me, and I couldn't tell if I was up or down.

Ken began to panic. "What if we run out of gas?" he said. "What if some other boat crashes into us? What if we drown?"

I might have gotten alarmed as well, but at that moment my eyes rested on an instrument in the middle of the dashboard.

"Relax," I said, pointing to the compass. All we needed to do was take our eyes off the fog and let a more reliable source guide us back to shore.

Thirty minutes later, we were back on the island.

That incident reminds me of how God guides and guards our lives. Paul and his crew also thought they'd be stranded. And they were sure they'd die. But just when the men lost all hope, God reminded them that He would lead the way and keep them safe.

Have courage. God will always direct you.

Discussion Starters:

1. How does God direct your path?
2. How can you cling to God when you're caught in storms?
3. What situation do you need God to direct you in right now?

Lifeline:

Memorize a verse that comforts and strengthens you so that when the storms of life come, you'll be able to hold on to God.

BE LOGICAL

"Until the day was about to dawn, Paul was encouraging them all to take some food, saying, 'Today is the fourteenth day that you have been constantly watching and going without eating, having taken nothing. Therefore I encourage you to take some food, for this is for your preservation, for not a hair from the head of any of you will perish.' Having said this, he took bread and gave thanks to God in the presence of all and he broke it and began to eat. And all of them were encouraged and they themselves also took food."

↪ Acts 27:33-36

Our society lacks logic. For all its technological breakthroughs and political correctness, the world is still backward in many ways. Scan the channels with me and you'll see what I mean....

In the drug war, some government officials tell us to "Just Say No" and then argue about whether we ought to legalize drugs.

The National Organization for Women claims that the majority of men are sexual harassers, yet I have a feeling it would be hard to find anyone in that organization committed to harassing the pornography industry.

The media call a baby a "fetus" when the mother wants to get an abortion, but when an expectant mother refuses on religious grounds to undergo a lifesaving operation, the "fetus" is suddenly depicted as a "child."

Psychologists routinely give tired people antidepressants and long-term psychotherapy without even considering that the only thing those people might need is sleep.

Paul kept his head on straight, however. Though his world was being turned upside down by a hurricane, he was still able to give the sailors sound advice. He said, "Eat! You'll feel a lot better." And they did. Sometimes an ordinary meal—or a clear head—is all you need to see the world in a new light.

Discussion Starters:

1. Why is it so important to keep a clear head when you're dealing with a crisis?

2. How can your belief in God enable you to become more rational in difficult situations?

Lifeline:

Describe a time in which you acted rationally, despite crazy circumstances. Then pray together that God would give your family the ability to think clearly during confusing and difficult times.

BACK FROM THE DARK AGES

"But when Paul had gathered a bundle of sticks and laid them on the fire, a viper came out because of the heat and fastened itself on his hand. When the natives saw the creature hanging from his hand, they began saying to one another, 'Undoubtedly this man is a murderer, and though he has been saved from the sea, justice has not allowed him to live.' However he shook the creature off into the fire and suffered no harm. But they were expecting that he was about to swell up or suddenly fall down dead. But after they had waited a long time and had seen nothing unusual happen to him, they changed their minds and began to say that he was a god."

⮌ Acts 28:3-6

Now, admit it. You probably chuckled a little as you read about those Maltese natives. One moment, they were convinced Paul was a murderer, and the next they glorified him as a divine snake charmer.

The Maltese thought bad things happened to bad people and that good people were blessed. They believed Paul's snakebite and the shipwreck he endured were punishments for his sins. They didn't know that Paul's sins were already forgiven and he was saved by grace.

The Maltese were primitive thinkers. Don't you agree?

A lot of Christians are equally primitive, though. We often doubt God's goodness when things go wrong. And, every so often, when times are tough, we wonder if God's punishing us for some long-ago sin.

It's easy to forget that God has saved us from our sins by His grace. Next time you doubt that, read the Bible. God's Word will welcome you back to the truth.

Discussion Starters:

1. The Maltese thought Paul's snakebite was God's judgment on him. What's wrong with that kind of simple cause-and-effect logic?

2. As the Maltese revealed, it's easy to let circumstances sway your convictions. Has any situation (or person) ever caused you to doubt God's Word or the goodness of His character? If so, when? Why?

3. Give some examples from society today in which people look past God's truth and rely instead on their own thinking. How do they let circumstances change their perspectives? Why is it so dangerous to do that?

Lifeline:

Read Romans 5:8-10. Thank God you're saved and forgiven in Christ and that nothing will ever separate you from His love.

IF THE DEVIL ASKED ME FOR A STRATEGY...

"Some were being persuaded by the things spoken, but others would not believe. And when they did not agree with one another, they began leaving after Paul had spoken one parting word, 'The Holy Spirit rightly spoke through Isaiah the prophet to your fathers, saying, "Go to this people and say, 'You will keep on hearing, but will not understand; and you will keep on seeing, but will not perceive; for the heart of this people has become dull, and with their ears they scarcely hear, and they have closed their eyes; otherwise they might see with their eyes, and hear with their ears, and understand with their heart and return, and I would heal them.'"'"

↜ Acts 28:24-27

An interesting sign was posted on the doors of one hot and undesirable work-place. It read: "Wanted—one devil. No management experience necessary."

Now, I definitely wouldn't want the job, but I don't think it would be too hard to do Satan's work. If I were him, I'd form a battle strategy, and it would focus on one simple thing: cutting Christians off from the home office. That's right. I'd sever all lines of communication between creation and the Creator. To do that, first I would blind their eyes so they couldn't see God. (That wouldn't be hard, since sin is such a convenient blindfold.) Then I'd plug their ears so they couldn't hear God. (To do that, I'd make prayer a burden and have Scripture seem as boring as a telephone book.) Finally, I'd gag their mouths so they couldn't praise God.

Paul certainly knew Satan's battle strategy. The Jews had been victims of the devil's wiles for thousands of years and were almost completely closed to God's Word. Paul tried to tell the Jews what was happening, but they wouldn't listen.

Paul's message should be a warning for you as well. Now that you know how Satan works, don't let him get the better of you.

Don't let the devil cut your lines of communication with God.

Discussion Starters:

1. Why was it so hard for the Jews to accept the gospel?

2. How can we be blind and deaf even while we have eyes and ears?

3. Even as you participate in this devotional book, have you been guilty of spiritual deafness or blindness? How can you remedy this problem?

Lifeline:

This passage is helpful in part because it explains why some people are closed to the gospel. Pray together for your unbelieving friends. Ask God to overcome Satan's battle strategy by opening their eyes and ears.

JaMes

Although there are four men named James in the New Testament, careful study leads most scholars to believe that the author of this letter was James, son of Mary and Joseph, the half-brother of Jesus.

Scholars think that James wrote this book between A.D. 45 and 50, only 10 to 15 years after he dramatically converted to Christianity when his brother, Jesus, was resurrected from the dead.

This letter is what I call "grace on wheels." It explains the practical aspects of the Christian faith—what a believer does (through grace) after he or she has been saved (by grace). The book of James teaches that faith works! God's grace doesn't sit still. A person who is full of God's grace will give it back to others. As you study this book together, your family will find tremendous joy in serving one another.

IT'S ALL JOY

"Consider it all joy, my brethren, when you encounter various trials, knowing that the testing of your faith produces endurance. And let endurance have its perfect result, so that you may be perfect and complete, lacking in nothing."

↜ James 1:2-4

My mom and dad had dreamed and prayed that they would have three children some day. Their first baby was a boy named Frank. Tragically, due to complications during childbirth, Frank lived for only one hour. My parents were heartbroken. They felt as if God had mercilessly allowed their son to be taken from them.

Gradually, though, Mom and Dad realized that Frank belonged to God and that He had a plan for their pain. They learned that "In [God's] presence is fullness of joy" (Psalm 16:11). Slowly, they began to heal. As the years went by, my parents had two more boys. Then they had me—the third son.

I know that my life is a part of God's plan. If Frank had lived, my parents wouldn't have tried to have another child after my other two brothers were born, and I probably wouldn't be here today.

Our family has had many bumps and bruises. We've cried, and we've clung to God in prayer, but we've learned to find joy in all circumstances.

Life is full of trials.

Your girlfriend cheats on you—with your best friend. Your boss falsely accuses you of stealing money at work. Everyone was asked to the homecoming dance except you. Someone breaks into your car and takes your new stereo. People make fun of you because you're a Christian.

When you feel as if the world is coming down on you, don't panic—pray. It may seem hard to believe, but God will work through your pain. He will give you endurance, hope, and eventually, joy.

My family knows that. With one baby in heaven and three sons on earth, God has shown us that He is sovereign—*especially* in difficult times.

Discussion Starters:

1. What's one trial you're experiencing in your life?

2. How can God turn this trial into a joyful experience?

3. When trials come, your reaction to them will make you either bitter or better. What kind of reaction makes you bitter? Better?

4. How do trials produce endurance? Why is endurance so important?

Lifeline:

Talk together about the different trials you've faced as a family. What did you learn from them? How did God allow those trials to shape you?

TACKLING TEMPTATION

"Let no one say when he is tempted, 'I am being tempted by God'; for God cannot be tempted by evil, and He Himself does not tempt anyone. But each one is tempted when he is carried away and enticed by his own lust. Then when lust has conceived, it gives birth to sin; and when sin is accomplished, it brings forth death. Do not be deceived, my beloved brethren."

↩ James 1:13-16

Two and a half months ago, our TV set broke. Boy, did that upset me! (Ha, ha, ha.) I'm so mad, I can't seem to find the phone number for the TV repairman. (Right!) I'm so mad, I keep forgetting to get it fixed!

Actually, I think it's one of the best things that's ever happened in our home. I like to call TV "Temptation Vision." Every year, TV pipes more than 180,000 rapes, murders, and acts of violence, beer commercials, and sexual innuendoes into the minds of each family member in the average American home. No wonder we're tempted to argue, lust, fight, and drink.

These messages from the media—these temptations—have had sweeping effects, too. One out of five Americans has a sexually transmitted disease (STD), the number of teenagers with AIDS doubles every 14 months, and more college students die alcohol-related deaths than those who will go on to graduate school.[1]

Those are just some of the problems TV and the movies have helped to foster in our culture. What about materialism and eating disorders? Hollywood stars drip money. They have rock-hard, lean bodies and killer clothes to match. We get tempted to try to look like them, so we spend dollar after dollar and go on diet after diet, attempting to model ourselves after the stars. Unfortunately, we often end up with eating obsessions and shopaholic tendencies. And our focus leaves God and settles on ourselves.

Be careful about what you fill your mind with when you watch the screen. No one wants to end up with a drinking problem, an eating disorder, a violent temper, or an STD, but those Temptation Visions can affect you far more than you realize. As James said, "Do not be deceived."

Avoid the things that lure you away from God.

Discussion Starters:

1. What do we mean when we pray, "Lead us not into temptation"?
2. Who tempts us? What part do we play in temptation?
3. Besides watching questionable TV shows and movies, how else do we expose ourselves to temptation?

Lifeline:

List some practical ways your family can help each other fight temptation.

JUST DO IT!

"But prove yourselves doers of the word, and not merely hearers who delude themselves. For if anyone is a hearer of the word and not a doer, he is like a man who looks at his natural face in a mirror; for once he has looked at himself and gone away, he has immediately forgotten what kind of person he was. But one who looks intently at the perfect law, the law of liberty, and abides by it, not having become a forgetful hearer but an effectual doer, this man will be blessed in what he does."

↪ James 1:22-25

If James, the author of the epistle we're studying, had worn tennis shoes back in the first century, I'll bet he would've worn Nikes. Why? Both James and the shoe company push the same slogan: Just Do It.

Nike sells in excess of $3.6 billion worth of shoes and sports accessories annually.[2] Nike's advertisements say, in effect, "Don't talk about going jogging—get yourself outside and exercise now."

Nike's ads sell shoes, but James's slogan guides souls. His "Just Do It" passage is the heartbeat of his epistle. James said, "Don't just read about giving; put some money in a piggy bank for the less fortunate. Don't just talk about wanting a better prayer life; start praying more consistently. Don't just talk about that overstuffed closet; give some clothes away."

My son Cooper learned at an early age how hard it is to be a "doer of the Word." One evening, Cooper, then five years old, told me he wanted to memorize a Bible verse.

"Well, Cooper, how about Ephesians 6:1?" I said, hiding my smile.

Cooper soon found out the verse reads, "Children, obey your parents in the Lord, for this is right." He innocently smiled and said, "Daad! That verse isn't there; you just made that up."

It's easy to ignore certain verses and commands in the Bible, isn't it? But as James said, over and over, you've got to take action for Christ. Let your faith show. And "Just Do It" for God—today.

Discussion Starters:

1. Why is it not enough to be just a "hearer of the word"?

2. It has been rightly stated, "When all is said and done, there's a lot more said than done." Why does that truth present a problem for Christians?

3. We're saved by faith in Christ, but our works are still important. Why?

4. In what areas of your faith do you need to be more action-oriented?

Lifeline:

Does anyone in your family have a project he or she needs help doing? In what ways can your family be better "doers of the Word"?

UP WITH THE UNDERDOG

"My brethren, do not hold your faith in our glorious Lord Jesus Christ with an attitude of personal favoritism. For if a man comes into your assembly with a gold ring and dressed in fine clothes, and there also comes in a poor man in dirty clothes, and you pay special attention to the one who is wearing the fine clothes, and say, 'You sit here in a good place,' and you say to the poor man, 'You stand over there, or sit down by my footstool,' have you not made distinctions among yourselves, and become judges with evil motives?"

↾ James 2:1-4

I've learned so much from my daddy that the encyclopedia couldn't contain it all. And 99 percent of what I've learned has been through his actions.

Dad never told me to love the underdog or those less fortunate, but I'll never forget watching him meet the garbage collectors at the back door of our house every Monday and Friday morning with a cup of hot coffee and a sweet roll for each worker, complete with a huge smile and a word of encouragement. When I was growing up, he often came home from work without his coat, shoes, or money because he'd met someone less fortunate who needed what he had. Even now, in church and at social gatherings, Dad automatically finds his way to the "lowest person on the totem pole." Those humble poor people are always Daddy's best friends.

You, too, are surrounded by the needy. The halls of junior high and high schools are filled with people who need love and support, like, for instance, that new girl with the shabby clothes who always sits by herself. Or the school mascot, the guy everyone loves to hate. Or Marshall, one of your childhood friends, the one your friends have nicknamed "Crater Face."

What do you do? Turn up your nose at them? Look past them in a crowd? Chime in with the insults?

James didn't mince words when he said we're to love all people. How good are you at loving those who don't have it as good as you?

Discussion Starters:

1. Why do we tend to push aside the less fortunate?
2. Why is it a sin to show partiality?
3. What is a Christian's responsibility toward the less fortunate? Are you carrying out Christ's command to help others? Why or why not?

Lifeline:

What opportunities do you have every day to help someone less fortunate? How you can show Christ's love to those needy people around you?

FAITH THAT WORKS

"What use is it, my brethren, if someone says he has faith but he has no works? Can that faith save him? If a brother or sister is without clothing and in need of daily food, and one of you says to them, 'Go in peace, be warmed and be filled,' and yet you do not give them what is necessary for their body, what use is that? Even so faith, if it has no works, is dead, being by itself."

⬿ James 2:14-17

An old friend of mine, Mr. Plummer, ran a sawmill where I used to buy my lumber for building projects. He was in his mid-80s, living out the final days of his life in the historic Ozark mountains.

Whenever I dropped by to buy lumber, I'd stop and chat with Mr. Plummer. We spent hours visiting together. Once, I asked the savvy old character where he went to church. He raised his white, bushy eyebrows, stomped his worn, black boot, and scowled.

"I'll never go to any ol' church!" he said gruffly. "Thirty years ago, some folks from that church down the road bought some lumber from me and cheated me out of my money."

Mr. Plummer quickly changed the subject, but his words stuck with me. Soon after our talk, he passed away—not knowing Christ.

What use was that church and all their beautiful prayers and hymns if they didn't show an old lumberjack the love of Jesus?

What good are 16 Bibles in a home if they're not read?

What good is a big savings account if it's not used for people in need?

What good is a smile that's not shared?

What use is a hug or an "I love you" that's not given?

And what use is faith when it doesn't have works?

Discussion Starters:

1. What does faith look like when it's coupled with works? Why is this kind of faith a true and sincere faith?

2. Why is faith dead if it doesn't have arms and legs?

3. How does faith work? What is an example of faith that works?

4. Who do you know that most connects actions with his or her faith? How is his or her faith evident?

Lifeline:

Yesterday we talked about helping those less fortunate than ourselves. Did anyone in the family put faith into action by loving a needy person? If so, describe the experience. If not, keep looking for opportunities to lend others a hand.

THE TERRIFIC, TERRIBLE TONGUE

"For every species of beasts and birds, of reptiles and creatures of the sea, is tamed and has been tamed by the human race. But no one can tame the tongue; it is a restless evil and full of deadly poison. With it we bless our Lord and Father, and with it we curse men, who have been made in the likeness of God."

⟿ James 3:7-9

Human beings have gotten pretty good at harnessing nature.

My friend "Snake" actually trains rattlesnakes. He doesn't exactly turn snakes into play toys, but he subdues them and makes them his pets.

Circus trainers tame lions, elephants, and bears.

My kids and I ride horses together, galloping across pastures and through the woods.

At our sports camps, the campers spend hours windsurfing. They love to catch the wind and skim speedily across the water.

It is impressive the way we've learned to control wild animals and the weather. But subduing a rattlesnake, training a wild beast, guiding a horse, and harnessing the wind take only time, patience, a bit on a horse's bridle, and a small rudder.

Our tongues are equally—if not more—powerful and destructive. Unfortunately, we don't focus our attention nearly enough on taming our tongues. Instead, we continue to hurt one another with our poorly chosen words.

Our words have the power to tear people down, but they can also be a great encouragement to others. Writing a love letter, saying "I'm proud of you," or complimenting a friend can bring sunshine to a cloudy day!

So what will it be? Gossip or encouragement? Cursing or enthusiasm? Negative comments or compliments? Sarcasm or praise?

The choice is yours.

Discussion Starters:

1. Why is it more difficult to "tame the tongue" than to tame a lion?

2. Why does the tongue work like a match that starts a forest fire?

3. When do you struggle most with taming your tongue? Why?

4. How can God help you guide your words?

Lifeline:

Try this exercise in your family: If you say one negative or cutting comment to someone, you immediately have to give that person five compliments.

ARE YOU A WISE GUY?

"Who among you is wise and understanding? Let him show by his good behavior his deeds in the gentleness of wisdom.... The wisdom from above is first pure, then peaceable, gentle, reasonable, full of mercy and good fruits, unwavering, without hypocrisy."

⌒ James 3:13,17

Do you value wisdom?

King Solomon sure did. His one request to God was for wisdom. Since Solomon's prayer was so noble and godly, God blessed him abundantly with both wisdom and wealth (see 2 Chronicles 1).

The gospel author Luke thought wisdom was important, too. The other gospel authors didn't mention Jesus' teenage years, but Luke noted that Jesus increased "in wisdom" (Luke 2:52). Luke didn't want us to overlook that significant detail.

Wisdom also enabled Ben Strong of Paducah, Kentucky, to act quickly and courageously. One school morning in December 1997, Strong and his high-school student prayer group, the Agape Club, looked up to see a freshman student holding a semiautomatic handgun. The boy began shooting, killing three girls and injuring several others.

My friend Steven Curtis Chapman and I talked after he returned from the funeral, where he sang and offered an invitation to receive Jesus Christ. Steven said the number of killings could have been far worse if Ben, the group's leader, hadn't disarmed the gunman before he pulled out the rest of his weaponry. God gave Ben, a devout Christian and star football player, the wisdom and words to convince the boy to stop shooting. Little did Ben Strong know as he studied the Bible that God was preparing him for a life-saving talk with a classmate whose life had gone awry.[3]

Solomon outlined a few great truths about wisdom in Proverbs 2: The Lord gives it, and if you seek wisdom from God's Word, you will find it. Wisdom is a treasure to be sought after, and the person who finds it will be blessed.

The Bible devotes a lot of space to the subject of wisdom. Are you seeking God for it?

Discussion Starters:

1. What is godly wisdom? How can we get it?

2. Why is wisdom one of the greatest things you can ask God for?

3. What's the difference between being smart and being wise?

Lifeline:

Since wisdom comes from God's truths, commit to spending more time in His Word.

WHOSE TEAM WILL YOU JOIN?

"You adulteresses, do you not know that friendship with the world is hostility toward God? Therefore whoever wishes to be a friend of the world makes himself an enemy of God.... Submit therefore to God. Resist the devil and he will flee from you. Draw near to God and He will draw near to you. Cleanse your hands, you sinners; and purify your hearts, you double-minded."

⤻ James 4:4,7-8

Michael Jordan and Shaquille O'Neal basketball cards get more valuable every year. Some Mickey Mantle baseball cards are worth hundreds of dollars today. An autograph from Joe Montana can generate huge amounts of money from folks in a football crowd.

Those cards and autographs are valuable because everybody loves winners. People always want to be on the winning side in a game or a war.

But what about in life?

You may not always win your track meets or debate competitions, but if you're a Christian, your life will be eternally victorious. God is *the* winner. He always coaches the winning team. He never fails.

Satan, on the other hand, is a loser. When the devil fights God and His team, Satan is always defeated in the end.

The devil often deceives people into thinking they're winning when they become friends with him. He gives temporary highs and fleeting satisfaction through partying, sex, power, and money. But Satan doesn't mention that the things you get from him will eventually destroy you.

You don't need to worry if you're on God's side, though. The Lord gives eternal, true happiness. If God lives in your heart, He'll help you deny the devil's temporary kicks and enable you to recognize counterfeit happiness.

Do you want to be a winner? Draw near to God. When you do, you'll find that He's already close beside you, guiding and coaching you every step of the way. No matter what the odds look like, God will always lead you to victory.

Discussion Starters:

1. How is God like the coach of a winning team?

2. How is Satan like the coach of a losing team?

3. How do you draw near to God? How do you resist the devil? Be specific.

Lifeline:

Family members should be accountable to one another. If someone in your family seems to be "befriending" Satan in an area of his or her life, lovingly tell that person. But also joyfully acknowledge God's work in his or her life.

THE MYSTERIOUS LADY

"Do not speak against one another, brethren. He who speaks against a brother or judges his brother, speaks against the law and judges the law; but if you judge the law, you are not a doer of the law, but a judge of it. There is only one Lawgiver and Judge, the One who is able to save and to destroy; but who are you who judge your neighbor?"

↩ James 4:11-12

Ruth Castillos always wore a bright red dress and dark sunglasses. Each Wednesday at 9:30 A.M., she'd meet a stocky, bearded man in front of the drugstore. Quietly, he would exchange a bottle of pills for her package of dollar bills. Then Ruth would quickly, mysteriously slip into her BMW and drive briskly away to her tiny house in the country.

Besides going to the drugstore each week, Ruth rarely left home.

She almost never had visitors, either. The only person who came to her house was a tall, handsome young man who stopped by each Friday afternoon—and stayed only an hour.

What do you think Ruth was doing? Drug dealing? Embezzling international funds? Holding hostages in her home?

Actually, Ruth wasn't doing any of the above. She was struggling to hold her life together. She had an eye disorder that made it difficult for her to see in broad daylight—and forced her to wear dark sunglasses. She only went out during the day to see the pharmacist because her mom was terminally ill and needed medicine. Her mom was so sick that neither she nor Ruth could have any visitors. So the only person who came by was a young doctor who made house calls on Friday.

Ruth's life was so dark, she wore red to cheer herself up.

Did you jump to conclusions when you first heard about Ruth? I did. It's easy to judge people when you don't know all the information.

It's easy, but it's dangerous. Most of the time we're mistaken about people. But even if we do come to the right conclusions, we're still wrong to judge.

Don't try to do God's job. He's the only One who has any business judging people.

Discussion Starters:

1. Why is it so dangerous to judge others? Why are we so quick to judge?

2. What did you first think Ruth was up to? Why?

3. Who have you judged unfairly? Why did you jump to conclusions?

Lifeline:

How can we help each other refrain from judging and slandering others but also be discerning about who we chose as friends?

ROTTING RICHES

"Come now, you rich, weep and howl for your miseries which are coming upon you. Your riches have rotted and your garments have become moth-eaten. Your gold and your silver have rusted; and their rust will be a witness against you and will consume your flesh like fire. It is in the last days that you have stored up your treasure!"

⤳ James 5:1-3

My friend "ol' Norm" owns a large corporation. He has lots of money and a big house. Anyone would say that ol' Norm is a rich man.

Norm's a great steward of his money, though. He gives to 1,600 different ministries. He pays his employees well and prays diligently for everyone he knows. In his spare time, he does mission work in impoverished countries around the world. He loves his wife, kids, and grandkids. But above all, Norm enjoys spending time with God.

My teenage friend Madeleine started a clothing company a few years ago. Mady's been very successful and now makes about $100,000 a year. But since the beginning, she's given every cent away to needy kids around the world. Mady has always had a generous heart. Even as a child she would give 25 to 50 percent of her small allowance to her church and to help alleviate world hunger.

Max, a dear 10-year-old I know, makes 25 cents a day by memorizing Bible verses. He puts each quarter into a piggy bank for poor inner-city kids.

Michael, an acquaintance of mine, inherited over $100 million when his father died. But he's selfish with his money and spends most of it on himself—his business and pleasures. Michael has lost more than 90 percent of his inheritance in the last 20 years, and if he doesn't become a better steward, he may lose it all. Even though right now he has virtually everything that money can buy, Michael's not happy. Most of the time, he looks nervous and stressed. In fact, I've never seen him smile.

Money won't make you happy, especially when you misuse or hoard it. But when you give it away—back to God—you'll be blessed with eternal riches.

Do you have the right attitude toward money?

Discussion Starters:

1. When is money a bad thing?

2. Jesus called the love of money "the root of all evil." In fact, He addressed the issue of wealth more than any other subject. Why?

3. How do you know when you're giving enough?

Lifeline:

As a family, how can you work together to give enough back to God and use your resources wisely?

PRAYER POWER

"Is anyone among you suffering? Then he must pray. Is anyone cheerful? He is to sing praises. Is anyone among you sick? Then he must call for the elders of the church and they are to pray over him, anointing him with oil in the name of the Lord; and the prayer offered in faith will restore the one who is sick, and the Lord will raise him up, and if he has committed sins, they will be forgiven him. Therefore, confess your sins to one another, and pray for one another so that you may be healed. The effective prayer of a righteous man can accomplish much."

⇜ James 5:13-16

Eight thousand kids shivered like wet puppies as the early spring rain turned the outdoor youth rally into an event that would've made only Noah rejoice. As our staff tried to make a final "go/no-go" decision about whether to have the music concert in the outdoor arena, I stood with a group of unbelieving technicians who were huddled around cups of coffee.

"Should we call 'er off, Joe?" they teased.

"Not yet," I said. "Elijah was a man with a nature like ours, and he prayed earnestly that it would not rain; and it did not rain on the earth for three years and six months," I said, quoting from James 5:17.

I continued, "Fellows, God says, 'The effective prayer of a righteous man accomplishes much.' I'm going to pray that the rain stops."

"Yeah, but you're not Elijah!" the technicians scoffed.

But Elijah's God is my God, I thought. I walked to the sound stage and asked God to let us hold the concert. Within 60 seconds, the rain stopped. We had the rally. And, for the record, that event hasn't been rained out once in 17 years. (Rained on, but not out!)

Does it rain or stop raining every time I pray? No. Does everyone get instantly healed each time I pray? No. But I've seen God answer every prayer faithfully. He'll say either "yes," "no," "now," or "later."

An old Southern preacher summed prayer up by saying, "God may not be there when you want Him, but He'll always get there right on time."

God will be faithful to your requests. Do you believe that?

Discussion Starters:

1. Why do you think God created prayer?

2. What prayer concerns do you have today?

3. What prayers have you seen answered in your life recently?

Lifeline:

Pray for each other right now. Keep a log of each family member's prayer requests, and then update the log when the requests have been answered. Doing that will reveal how God is working in your family.

Revelation

While most of Jesus' original 12 disciples died heroic martyrs' deaths, John was exiled to the tiny Mediterranean island of Patmos. During his latter years, God appeared to him with the prophecy of His final works on earth, which, written, became the book of Revelation.

This glorious and sometimes confusing book contains highly symbolic pictures describing the people and events surrounding the fall of humankind; the banishment of Satan; the second coming of Christ; His millennial, peaceful reign on earth; and the eternal home of all believers. These passages bring the assurance of our salvation, the encouragement we need to overcome all of Satan's ploys, and the hope of Christ's ultimate victory.

THE SECOND HAND

"Blessed is he who reads and those who hear the words of the prophecy, and heed the things which are written in it; for the time is near."

⮑ Revelation 1:3

Angela wound her car around the narrow country road, excitedly anticipating her first trip home from college. She peered out the window, lost in memories. She couldn't wait to be talking with her parents, surrounded by the tick-tocking of the clocks that filled the house.

Angela had grown up listening to the sound of dozens of pendulum clocks that echoed throughout the house. Her parents had collected the antique timepieces while they were overseas in Frankfurt, West Germany, during the Vietnam War. Every stately room resounded to the song of each clock's unique chime—some at the hour, some at the half hour, and with the great-grandfather clock in the entryway, every quarter hour as well.

She thought back to how her father would make the rounds once a week, winding the clocks and checking the accuracy of his beloved timepieces. The only time it was silent in the house was when the family left for vacation and the clocks ran down. It always struck Angela as rather odd that the sound of passing time could be so comforting.

Time is important, and it's constantly urging us forward. Our alarm clocks, watches, and even calendars remind us that time is precious—and short.

The Bible is like an alarm clock in some ways. The New Testament—and especially Revelation—always ticks away, pointing to Jesus' imminent return. Each word urges Christians forward, encouraging us to persevere, hold fast, and overcome.

We don't have an indefinite amount of time in our lives. Each day is significant. Each person we meet is important. And everything matters.

Jesus is coming back—soon. We shouldn't let one word of Scripture slip by us. We'll want to be ready when the final trumpet blows and the clock winds down for good.

Discussion Starters:

1. Why do you think God didn't give a definite time for Jesus' return?
2. What are some things you would do today if you knew Jesus was coming back tomorrow? Would you be ready for His return? Explain.
3. How can you make the most of each day?

Lifeline:

What are some practical ways your family can encourage one another to take advantage of today, especially if it turns out to be *the* day?

LOCKED OUT

"When I saw Him, I fell at His feet like a dead man. And He placed His right hand on me, saying, 'Do not be afraid; I am the first and the last, and the living One; and I was dead, and behold, I am alive forevermore, and I have the keys of death and of Hades.'"

↪ Revelation 1:17-18

The door made an ominous "click" as it swung shut, locking Becky, the baby-sitter, outside in the cool evening and locking the sleeping Adam, a six-month-old baby, inside. The house was locked up tighter than Fort Knox. *Great. What am I going to do? I don't have a key*, Becky thought.

She couldn't believe it. This was only her second time to baby-sit for the Jensens—and they were brand-spanking-new parents. Worse still, they were out for the evening with two famous entertainers, having a prestigious dinner. It was a black-tie affair, *of course*, where a waiter would have to scurry in and conspicuously interrupt their dinner to say, "Your baby-sitter is on the phone. It's an emergency." Quadruple-whammy. Becky ran her hands through her hair, trying not to panic. She checked all the doors and windows again, then went door to door, looking for a spare key. *No luck. I'll have to bite the bullet hard*, she told herself.

After two embarrassing phone calls to the parents, Becky flagged down the development security guard and explained her dilemma. Finally, with the help of his credit card, Becky got inside.

Next time, I'll carry a house key with me, she vowed, determined never to be caught in that situation again.

As Becky found, being locked out of the house is a frustrating experience. It makes you feel alone and helpless.

Getting shut out of heaven's gates will be even worse.

Fortunately, Jesus holds the keys to God's kingdom. He transcends life and death. He's the "living One." The blood Christ shed for you on the cross gives you the opportunity to have eternal life with God in heaven.

If you develop a relationship with Him, I guarantee you won't be left out in the cold.

Discussion Starters:

1. What did Jesus mean when He called Himself the "first and the last" and the "living One"?

2. On a scale from 0 to 100 percent, how confident are you of your salvation? Explain your answer.

3. If you aren't 100 percent confident, what are some things that keep you from feeling secure in your faith? How can you work through those issues?

Lifeline:

As a family, begin memorizing Bible verses that will help you be 100 percent sure of your salvation. (Start with John 1:12 and Acts 4:12.)

FIRST LOVE

"'But I have this against you, that you have left your first love. Therefore remember from where you have fallen, and repent and do the deeds you did at first; or else I am coming to you and will remove your lampstand out of its place—unless you repent.'"

↪ Revelation 2:4-5

The first love of Leah's life was Shane—a brawny, brown-faced, tempestuous Irish boy. Leah and Shane immediately fell in love the moment they gazed at each other across the park playground.

"What's yer name?" Shane asked Leah.

"Leah," she said, gazing shyly at him as she sat on a swing.

That meeting began their lovestruck friendship. And soon after, they decided to get married sometime in the future.

"I'll work on the highway crew, and you can stay home and take care of the family," Shane confidently told Leah.

"OK. I'll put cookies in your lunch every day," Leah said, giggling.

The young lovebirds were inseparable. All day they played games, climbed trees, rode bikes, dug for buried treasure, and captured bad guys.

They talked about everything and made important decisions together.

Shane and Leah were in love. (As much as six-year-olds can be.)

The first time you fall in love—no matter what your age—it's unforgettable! In the Bible, God speaks of having a "first love." But He isn't talking about small schooltime crushes.

God says our first love should be for Him—*and He means business.*

That's the message God was trying to get across to the church at Ephesus—that He deserves be loved above all things and all people. God should be more important in your life than your friends, activities, favorite things, and yes, even your family. God is to be your highest, most treasured, *forever* love.

Does your life reflect that God is your first love?

Discussion Starters:

1. Who was your first love? How did you feel? How did you act?

2. Is Jesus your first love now? Why or why not?

3. What choices do you make that cause your love for God to grow cold?

4. How can you keep your first love for Jesus Christ passionate and alive?

Lifeline:

Parents, when you first knew Christ, how was your faith "on fire" for Jesus? What did you do for Him? What have you done to maintain your love for Christ?

PASSING STORM

"'Do not fear what you are about to suffer. Behold, the devil is about to cast some of you into prison, so that you will be tested, and you will have tribulation for ten days. Be faithful until death, and I will give you the crown of life.'"

↩ Revelation 2:10

There's something romantic and delightfully scary about thunderstorm blackouts, especially when you're a kid. There's a certain giddy excitement about the darkness and the mad dash for candles and flashlights. But eventually the lights flicker and come back on, and the storm clouds roll away to reveal a vivid, rain-drenched world.

During World War II, thousands of British children sat in the flicker of candlelight in darkened London bunkers amidst the storm of war—but without giddy excitement. Air-raid sirens pierced the air, engines hummed, and booming explosions drew nearer each day. Parents and children alike huddled in fear, not knowing if the storm would pass them by or if the light of freedom and truth would be extinguished by Nazi Germany.

The storm of war was clouding their world.

You may not have experienced the terrors of war, but chances are you've weathered other storms—especially the trials of growing up.

I did. When I was in junior high, my best friend, Paul (the one who stole my eighth grade girlfriend), made the varsity junior high football team, while I had to be a bench warmer on the "B team."

Another painful moment occurred when I was a junior in high school. Sue, a girl in typing class whom I'd asked to the movies, decided during fourth period on Friday that she didn't want to go..."Just because."

Some storms will be huge, and others will be small. But they're an inevitable, unavoidable part of life. The Bible doesn't say, "If you suffer." Instead, Revelation predicts, "You *will* suffer"—maybe even more than unbelievers. God tells us that during stormy times, we must persevere, have faith, and be courageous. No storm will last forever, but our *faithful response* to difficulty will have eternal significance.

And that's God's promise.

Discussion Starters:

1. What "storms of life" are you experiencing right now?

2. How are you responding? How do tough times affect your relationship with God? Do you become angry or confused with Him? Explain.

3. How do God's promises bring comfort and understanding to our trials?

Lifeline:

Pray together for any family members who are going through storms.

"TORNADO HEAD"

" ' "He who has an ear, let him hear what the Spirit says to the churches. To him who overcomes, to him I will give some of the hidden manna, and I will give him a white stone, and a new name written on the stone which no one knows but he who receives it." ' "

⮌ Revelation 2:17

Do you have a nickname? Elizabeth, an old friend of mine, had a hodge-podge of them when she was little. Her family called her "B" for short. (We're still not sure why.) Todd, a neighborhood boy, affectionately called her "Lizard" because she once saved a baby lizard from her brother's fang-toothed cat. For the same reason, her uncle nicknamed her "Lizardo." Other pals called her "Monkey" for her prowess in tree climbing, and her camp buddies dubbed her "Pony" because she was so horse-crazy.

Still another nickname Elizabeth had was "Tornado Head," which came from her incessant habit of sucking her left thumb and twirling the hair on top of her head into...well, into a tornado. The nickname and the habit stuck all the way into the fourth grade. Without a doubt, of all the nicknames she had, "Tornado Head" was the one she most wanted to outgrow, and the older she got, the more she wanted to be just Elizabeth.

Names are important, especially to God. Throughout the Bible, God nicknamed His followers when they turned to Him. It was like a sign of a covenant He'd made with His children. Abram became Abraham, Sarai was called Sarah, and Saul was named Paul. When Jesus renamed Simon, He called him Peter, meaning "rock," because Peter had just professed that Christ was the divine Son of God. Christ said He'd build His church upon Peter's solid declaration.

This passage in Revelation tells us that God will give us new names when we go to heaven, to reflect our new life with the Lord. Chances are, His nickname for us will reveal a lot about our character. What do you want God to notice about you? Your kindness? Joy? Generosity? Faithfulness? Patience?

If Christ gave you a new name right now, what would it be?

Discussion Starters:

1. Why are names so significant? Why are they important to God?
2. What did a name change signify in the Bible?
3. Most parents pass along a family name or pore over name books to find the perfect name. What's the story behind your birth name?

Lifeline:

If you had to choose a new name to represent what God has done in your life and how you identify with Him, what would it be, and why?

THE SNOOZE BUTTON

"'"Wake up, and strengthen the things that remain, which were about to die; for I have not found your deeds completed in the sight of My God. So remember what you have received and heard; and keep it, and repent. Therefore if you do not wake up, I will come like a thief, and you will not know at what hour I will come to you."'"

↪ Revelation 3:2-3

Alarm clocks used to be so simple. They'd ring until you woke up, shut them off, and bounded out of bed. Alarms were simple but effective.

Then something happened. A mad scientist type, tinkering away in a laboratory somewhere, invented the "snooze button" and, in one swoop, changed the face of mornings and altered the wake-up ritual forever.

Some stalwart men and women still leaped out of bed at the first ring, ready to face the day. But thousands of sleepers rejected the old ways and embraced the new mechanism with delight. With the snooze button, they could retreat into the warmth of sleep for a few more minutes. All it took was a quick swipe of the hand to silence the clock's noisy protest and snooze until the last possible moment.

A few wise people sounded their warnings—in vain. "Mornings will be shattered," they said. "Precious time will be stolen forever."

But no one listened. They'd slept too long and were rushing around as fast as they could, scrambling to get to places on time.

The church at Sardis had been snoozing too long as well. The people had become spiritually sluggish, devoid of spiritual life and power.

"You snooze—you lose," God said (in effect) to the church. God's revelation to the people was supposed to be a wake-up call, reminding them to remember Him, to repent, and to change their ways.

God let the people of Sardis know they could be in for a rude awakening. "If you're not ready—if you're sleeping—I'll come back when you least expect Me," He warned.

Would He give the same urgent message to you?

Discussion Starters:

1. What does it mean to be spiritually awake? Spiritually asleep?
2. What kinds of "alarms" does God use to get our attention?
3. How do you "hit the snooze button" in your spiritual life? What has God been calling you to wake up and do?

Lifeline:

Are you sleepy, wide awake, or in between? List some practical ways your family can encourage one another to stay wide awake spiritually.

LOVING DISCIPLINE

""""Those whom I love, I reprove and discipline; therefore be zealous and repent."""

⬳ Revelation 3:19

Alison had a frightening temper. It was bad enough when she was a little girl, but once she crossed the hormone line of adolescence, she ruthlessly declared war on her entire family. And it didn't seem to matter that the other side had voted for peace.

Alison would throw some tremendously colorful tantrums, yelling and flinging books, pillows, and pans against the wall. Then she'd hurl her last comment into the air, stomp through the house, and pound her feet up the stairs to her bedroom. Furiously, she'd slam her bedroom door with such vengeance that the walls trembled.

Her dad had little patience with her tantrums. After a few gentle warnings, he took his creativity and hammer upstairs, knocked the hinge pins from her bedroom door, and carried the door to the basement for a rest from Alison's violent exertions. She quickly learned a lesson in self-control.

When my youngest son, Cooper, was about four, he threw a rock at his brother and connected perfectly with Brady's nose. Blood flew everywhere. They both ran to the house—Brady in tears, Cooper in fear.

"Cooper," I interrogated, "what happened?"

"I hit Bwady with a wock," he said, his lip quivering.

"Well, I'm going to have to punish you for that," I said.

His big, brown eyes filled with tears. "I can take it," Cooper said.

I had to turn around to hold back the laughter. It was tough to discipline him after hearing that comment, but I knew it was important.

Parents lovingly direct and shape their kids through encouragement and discipline, and God does the same thing with His children. He reproves us because He loves us! The Lord doesn't want us to be spoiled and selfish but mature in our faith, walking on the right path.

It isn't fun to be corrected—but the benefits we gain from receiving God's loving discipline will be everlasting.

Discussion Starters:

1. What's the purpose of discipline? What are the benefits? How does the Lord discipline us?

2. Does God's discipline range in severity? What are some examples from God's Word? From your own life?

Lifeline:

Is God disciplining you in an area of your life? Take some time to pray for the strength to submit to God's authority today.

VIRTUAL REALITY

"After these things I looked, and behold, a door standing open in heaven, and the first voice which I had heard, like the sound of a trumpet speaking with me, said, 'Come up here, and I will show you what must take place after these things.' Immediately I was in the Spirit; and behold, a throne was standing in heaven, and One sitting on the throne. And He who was sitting was like a jasper stone and a sardius in appearance; and there was a rainbow around the throne, like an emerald in appearance."

⟿ Revelation 4:1-3

As human beings, we have an unquenchable spirit of adventure and exploration inside us. We're always longing to turn a corner and unexpectedly tumble into another world through a black hole in outer space, the doorway of a wardrobe, or a rabbit hole.

Virtual reality creates technological rabbit holes that will allow you to tumble into three-dimensional computer worlds. Have you always wanted to explore outer space, discover new worlds, and battle alien enemies? With a pair of goggles and some pocket change, you'll be able to do all that and more. Virtual reality leads you to feel as if you're living inside a vision. Only once the time has run out and the goggles are off, the real world is always waiting outside.

The apostle John's adventure into his own "virtual reality" was incredibly different. He saw a real doorway in his dreams, and, through that opening, he saw unbelievable new worlds. It was the adventure of a lifetime and beyond, and it was real—real for life today and for the distant tomorrow. Nineteen hundred years have passed since John received his heavenly vision, but it's still as relevant now as it was then. The future times John saw seem a lot like the times in which we live today. His words of warning should speak soberly to our morally corrupt generation, which continuously turns its back on God.

But for those of us who strive to follow Him, God's words of hope and encouragement have never been as needed and welcome as they are today.

Discussion Starters:

1. What does today's glimpse through John's doorway of revelation tell us about God? About heaven?

2. What do you think eternal life is going to be like?

3. How does knowing you'll spend eternity with God in heaven affect the way you live now? Why?

Lifeline:

Many people want to ignore the realities of heaven and hell. How can you live in the present yet still be aware that your eternal life in heaven is of utmost significance?

LOVE, DAD

"And they sang a new song, saying, 'Worthy are You to take the book and to break its seals; for You were slain, and purchased for God with Your blood men from every tribe and tongue and people and nation. You have made them to be a kingdom and priests to our God; and they will reign upon the earth.'"

↪ Revelation 5:9-10

Sophie was terribly inept at handling her money. All through high school and college, her dad bailed her out of financial trouble or extended an extra "line of credit" if she was short for the month. Once, while she was in college, Sophie bounced so many checks that the return check fees were quadruple the face value of the checks.

Things got better after she closed her checking account, but then Sophie got herself into a couple thousand dollars of credit card debt. Once again, when Sophie's dad found out, he gave his daughter money.

Even when she got older and wanted to invest in a piece of furniture and had only half the amount, a check from Dad would show up in the mail. Sometimes Sophie paid him back, but more often than not, when her birthday, Christmas, or another convenient holiday rolled around, she would find the remainder of her debt listed inside a card with a small note that said, "Debt forgiven. Love, Dad."

Sophie's dad was generous to a fault. He should have made his daughter own up to her debts. Good parents know that if they don't make their kids "face the music" once in a while, their children will become emotionally insecure and morally crippled. But good parents will also find ways to help their kids just when they need it the most.

That's how our heavenly Father treats us. He sent His Son, Jesus, to pay our sin-debt with His blood. It doesn't matter how many mistakes we make or how bad they are—if we ask God for forgiveness, He will erase our sin-debts, once and for all.

Discussion Starters:

1. What does today's scripture mean by saying that Jesus "purchased" us by His blood?

2. What does it mean to have a sin-debt?

3. How does God make us face up to our mistakes while, at the same time, forgiving us?

Lifeline:

How can your family encourage each other to forgive from the heart, no matter how large the other person's debt is? At the same time, how can you help one another own up to mistakes?

HE'S GOT PLANS FOR YOU

"When the Lamb broke the fifth seal, I saw underneath the altar the souls of those who had been slain because of the word of God, and because of the testimony which they had maintained; and they cried out with a loud voice, saying, 'How long, O Lord, holy and true, will You refrain from judging and avenging our blood on those who dwell on the earth?' ...And they were told that they should rest for a little while longer, until the number of their fellow servants and their brethren who were to be killed even as they had been, would be completed also."

↪ Revelation 6:9-11

In *The Scarlet Pimpernel*, an adventure story set in the late 1700s, an English nobleman and his friends work during the French Revolution to save the lives of French noblemen and their families who have been sentenced to death. Using disguises and clever schemes, the Pimpernel and his band smuggle the innocent out of Paris and on to safety in England.

At one point in the story, it looks as though the Pimpernel is going to be captured by French soldiers. Posing as an old woman driving a farm wagon (in which a family he's helping is hiding), he passes through a Paris gate. All seems well. But a few minutes later, a troop of French cavalry rides through that same gate in hot pursuit.

A spirited chase follows. Soon the Frenchmen overtake the Pimpernel, forcing his wagon to a halt. It seems his luck is finally gone.

It turns out, however, that these soldiers are actually part of the Pimpernel's band! Once again, the Pimpernel was in control of the situation the whole time, even when all appearances seemed to the contrary.

In today's scripture, Christian martyrs impatiently ask God why He hasn't yet avenged their terrible deaths. His answer, while it's a little hard for us to understand, indicates that appearances to the contrary, He is very much in control of the situation. Even when His people are dying, it's all somehow a part of His sovereign plan. And in the end, things will work out exactly as He intended.

Because we know He loves us, and that ultimately He is always in control, we can find comfort and hope even in the worst of times.

Discussion Starters:

1. Why do we so often struggle to trust God's plan in our lives?

2. Practically speaking, how can we learn to place all our hope in Christ?

Lifeline:

Often we can see God's hand in circumstances only after the difficulty has already passed. Have each family member describe a time in which he or she saw how God worked through a trial *after* the event was over.

THE FOUNTAIN OF YOUTH

"'They will hunger no longer, nor thirst anymore; nor will the sun beat down on them, nor any heat; for the Lamb in the center of the throne will be their shepherd, and will guide them to springs of the water of life; and God will wipe every tear from their eyes.'"

↪ Revelation 7:16-17

The earth was still deeply shrouded in mystery. In the eyes of the masses, most still thought the world was flat, its vast oceans running off the edges. It was a time of great thought, reform, adventure—and superstition.

Around the beginning of the sixteenth century, the famous Spanish explorer Juan Ponce de León embarked on the high seas once again to search for the island of Bimini. The Spanish crown had a lot of faith in him; he had a remarkable track record for discoveries. In 1493, he had accompanied Christopher Columbus on his second voyage to America. Then in 1508, he discovered and settled in Puerto Rico.

Twenty years after he traveled with Columbus to the New World, Ponce de León sailed westward again, seeking to add rich new lands to Spain. But supposedly by royal decree, he was commanded to expend a great portion of his energy toward discovering the island of Bimini, home of the legendary fountain of youth.

The story had it that the fountain's waters would restore an old person's vitality and strength forever. To the Spanish crown and Ponce de León, one sip was worth any risk. It was the quest for eternal youth.

As Christians, we've got something even better than a fountain of youth. When we get to heaven, Jesus will give us a fountain of eternal life. There, we'll experience true, complete joy and everlasting life as we celebrate an eternal union with our heavenly Father.

People are constantly trying to extend their lives—through diets, exercise, vitamins, and medicine. There's nothing wrong with trying to live longer, healthier lives, but we should be concentrating on things that last—namely, our relationship with God, which will *really* lead us to the waters of life.

Discussion Starters:

1. What are the "springs of the water of life" to which the Bible refers?

2. What are some modern day quests to find a "fountain of youth"?

3. Today's passage in Revelation offers a glimpse through heaven's gates. What else do you think heaven will be like?

Lifeline:

Focus on your relationship with God. It's the only thing that'll last.

WOE, WOE, WOE!

"Then I looked, and I heard an eagle flying in midheaven, saying with a loud voice, 'Woe, woe, woe to those who dwell on the earth, because of the remaining blasts of the trumpet of the three angels who are about to sound!'"

⮑ Revelation 8:13

For weeks Mindy, a 16-year-old Missouri teen, had dreamed of getting a phone call from Jake, the handsome running back on the high school football team. On Saturday morning, the phone rang.

"Want to go out tonight, Mindy?" Jake asked, his deep voice booming.

Mindy's heart pounded. She knew Jake's reputation with girls was shaky at best, but how could she pass up this opportunity? "Yeah! I'd love to," Mindy told him, ignoring the warning signal that went off in her head.

Jake picked her up and told Mindy they were going to a movie. But when they arrived at the theater, he said he didn't like any of the shows that were playing. "We'll go to the lake instead. Okay?" Jake told Mindy.

Another warning sounded in Mindy's head, but she said, "Uh, sure."

"Lots of my friends will be there having bonfires," Jake assured her.

But when they arrived at the lake, it was dark and desolate. Mindy's eyes grew large with worry, but Jake said they'd only sit and talk.

Again, the alarm sounded—louder this time—but she agreed to stay.

Jake leaned over Mindy, and she shrank back. "Relax. It's just a kiss," he said. Another alarm rang in her head, but she kissed him back. Soon things heated up, and the kiss went much further than Mindy had intended.

Two months later, Mindy took a pregnancy test and realized her biggest fear had come true: She was carrying Jake's baby.

God fills our minds and His Word with warnings designed to lead us in the right direction. Mindy ignored God's warning voice and ended up pregnant. The book of Revelation depicts what will *ultimately* happen to those who don't heed God's warnings to turn back to Him. Some day, wayward people will undergo God's final, terrible judgment as described in Revelation 8. When it happens, they will wish they'd listened to God.

Pay attention to God's alarms. Don't let disaster creep up on you!

Discussion Starters:

1. What warning signs have caused you to stop and think about something you were doing wrong?

2. How does your commitment to Christ remove the fear from today's passage?

Lifeline:

Warnings given in the home help all of us avoid trumpets of disaster.

WHODUNIT?

"But in the days of the voice of the seventh angel, when he is about to sound, then the mystery of God is finished, as He preached to His servants the prophets."

↪ Revelation 10:7

Perry Mason always knew the answer. Of course, you had to wait through the entire episode for the suspense-filled courtroom conclusion before you finally knew "whodunit." Perry Mason always had his mental machinery going full steam, and it was his calm logic that solved the mystery and made the criminals confess.

Among the ancient Greeks, mysteries were religious rites and ceremonies practiced by secret societies. Those who wanted to be a member of the societies (and who were selected) could be initiated and then would possess this special and coveted knowledge.

The mysteries of the Bible, however, can't be figured out on your own. And they can't be disclosed by other people. Only the Holy Spirit can reveal the secret things of God and enable us to understand some of the mysteries of His Word.

No matter how much we know, there'll always be things we won't be able to comprehend about God. Some issues just can't be resolved by human beings. So we can only do our best to explain the unexplainable—like, how the Trinity works or how Jesus can be both God and man. We can try to debate our nonbelieving friends over why a good, powerful God would allow evil in the world. But until the Lord reveals mysteries like these, we'll never know for sure if we've got it right.

The book of Revelation speaks of a time when all things will be made known. But until then, we've got to wait for the Holy Spirit to unveil the truth—and we must take the rest of it (what we don't understand) on faith.

Discussion Starters:

1. Why can't we understand God's Word just by applying our own mental abilities or logically reasoning our way to an answer? What's the difference between having understanding and receiving revelation?

2. What are some good ways to tackle the difficulties and questions you have about God's Word?

3. What was one "unknown" the Holy Spirit revealed to His believers in the first-century church? (Hint: Look in the book of Acts.)

Lifeline:

Unless the Holy Spirit is working in an unbeliever's heart, most of the mysteries of the Bible won't seem logical or likely to him or her. If you have a pre-Christian friend, pray that God would make Himself known in your friend's heart, just as He reveals truth about Himself to you.

ANYTHING BUT BORING

"'And I will grant authority to my two witnesses, and they will prophesy for twelve hundred and sixty days, clothed in sackcloth.' These are the two olive trees and the two lampstands that stand before the Lord of the earth."

↩ Revelation 11:3-4

Robyn was no stranger to the church. As an infant, she had been consecrated at the marble baptismal of her family's church. As a child, she had sung the "Great Big Purple People Eater" song in Sunday school, gone on dozens of retreats at Camp Whatchamacallit, and daydreamed through a thousand sermons.

Then when she was 12, Robyn had to memorize the shorter catechism. It was the rite of passage into the ranks of church membership. Trembling and fearful, she recited them before the elders of the church.

She passed and became an official church member, but that wasn't important to her. To Robyn, everything about God was boring.

Her attitude soon changed. One night, Robyn's next-door neighbors invited her to their church down the street for a youth encounter weekend. Wanting to meet other kids her age, she went. She sat in the dark that night, electrified by the speaker and his message.

Filled with the Holy Spirit like the two witnesses in today's scripture, this speaker let life and laughter tumble out of him like a river. For the first time, Robyn saw someone who wasn't just talking about Jesus. The speaker was obviously someone who *knew* Jesus and lived by His power. Finally, she'd heard and met the gospel message—and it was anything but boring.

If you believe in Jesus, you *can* be a witness for Him. Once you accept Him into your heart, His Spirit lives in you. The Holy Spirit will give you the words to say and the courage to stand up for God.

Let your words and life reveal His power and vitality in you!

Discussion Starters:

1. Who made a significant impact on your decision to follow Jesus Christ? Why was this person such a strong influence in your life?

2. Why is it so important to present the gospel to others?

3. What keeps you from witnessing for Jesus? How can you be a more effective witness?

Lifeline:

Have everyone in the family take turns presenting his or her testimony. Pretend this is the last opportunity to tell others about Jesus!

THE UNDERDOG

"'And the nations were enraged, and Your wrath came, and the time came for the dead to be judged, and the time to reward to Your bond-servants the prophets and the saints and those who fear Your name, the small and the great, and to destroy those who destroy the earth.'"

↩ Revelation 11:18

People in our day love the underdog. We cheer ourselves hoarse when a small, scrappy hometown team unexpectedly beats the strutting big-town players to win its way to the top of the heap. We roar with excitement when a bag-of-bones workhorse can outrun the finest racehorses in the world. We admire grit and verve and a stick-to-it heart. We have a passion for fairy tales come true—for Cinderella stories, which tell about those who go from rags to riches. It does us a world of good to see the humble and pure of heart win the day. We're *glad* David walloped Goliath. Our souls sing inside when we see great self-sacrifice, integrity, honesty, and justice.

Hurrah! The underdog overcame!

But did you ever think about the fact that Christians are the underdogs of this world?

We are. Both Jesus' words and the book of Revelation reveal that during the end times, we'll be treated as the lowest of the low. Christians will be persecuted, mocked, put through unbelievable trials, and even martyred because we claim Christ's name. But, as today's passage of scripture states, Christians will ultimately win. Nothing in all of creation will separate us from God's love (Roman 8:38-39). Eventually, God will judge everyone, and if we've accepted Him as our Savior, we'll be victorious.

It'll be an authentic rags-to-eternal-riches story.

Discussion Starters:

1. How can you hold on to the truth that one day all the injustices Christians face in this devil-dominated world will be reversed, and we'll reign victorious?

2. What do you think that day of judgment will be like? Which passages in Revelation add to your understanding?

3. A pebble hurled in faith can topple a giant any day. How can you fight back against society's worldly, anti-Christian "giant"?

Lifeline:

Which other people do you know who are despised and rejected by the world? How can your family better love those underdogs?

GRIT YOUR MENTAL TEETH

"'And they overcame [the accuser] because of the blood of the Lamb and because of the word of their testimony, and they did not love their life even when faced with death.'"

↩ Revelation 12:11

The Kansas state motto proudly proclaims, *Ad astra per aspera*—"To the stars through hardship." It's a noble thought, but most people don't buy it. Sadly, most of us live by the world's motto, "Whoever has the most toys wins." If you have money and power, you've "made it." You've won.

Often it seems that those who have "made it"—the rich, popular, successful types—reach the stars just fine, without hardship. But a lot of times, those "successful" people are reaching for stars that will fade, not ones that will last forever.

Don't get discouraged if you feel as though you'll never succeed in the world's eyes. Your difficulties can actually be assets to your spiritual life. An old Spanish proverb says, "From a fallen tree, all make kindling." Hardship won't bring you any worldly good, but it can build character, strengthen family ties, and mature your faith.

Difficulty often brings spiritual gain.

But to find spiritual success, you must grit your teeth in the face of adversity and see obstacles as challenges, failures as opportunities. Sports psychologists call it mental toughness; God calls it faith.

The saints from Revelation had so much faith that they *lived* for eternal triumph. They didn't win in the world's eyes, but their spirits prevailed over "the accuser." These saints reached for the right stars—seeking to tell others about Jesus and please God in everything—and were willing to give up anything, even their lives, to gain heavenly victory.

It's not easy to place finding victory in God's eyes above winning on this earth. You need to have a long-term perspective, a ton of perseverance, and unshakable faith in God's promise of eternal glory.

Are you obsessed with obtaining what the world defines to be success? Which crown do you want? An earthly, flimsy Burger King crown or a solid, priceless one that lasts forever?

Discussion Starters:

1. How can you focus solely on having eternal victory in Christ?

2. What does it take to be successful and popular in your school, workplace, or home? Do you place more importance on earthly "wins" or heavenly victories? Explain your answers.

Lifeline:

How can your family learn to keep a sense of humor when facing "failure"?

THE FINAL SHOWDOWN

"And when the dragon saw that he was thrown down to the earth, he persecuted the woman who gave birth to the male child. But the two wings of the great eagle were given to the woman, so that she could fly into the wilderness to her place, where she was nourished for a time and times and half a time, from the presence of the serpent."

↪ Revelation 12:13-14

Okay, let's face it. A great deal of John's end-times prophecy in Revelation is difficult to understand. Theologians still debate the meanings of all the word pictures John uses to describe the coming events.

One thing is clear, though: As Daniel prophesied almost 600 years before the time of Christ, there *will* be a Great Tribulation. Then the slang expression "all hell will break loose" will be a reality, and Satan's final battle will be fought on this earth (see Daniel 11). The battle will be fought in the Middle East; all of the world's armies will engage; Satan will use the armies to try to destroy Israel; and God will prevail and defeat them all (see Revelation 20:7-10).

Many sound biblical scholars agree that the prophetic signs pointing to Jesus' second coming suggest that Christ could return any day. What does that mean for you? Are you counting on "having fun" now and then shaping up your spiritual life later? Do you blow off the fact that your day-to-day choices matter?

Those prophecies should cause you to think about your life and the decisions you make, but the end times shouldn't scare you. If you're living for Christ, it won't ultimately matter if He comes back tomorrow or 100 years from now. As the apostle Paul wrote, "For to me, to live is Christ and to die is gain" (Philippians 1:21).

No matter what, you'll be a winner in the end.

Discussion Starters:

1. What confuses you most about the end times? (Parents, try to help answer your kids' questions.)
2. Why is it important to study the end times? What benefits can Christians glean from learning about the end times?
3. What did Paul mean when he said, "To live is Christ and to die is gain"? How should that encourage you as you face the thought of tribulation?

Lifeline:

Ask God to show your family how to live each day as if His return will be tomorrow.

COUNTERFEITS

"I saw one of his heads as if it had been slain, and his fatal wound was healed. And the whole earth was amazed and followed after the beast; they worshiped the dragon because he gave his authority to the beast; and they worshiped the beast, saying, 'Who is like the beast, and who is able to wage war with him?'"

↪ Revelation 13:3-4

According to the book of Revelation, the antichrist (the beast) will be high profile—but tough to spot. At first, most people won't be able to tell he's a fake.

Satan will give this man tremendous power and will enthrone him as a temporary world dictator prior to the second coming of Jesus Christ. The antichrist will be very winsome, and initially the world will love him. USA *Today, Time, Newsweek,* and CNN will rave about his political genius.

His heart will be cold, though. He'll support abortion, euthanasia, pornography, homosexual conduct, and everything else that God is against. The beast will blaspheme God's name and persecute Christians.

But because he'll look so appealing on the surface, many people—including Christians—won't recognize that the antichrist is a counterfeit. Only those who intimately know Jesus Christ, who worship Him as Lord and desire to put Jesus above everything else, will see the truth and refuse to worship the beast.

How can we ensure that we'll recognize a fake leader when we see one? The same way bankers and FBI agents spot counterfeit money: They study the real thing, spending hours carefully inspecting authentic cash so they can spot a fraudulent copy in a second.

Spend time getting to know Jesus. Talk to Him, read about Him, study His ways, and ask questions of others who know Him intimately. That way, if the antichrist rises to power in your lifetime, you'll be able to detect this phony leader at a glance.

Discussion Starters:

1. What's the difference between knowing about Jesus and truly knowing Him? Do you know Him well? Explain.

2. Why are counterfeits so hard to spot? Why can't you spot them just by intuition?

Lifeline:

Adolf Hitler was a great counterfeit. At one point, both the United States and Great Britain supported him, and in his own free elections, he received 98.8 percent of the German vote. Take time to learn the scriptural qualities of a genuine Christian so you won't be fooled by a false one.

BOOKMARKED

"And he causes all, the small and the great, and the rich and the poor, and the free men and the slaves, to be given a mark on their right hand or on their forehead, and he provides that no one will be able to buy or to sell, except the one who has the mark, either the name of the beast or the number of his name."

↶ Revelation 13:16-17

Libraries have forged into the computer age, leaving behind a trail of index cards. The old card catalog indexes have been dumped for the neon glow of computer monitors that reference and cross-reference an array of newspapers, journals, films, music, microfiche, and books. The system then reveals important pieces of information about each item.

Library cards have followed suit. One swipe of the card's magnetic strip and the account appears on screen with a list of current information: which books the cardholder checked out, how many are overdue, how much the fine costs, and that person's personal history.

But not only libraries have become computerized. Almost all the merchandise we buy is marked with a bar code and scanned in a flash at the checkout counter. Entire inventories of nationwide chains like Wal-Mart are available to the company president via computer.

This computerized system has gotten so sophisticated that for tax and merchandising purposes, the government holds information on individuals and their bank accounts, too. These officials get the scoop on our lives through our social security numbers, bank card numbers, and personal identification numbers (PINs).

In the last 20 years, a significant marketing, banking, governing, and control system has been put into place. Now, I don't mean to be sensational, but I think this system will enable the future antichrist to control all purchases and limit sales to those who bear his laser-tattooed mark on their hand or forehead. It's a terrifying thought, but don't be too concerned—the Bible already predicted this would happen.

As this system unfolds, keep reminding yourself that you belong to God. He'll be with you in all the days that lie ahead.

Discussion Starters:

1. What does a mark signify?
2. What are some spiritual marks of being a Christian? What physical symbols do Christians mark themselves with to represent their beliefs?
3. If we were physically marked when we accepted Jesus, would it affect the way we acted or how we represented Him? Why or why not?

Lifeline:

Pray that you'll be so close to Jesus Christ that others will know you're a Christian—even without being physically marked.

THE GOLDEN DOOR

"Here is the perseverance of the saints who keep the commandments of God and their faith in Jesus. And I heard a voice from heaven, saying, 'Write, "Blessed are the dead who die in the Lord from now on!" 'Yes,' says the Spirit, 'so that they may rest from their labors, for their deeds follow with them.'"

↩ Revelation 14:12-13

She was born in 1886. In portraits she stands alone, crowned and regal, with lamp in hand. Her father was Frédéric-Auguste Bartholdi, a Frenchman. But her birthplace was America, and in some American hearts, she still reigns. She is called the Mother of Exiles—the Statue of Liberty.

At her dedication, a sonnet by Emma Lazarus was inscribed on a plaque, which reads in part:

> "Keep, ancient lands, your storied pomp!" cried she
> With silent lips. "Give me your tired, your poor,
> Your huddled masses yearning to breathe free,
> The wretched refuse of your teeming shore.
> Send these, the homeless, tempest-tossed to me,
> I lift my lamp beside the golden door."

She holds her beacon 151 feet aloft to welcome refugees to the land of the free and the home of brave. She welcomes them home.

Life can be wearisome, and growing up can be one of the most tiring aspects of life. It's hard work to be a Christian in a sometimes ugly, non-believing world. But when you feel like giving up, remember: This world is not where you belong.

One day, those of us who have yearned and dreamed and waited all our lives to reach the shores of God's kingdom will find our way to the golden door. The Prince of the Exiles, with lamp in hand, will welcome us home. As the book of Revelation states, we will "rest from our labors" because in Jesus Christ, we'll finally find peace, hope, and joy in our *true* home—heaven.

Discussion Starters:

1. What does it mean to be an exile?
2. Why do you think so many tens of thousands of families immigrated to the United States in the nineteenth century?
3. The Bible frequently says that a Christian's true home is heaven. What does that mean?
4. Why does Revelation say we will "rest from our labors"?

Lifeline:

Do you feel more "at home" living on earth than you should?

WORSHIP HIM

"And they sang..., 'Great and marvelous are Your works, O Lord God, the Almighty; righteous and true are Your ways, King of the nations! Who will not fear, O Lord, and glorify Your name? For You alone are holy; for all the nations will come and worship before You, for Your righteous acts have been revealed.'"

↩ Revelation 15:3-4

I know it's hard to believe, but thousands of people think Elvis Presley is still alive. Some folks say they spotted him in New York City at Balducci's Grocery in Greenwich Village. Others claim that Elvis frequents the Piggly Wiggly in Manhattan, Kansas. It seems as if every week, the tabloids run a new article on yet another Elvis sighting.

Well, I say that if Elvis is alive (which is a mighty long shot), he's living "high on the hog" on profits from Graceland, his previous home and grave site. If you haven't been there, it's worth the trip to Memphis, Tennessee. At the time I'm writing this, tours leave every five minutes from 8:30 A.M. to 5:00 P.M. There are four tours available: $8.00 for Graceland mansion, $4.50 for the Elvis Car Museum, $4.25 to see his private airplanes, and $2.25 for Sincerely Elvis, a small museum that stores his personal items. You can also get a package deal to see all four museums for $16.00. Graceland does great business because there are a bazillion Elvis worshipers still around.

But Elvis isn't the only person who gets false glory. Many movie stars, musicians, supermodels, and multi-millionaires bask in the riches, praise, and worship they get from countless numbers of people worldwide.

The glory these stars receive is fleeting, though—nothing compared to the worship Jesus will get when His people gather together to praise Him. That heavenly scene will be indescribable. Imagine seeing God in all His awesome power, holiness, and love. No teen idol or rock star will ever bring you the lasting joy and victory that come with praising God.

Who gets more of your attention? The stars who gaze from posters on your wall or the living God?

Discussion Starters:

1. Why do people worship famous stars? What's the pitfall in worshiping the created rather than the Creator?

2. What is worship? Why is it necessary to your faith?

3. What are some of your favorite ways to worship God? Why?

Lifeline:

Plan a family worship service one Sunday. Include everyone's favorite ways to worship, whether it's through song, silence, or Scripture reading.

THAT WILL BE $109, PLEASE

"And I heard the angel of the waters saying, 'Righteous are You, who are and who were, O Holy One, because You judged these things; for they poured out the blood of saints and prophets, and You have given them blood to drink. They deserve it.' And I heard the altar saying, 'Yes, O Lord God, the Almighty, true and righteous are Your judgments.'"

↩ Revelation 16:5-7

Jessica sat in the Sumner County courthouse, her hands clasped firmly together to keep them from trembling. There was no backing out this time. She'd already pushed back her court date once to accommodate her travel schedule to and from college. Jessica was just hoping the judge would reduce the amount on her speeding ticket and waive the mark against her license. After all, it was her first speeding ticket. Hopefully she'd only have to pay a small fine and watch one of the "gore" films on reckless driving.

The judge called her up to the bench. He peered through his glasses at her, raised his white, bushy eyebrows, and sharply queried, "Guilty or not guilty?"

Jessica meekly croaked out, "Guilty."

The bailiff escorted her out of the courtroom, and Jessica found herself handing $109 to the cashier. She drove the speed limit on her way home.

Because of our sin, we were destined to appear in a type of "divine courtroom." With weak knees and raspy voices, we came to God, begging His forgiveness. But unlike in a courtroom scene, we never had to worry whether God would forgive our sins. He wiped our record clean as soon as we humbly believed in Jesus.

God makes His truly amazing grace readily available to anyone who asks forgiveness for his or her sins. Sadly, though, not everyone accepts His offer. Today's passage in Revelation depicts those who not only rejected God's grace, but who also persecuted His prophets and saints. As this scripture shows, God's grace is abundant—but to those who repeatedly reject it, His final judgment will be severe.

Discussion Starters:

1. Why does God graciously choose to forgive us?
2. Why is His punishment so severe in Revelation?
3. When have you experienced God's saving grace? Did you feel you deserved to be forgiven? Why or why not?

Lifeline:

Discuss together the meaning of grace. Talk about the difference between God's forgiveness and people's forgiveness. Remember—God forgives and *forgets*. If you accept His grace, you're clean in His sight.

HE WILL OVERCOME

" 'These will wage war against the Lamb, and the Lamb will overcome them, because He is Lord of lords and King of kings, and those who are with Him are the called and chosen and faithful.' "

~ Revelation 17:14

It was 1836, and about 180 dirty, tired soldiers were stationed in the Alamo, a mission near San Antonio, Texas. The odds seemed hopeless. The men faced a Mexican army of thousands. The only things these Texans possessed were courage and determination.

Knowing the inevitable slaughter that lay ahead, Texas commander William B. Travis drew his sword and slashed a deep line in the southwest Texas sand. Each fighter who crossed the line knew he'd die if he stayed to fight. All but one made the gallant move.

The Texans believed that even death was not too high a price to pay for their sons', grandsons', and families' futures. And it wasn't. Though the Alamo fell, Texas later gained her freedom in the Battle of San Jacinto. In part, because the freedom fighters possessed such courage, the people of Texas eventually enjoyed freedom and ensuing membership in the United States of America.

Do *you* know how to fight?

Now, more than a century later, the well-entrenched army of pornography, violence, drugs and alcohol, rape, and lewd movies and TV programs surrounds Christians as we fight to be free from Satan's ever-tightening grip on earth. If we're following Christ, we will step across the line and fight for God.

But the cost will be high.

Friends will laugh, girlfriends will turn their backs, and Saturday nights will be lonely as you battle for Christ. But hold on to this: Jesus will come back and redeem you. He'll reward your faithfulness to Him.

Today, Christians are sacrificing, suffering, and even dying for their faith. But Revelation states that some day—maybe soon—"the Lamb" will overcome Satan and his army, and the world's forces of darkness will be crushed.

Will you be strong and faithful enough to fight on God's side until He claims the victory?

Discussion Starters:

1. Why must we as Christians be prepared to fight for our faith?

2. How can we get ready for spiritual battle?

3. How will you step across the line for God this week? Be specific.

Lifeline:

Though we live in the Alamo, we'll see the victory of San Jacinto!

CARRIER OF TRUTH

"'And the kings of the earth, who committed acts of immorality and lived sensuously with her, will weep and lament over her when they see the smoke of her burning, standing at a distance because of the fear of her torment, saying, "Woe, woe, the great city, Babylon, the strong city! For in one hour your judgment has come."'"

↪ Revelation 18:9-10

During World War II, Adelaide wrote frequent letters to her husband, Arthur, who was serving overseas in the army. Both enlisted men and officers moved around frequently, which made the overseas mail service erratic at best. It was a frustrating problem, and Adelaide could never be sure when her letters would actually arrive. Some of them were delivered within a couple of weeks, some were received months after they'd been posted, and some even came back home. So she numbered each letter in sequence so that Arthur would have some idea of what was happening and in what order.

One afternoon, a letter addressed to her husband was returned. When Adelaide opened the letter, she gasped. With trembling hands, she read, *Dearest Arthur, I miss you so much and constantly think of the wonderful times we spent together. Please write me soon. Love, Frances.*

This letter was numbered, just like Adelaide's, apparently written by Arthur's secret mistress. A horrible truth was resting in her hands, accidentally delivered to her by the U.S. Postal Service. Adelaide got a fresh envelope and slip of paper; wrote Arthur a quick, questioning note; and slipped Frances's letter in with hers.

Deception and immorality will always catch up with you, Arthur, Adelaide thought sadly.

The kings portrayed in today's passage of Revelation find out much the same truth. They've been shamelessly living in sin, and, because they haven't admitted and dealt with their acts of immorality, the consequences all quickly catch up with them. They weep, lament, and mourn over their beloved sinful city, Babylon. Their revelry is quickly over.

As you make choices each day, remember that nothing you do is neutral. Everything matters. Make it a habit to prize purity and integrity.

Discussion Starters:

1. What are some of the consequences of sin?

2. What tempts you to compromise your integrity?

3. How can you avoid getting caught in the trap of immorality?

Lifeline:

How can your family make honesty and integrity a priority in its relationships?

BLACK THURSDAY

" 'The fruit you long for has gone from you, and all things that were luxurious and splendid have passed away from you and men will no longer find them. The merchants of these things, who became rich from her, will stand at a distance because of the fear of her torment, weeping and mourning, saying, "Woe, woe, the great city, she who was clothed in fine linen and purple and scarlet, and adorned with gold and precious stones and pearls; for in one hour such great wealth has been laid waste!" ' "

⟿ Revelation 18:14-17

In 1918, the United States emerged from World War I virtually untouched. Not only that, but most of western Europe was deeply in debt to her. As industry flourished and the 1920s roared in, a feverish attitude of prosperity and affluence swept the country. From mob bosses to shoe shine boys, big spenders to conservative investors, people were speculating wildly in the stock market, looking to cash in on the boom. By late summer of 1929, millionaires were being made overnight as stock prices rose to unprecedented heights. But reality eventually hit the New York Stock Exchange.

On Thursday, October 24, 1929, an unprecedented 16 million shares traded hands, sending the stock market into an unstoppable decline. Wealthy financiers moved quickly to obtain large blocks of shares—hoping to abate the crisis. But the market crashed the following Tuesday, and when the dust had settled, $15 billion worth of stock value had vaporized. Vast fortunes and small savings alike were wiped out.

Thousands of people in the 1920s invested their money poorly. The Bible says millions more in the end times will foolishly invest their souls. They'll buy into the ungodliness of the world. At first, these misguided people will find wealth and power in their sinful investments. But as the book of Revelation says, in one hour their glory will lie in ruins.

Think before you buy into the temporary things the world has to offer. Instead, invest your time, money, and soul in God. He'll multiply your investments and give you something far more important than wealth—eternal life.

Discussion Starters:

1. Why is your investment in Jesus in some ways a no-risk investment in the end? Why is it also costly to build a relationship with Him?

2. What spiritual investments are you making in your life?

Lifeline:

Read Matthew 16:24. What's the cost of discipleship? Be specific.

THE BRIDE

"'Let us rejoice and be glad and give the glory to Him, for the marriage of the Lamb has come and His bride has made herself ready.' It was given to her to clothe herself in fine linen, bright and clean; for the fine linen is the righteous acts of the saints. Then he said to me, 'Write, "Blessed are those who are invited to the marriage supper of the Lamb."' And he said to me, 'These are true words of God.'"

⮑ Revelation 19:7-9

It happened. I can't believe it—but it finally happened! My "little" girl Jamie (who is now 5'6" and 22 years old) just made the most graceful walk of her life down the wedding aisle, into the arms of the only boy she ever loved. It was a dream come true. The beauty, excitement, and splendor that surrounded that awesome walk were indescribable.

Walking the road of purity wasn't always easy for Jamie, though.

One summer when she was in junior high, she and I and her little sister, Courtney, were driving to town. I was happily reminiscing about the wonderful summer we had shared and all the fun stuff we had done.

Or so I thought.

Jamie just stared out the window. After a few tense moments, she said, "My friends can see any movie they want, and I can't. They can go to all the parties, and I can't. You're mean. You don't let me do anything."

I pondered this, then said, "Jamie, my first job isn't to be your friend, but to be your dad. If you don't like me for the next few years, that's okay. Some day when you get married, I want you to be able to walk down the aisle as a pure young woman. Then I hope you'll say you love your dad."

Jamie's dislike for me didn't last long. Soon after eighth grade, she realized she was making valuable sacrifices. On her wedding day, she had no regrets. Now, her honeymoon with her husband will last a lifetime.

Her story is wonderful, but it's a mere shadow of the real wedding walk that God's children will take when we see Christ face to face. You are Christ's bride. Make every effort to pursue purity and righteousness.

The sacrifice will be well worth it.

Discussion Starters:

1. What do you think it will be like to meet Christ face to face?

2. Why does Jesus call us, His believers, His bride?

3. What sacrifices are you making in your life right now to live for Him?

Lifeline:

Look around your house. Is there anything that's getting in the way of your family's pursuit of righteousness for the wedding day? If so, toss it.

INDEPENDENCE DAY

"He is clothed with a robe dipped in blood, and His name is called The Word of God. And the armies which are in heaven, clothed in fine linen, white and clean, were following Him on white horses. From His mouth comes a sharp sword, so that with it He may strike down the nations, and He will rule them with a rod of iron; and He treads the wine press of the fierce wrath of God, the Almighty."

↪ Revelation 19:13-15

Commonwealth Stadium was just over the hill a mile or so, and from his rooftop, Billy had a great view of the July fourth fireworks. Each explosion skyrocketed heavenward, then burst and cascaded in a waterfall of colors. Billy felt a rush of memories swell within him—parents sitting on the front stoop on warm summer nights, neighborhood kids running through the dark with sparklers in hand, potlucks in the park...

Billy knew that thousands of people in the last two centuries had celebrated every Fourth of July just like him, enjoying their freedom and remembering the boldness of the Declaration of Independence. He wished he could've been alive to witness that first July fourth holiday—and wondered whether he'd be there for the last Independence Day, when a heavenly shot would echo around the world, heralding God's Great War of Final Independence.

Can you even fathom it? Jesus Himself, the ultimate King of kings, will ride into battle, victorious on His white horse, followed by His children. And this battle will be different from any other. Christ alone will fight. His only weapon will be His Word. He'll simply speak—and conquer.

Do you ever doubt that Christ has the power to work in your life? Do you sometimes get discouraged, feeling as if the world's winning and God's losing? Have you ever thought some prayers are too hard for God to answer or some things are too much for Him to handle?

Well, think again.

God is more powerful than you realize. If He can flatten the nations of the world with His Word, He can handle the details of your life. All He asks is that you have faith...and that you're prepared for spiritual battle.

Discussion Starters:

1. What do you see when you picture the final battle?

2. What kinds of spiritual battles do you face in your school or workplace?

3. How can you enlist God's power in your daily battles?

Lifeline:

Discuss how your family can gear up and get ready for the spiritual fights that lie ahead. (Hint: Read Ephesians 6:10-18.)

ALL ACCESS

"And I saw the dead, the great and the small, standing before the throne, and books were opened; and another book was opened, which is the book of life; and the dead were judged from the things which were written in the books, according to their deeds. And the sea gave up the dead which were in it, and death and Hades gave up the dead which were in them; and they were judged, every one of them according to their deeds. Then death and Hades were thrown into the lake of fire. This is the second death, the lake of fire. And if anyone's name was not found written in the book of life, he was thrown into the lake of fire."

⮑ Revelation 20:12-15

As a camp director, I've had the privilege of befriending a lot of famous Christian artists. My kids love that part of my job.

"Dad! Can you get us backstage passes to the concert?" they plead. They know that since I'm friends with various artists, I can usually get them "all access" passes to see the stars after the show.

When that happens, my kids become the envy of all their friends, who know that there's no earthly way to get backstage and meet the musicians without a pass.

Not only have my kids been able to meet musicians, but my job once enabled them to get a similar "all-access" pass into the Atlanta Braves' locker room. I'll never forget the wide-eyed look on my two sons' faces (then ages 8 and 10) as they sat in the room, listening while I addressed the Braves' chapel service. Brady's and Cooper's eyes got even wider when one of the star players walked over to them, shook their hands, and introduced himself.

Meeting the stars is exciting, but it's nothing compared to what it'll be like to "walk backstage" and hang with Jesus. Some day, every worldly superstar will yearn to have the pass you possess—the relationship you have with Christ, which puts your name in the book of life and allows you to enter heaven. Time is short. Don't wait to tell your friends about God.

Discussion Starters:

1. How does God provide everyone the opportunity to have access to Him?

2. Why is absolute justice so important to God? Why can't everyone—or at least those who've led a good life—have their name in the book of life?

Lifeline:

If you knew how to get a backstage pass to meet your favorite star, you would probably tell your friends how they could get one, too. So why wouldn't you tell them how to get an "all-access" pass into heaven?

NO PAIN

"And I heard a loud voice from the throne, saying, 'Behold, the tabernacle of God is among men, and He will dwell among them, and they shall be His people, and God Himself will be among them, and He will wipe away every tear from their eyes; and there will no longer be any death; there will no longer be any mourning, or crying, or pain; the first things have passed away.'"

⌒ Revelation 21:3-4

Tim's funeral was one of the most difficult days of my life. *Why did it have to be Tim, God?* I kept asking the Lord.

My dear friend Tim was only 19. We laughed together, went fishing, and talked about the struggles of being a teenager. Tim smoked a little pot in high school and tried LSD once.

It was one time too many.

From that day on, Tim's mind became his enemy. He began having violent, haunting flashbacks. They must have been excruciating because soon after he experimented with LSD, Tim decided he couldn't bear life any longer. He grabbed his father's shotgun, loaded it, aimed it at his own head, and pulled the trigger. One thundering blast later, it was all over.

At the funeral, his druggie friends acted aloof and in control.

"I guess Tim couldn't handle it. We can," they said to me, scoffing.

What a waste, I thought. *What a pitiful waste. Why can't his friends learn from this? Why did Tim feel he had to take his life?*

Why is there so much pain in the world? Last spring, my friend Dennis and his baby were killed by a drunk driver. Rachel's husband left her after 22 years of marriage. Julia died of a rare heart disease just after her 16th birthday. And you've probably suffered as well.

Fortunately, this passage from Revelation offers hope. Scripture tells us the pain of this world is temporary. Some day, God will wipe all the tears from our faces. We'll be full of smiles and joy—all the time.

Be encouraged. God will fulfill that promise.

Discussion Starters:

1. How does the world handle grief? Why should Christians handle death differently? Do they?

2. What do you think causes God the most grief? Explain your answer.

Lifeline:

In this passage from Revelation, God offers one of many promises of hope to His people. Discuss: Where else in the Bible does God give His children encouraging promises? How did those biblical figures hold on to that hope?

ALL IN WHITE

"Then one of the seven angels who had the seven bowls full of the seven last plagues came and spoke with me, saying, 'Come here, I will show you the bride, the wife of the Lamb.' And he carried me away in the Spirit to a great and high mountain, and showed me the holy city, Jerusalem, coming down out of heaven from God, having the glory of God. Her brilliance was like a very costly stone, as a stone of crystal-clear jasper."

⌐ Revelation 21:9-11

As a pastor, I've performed many weddings for my close friends over the past 20 years. Some have been formal and expensive, costing the father of the bride thousands of dollars. (Poor fellow!) Some have been very simple—and equally fantastic.

Of all the brides I've ever seen, few have been as beautiful as Candy, a friend of mine who only had $100 to spend on her wedding day.

She chose to hold the ceremony on a lush, green hillside, overlooking a silver-blue lake. Then Candy invested the entire $100 in her wedding gown, the least expensive one she could find. She labored for three months, sewing tiny costume pearls and white sequins to the gown.

The effect was breathtaking.

As Candy floated to the altar to meet her bridegroom, a gentle October breeze blew brilliant star-shaped maple leaves to the ground, paving her path with gold, red, and orange hues. When Andy, her bridegroom, saw her, his face lit up with joy. For three years, he'd waited patiently for Candy while she took care of her ailing grandmother.

I was so moved by the beauty of the moment that I forgot to have the couple say "I do" and seal the vow with a kiss. Awkwardly, I regained my composure and added this important part of the ceremony to the wedding script.

God intends your wedding day—both on earth and in heaven—to be just as pure and beautiful. Start praying for your future spouse. Ask God to keep him or her pure and mature in the faith. Then pray that God would work in your heart so that when that day comes, you'll be ready, too.

Discussion Starters:

1. The Bible states that Christians are the bride of Christ. What does that reveal about our relationship with God?

2. What character qualities would you like to see in your future mate? What virtues are you building in your own life right now...both for your earthly husband or wife and for Jesus Christ?

3. Mom and Dad: How did you meet and fall in love? What first attracted you to each other?

Lifeline:

As a family, come up with a list of biblically based character qualities that are important to a healthy marriage relationship.

OPEN 24 HOURS

"And the city has no need of the sun or of the moon to shine on it, for the glory of God has illumined it, and its lamp is the Lamb. The nations will walk by its light, and the kings of the earth will bring their glory into it. In the daytime (for there will be no night there) its gates will never be closed."

↪ Revelation 21:23-25

Wal-Mart is an amazing place. It started out as a simple discount store but has become its own mecca, where millions of people shop every day. In fact, the latest Wal-Marts include grocery stores, photo shops, outdoor and garden centers, pharmacies, hair salons, banks, dry cleaning establishments, and a McDonald's...all under one roof. Not only can you get a haircut, eat lunch, clean your clothes, and buy a chain saw, but you can do it 24 hours a day. The doors never shut! In the field of merchandising, that's called an "open-door" policy. This policy makes shopping convenient for customers.

Wal-Mart's open-door service is great, but wouldn't it be even better if it were applied to friendship? If we always focused on having open-door hearts, we would drop everything to make our friends and family a priority and listen to their concerns. We'd be available to open our ears and hearts to family members and friends who need support.

Jesus had an open heart, and His kingdom will have open-door availability, too. Today's passage in Revelation tells us that, for God's children, heaven's gates will always be open wide. And it's not because of anything we've done. God's grace is accessible to everyone, enabling all people to enter His kingdom.

His open heart gives us a never-ending welcome into heaven's gates.

Discussion Starters:

1. Describe in your own words what it means for God to have an open-heart policy with His believers.
2. What's the difference between an open-heart and a closed-heart policy?
3. What are some characteristics of an approachable person? How do his or her facial expressions and mannerisms reflect openness and availability?
4. Why do we often close our emotional doors and shut others out of our lives? How can we change that?

Lifeline:

List some ways in which your family can have an open-heart policy around one another and with your friends and neighbors.

FREIHEIT!

"There will no longer be any curse; and the throne of God and of the Lamb will be in it, and His bond-servants will serve Him; they will see His face, and His name will be on their foreheads. And there will no longer be any night; and they will not have need of the light of a lamp nor the light of the sun, because the Lord God will illumine them; and they will reign forever and ever."

↪ Revelation 22:3-5

The infamous Berlin Wall was built in 1961 to stem the flood of refugees streaming from Communist East Berlin into the west after the Allies defeated Germany in World War II. But many people, hungry for freedom, still continued to risk their lives trying to cross the border.

Thirty years later, the world gasped in disbelief when democratic reform swept through the Eastern bloc countries, and the wall crumbled to deafening cries of *freiheit!* People everywhere cried out, "Free at last!"

You may not lack physical freedom, but as a fallen young man or woman, your soul is in bondage, longing to be freed from sin.

My friend "Ben" could tell you that. Ben, a talented young athlete I've been close to for the past four years, recently called to tell me he was fasting and praying that that particular day would be the day he would break free from the grip of pornography forever.

"Today," Ben said, "I no longer want to stop looking at those pictures. I *will* to quit. There's a big difference between willing to and just wanting to do something."

Ben's fight was too big for him to fight on his own. So he fasted and prayed. With God's help, Ben was released from his sin.

Although God has the power to free us from our sins, the reality is that we're still fallen people. We continue to mess up, think bad thoughts, lie, steal, and hurt God. Fortunately, though, the Bible tells us that one day all of God's children will be freed from sin forever. We will be reunited with the Lord and enjoy perfect communion with Him in heaven.

Discussion Starters:

1. What did the Berlin Wall represent? How do you think it felt to live on the East (Communist) side of the wall?

2. How does sin enslave us?

3. How does God give us freedom from sin each day? How will He give us ultimate freedom in heaven?

Lifeline:

Discuss some ways your family can minister to those who have lost their freedom (for example, prison inmates, hospital patients, or nursing home residents).

THE 100 BIBLE MEMORY VERSES
EVERY CHRISTIAN TEENAGER NEEDS TO KNOW

(2 *each week for* 50 *weeks*)

Your word I have treasured in my heart, that I may not sin against You.

↜ Psalm 119:11

1. Psalm 1:1
2. Psalm 1:2
3. Psalm 1:3
4. Psalm 1:4-5
5. Psalm 1:6
6. Psalm 119:1-2
7. Psalm 119:3-4
8. Psalm 119:5-6
9. Psalm 119:7-8
10. Psalm 119:9
11. Psalm 119:10-11
12. Proverbs 1:8-9
13. Proverbs 4:23
14. Proverbs 6:16
15. Proverbs 6:17-19
16. Proverbs 10:1
17. Proverbs 10:19
18. Proverbs 12:1
19. Proverbs 15:1
20. Proverbs 22:1
21. Proverbs 22:6
22. Proverbs 23:31-32
23. Proverbs 29:1
24. Proverbs 31:30
25. Matthew 5:11-12
26. Matthew 5:16
27. Matthew 5:27-28
28. Matthew 6:22
29. Matthew 6:23
30. Matthew 6:28-29
31. Matthew 6:33
32. Matthew 7:2-4
33. Matthew 7:13
34. Matthew 16:24-25
35. Matthew 18:3
36. Matthew 18:12
37. Matthew 19:24
38. Matthew 22:36-38
39. Matthew 22:39-40
40. Matthew 24:44
41. Matthew 25:40
42. Matthew 26:26-29
43. Luke 2:52
44. Luke 6:31
45. Luke 6:38
46. Luke 9:62
47. Luke 11:9-10
48. Luke 11:17
49. Luke 14:27
50. Luke 14:28
51. Luke 15:7
52. John 1:1-2
53. John 1:3-4
54. John 1:5
55. John 1:6-8
56. John 1:9-10
57. John 1:11-12
58. John 3:3
59. John 3:16
60. John 6:35
61. John 6:40
62. John 8:32
63. John 8:34,36
64. John 10:10
65. John 11:25
66. John 13:14
67. John 14:2
68. John 14:6
69. John 14:13
70. John 14:16
71. John 14:17
72. John 14:18-19
73. John 14:20
74. John 14:21
75. John 15:4
76. John 15:5
77. John 16:33
78. John 20:29
79. Acts 1:8
80. James 1:2-3
81. James 1:4
82. James 1:5
83. James 1:6
84. James 1:7-8
85. James 1:13
86. James 1:14-15
87. James 1:22
88. James 1:25
89. James 2:17
90. James 3:2
91. James 3:5
92. James 4:4
93. James 4:7
94. James 4:10
95. James 5:16
96. Revelation 3:15-16
97. Revelation 3:20
98. Revelation 21:1-2
99. Revelation 21:3
100. Revelation 21:4

NOTES

Matthew:

1. Brigham Young, *Journal of Discourses* (Salt Lake City: The Church of Jesus Christ of Latter-Day Saints, 1966), 1:50-51.

2. *Rolling Stone.*

3. *USA Today*, April 24, 1987, p. 1D.

4. *Dallas Morning News*, October 11, 1987.

5. *The New Research*, published by the Rockford Institute, November 1990, pp. 2-4.

6. Peggy Anderson, *Great Quotes from Great Leaders* (Lombard, IL: Celebrating Excellence Publishing, 1990), p. 102.

7. Robert Wright, "Our Cheating Hearts," *Time*, 15 August 1994: 45.

8. William J. Federer, *America's God and Country* (Coppell, TX: Fame Publishing, 1994), p. 657.

9. Federer, p. 275.

10. Gideon Hausner, *Justice in Jerusalem* (New York: Harper & Row, 1966), pp. 354, 366, 446.

11. Joseph Smith, *The Pearl of Great Price* (Salt Lake City: The Church of Jesus Christ of Latter-Day Saints, 1952), 2:18-19.

12. Bruce R. McConkie, *Mormon Doctrine* (Salt Lake City: Bookcraft, 1979), pp. 238-39; Joseph Smith, Jr., *History of the Church* (Salt Lake City: The Church of Jesus Christ of Latter-Day Saints, n.d.), 6:310-12.

13. *Let God Be True* (Brooklyn: Watchtower Bible and Tract Society, 1946), p. 111.

14. *Encyclopaedia Britannica*, Vol. 4, p. 294.

15. Topps Baseball Card, "Jim Abbott."

16. George Currie, *The Military Discipline of the Romans from the Founding of the City to the Close of the Republic.* An abstract of a thesis published under the auspices of the Graduate Council of Indiana University, 1928.

17. Josh McDowell, *Evidence That Demands a Verdict*, (San Bernardino, CA: Campus Crusade for Christ International,1972), p. 217.

18. Ibid, p. 231.

Luke:

1. Panatti, *Book of Origins.*

2. Ibid.

3. *William Barclay's Commentary on Luke.*

John:

1. Donald M. Bowman, "Number One Killer of Teenagers—Drunk Driving," *California Capitol Report*, Dec. 1990. Mike Snider, "Alcohol Is Leading U.S. Drug Worry," *USA Today*, Tuesday, April 14, 1992, p. 1D. "It Is Time to Ban the Advertising of Alcohol from Broadcasting," *AFA Journal*, January 1990, p. 12. Andrea Stone and Conner Chance, "Courts Must Address Unborn's Rights," *USA Today*, Feb. 2, 1990, p. 3A.

2. Josh McDowell, *Evidence That Demands a Verdict* (San Bernardino, CA: Here's Life, 1979-81).

3. Ibid.

4. Joseph Smith, *The Pearl of Great Price* (Salt Lake City: Church of Jesus Christ of Latter-Day Saints, 1952), 2:18,19.

5. Joseph Fielding Smith, *Doctrines of Salvation* (Salt Lake City: Church of Jesus Christ of Latter-Day Saints, n.d.), pp. 189-90.

6. Shirley MacLaine, *Dancing in the Light* (New York: Bantam, 1985), p. 420.

7. Mary Baker Eddy, *Science and Health: With Key to the Scriptures* (Boston: Allison V. Stewart, 1906), 25:6-8.

8. *Make Sure of All Things* (Brooklyn: Watchtower Bible and Tract Society, 1953), p. 207; *Let God Be True*, pp. 33,88.

Acts:

1. Dr. David Barrett, ed., *World Christian Encyclopedia*, 2nd ed. (Oxford University Press, 1998).

2. *Compass Direct*, Sep. 26, 1997, p. 7.

3. Panatti, *Book of Origins*.

James:

1. Patricia Hersch, "Sexually Transmitted Diseases Are Ravaging Our Children," *American Health* (May 1991): 44; Hersch, "Teen Epidemic," *American Health* (May 1991): 42-45; Jeff Kleinhuizen, "Campus Drinking Targeted," *USA Today*, Mar. 6, 1991, p. 1.

2. Nike annual sales for 1993, in *Moody's Industrial News Report* 65, 50 (Feb. 1, 1994): 3277.

3. Jonah Blank and Warren Cohen, "Prayer-Circle Murders," *U.S. News & World Report*, December 15, 1997, pp. 25-27.

BOOST YOUR FAMILY'S FAITH

More Great Resources from Joe White and Focus on the Family

FaithTraining

You can pass the baton of faith to your kids, and this collection of practical insights and creative ideas shows you how! With ways to spark incredible prayer times, memorize Scripture more easily, and make Bible study times something to look forward to, it's an ideal guide for helping your children develop a close, personal relationship with the Lord. Paperback.

Pure Excitement

How can you steer teens away from promiscuity when it's at the movies, on TV... even in bright lights on billboards? By getting a copy of this book into each of their hands! It's packed with success stories of many young adults who remained virgins until their wedding nights (and survived!), and heartrending letters from teens who didn't and regret it. Plus, it outlines God's intentions for sexual pleasure and how all guys and girls can decide now to save sex for later, when they can fully and completely enjoy it. Paperback.

╰╮

Plugged In

Today's youth culture can make even the most "with it" parent's head spin! That's why Focus on the Family created this monthly publication. It's filled with news, reviews and commentary on what's being sung on the latest music releases, and what's now showing on both the big and small screen. Best of all, it offers parents entertaining, uplifting alternatives to build up your teens, not tear them down.

The "Life on the Edge Tour"—Coming Soon to a Community Near You!

Does a day and a half with your teens, learning ways to enhance communication, build your faith, and strengthen family unity, sound too good to be true? It's not, and it's exactly what you'll experience at Focus on the Family's "Life on the Edge Tour." Featuring such captivating speakers as Joe White, *Brio* editor Susie Shellenberger, Miles McPherson, and many others, it's the weekend conference your family will never forget!

Tune Your Teens Into "Life on the Edge LIVE"!

You give them the best advice. But sometimes counsel is better taken when it comes from an unbiased, outside but trusted source—like Focus on the Family's "Life on the Edge LIVE." Co-hosted by none other than author, family counselor, and teen authority Joe White, this nationally syndicated live call-in radio show gives teens a safe place to talk about the issues on their minds and hearts. Listen along with them and spark conversations you never thought possible!

╰╮

For more information, or if we can be of help to your family, simply write to Focus on the Family, Colorado Springs, CO 80995 or call 1-800-A-FAMILY (1-800-232-6459). Friends in Canada may write Focus on the Family, P.O. Box 9800, Stn. Terminal, Vancouver, B.C. V6B 4G3 or call 1-800-661-9800. You may also visit our website: www.family.org, to learn more about the ministry or to find out if there is a Focus on the Family office in your country.

We are here for you!

Check your local Christian bookstore for these and other Focus on the Family resources.

8BPXMP

WELCOME TO THE FAMILY!

Whether you received this book as a gift, borrowed it from a friend, or purchased it yourself, we're glad you read it! It's just one of the many helpful, insightful, and encouraging resources produced by Focus on the Family.

In fact, that's what Focus on the Family is all about—providing inspiration, information, and biblically based advice to people in all stages of life.

It began in 1977 with the vision of one man, Dr. James Dobson, a licensed psychologist and author of 16 best-selling books on marriage, parenting, and family. Alarmed by the societal, political, and economic pressures that were threatening the existence of the American family, Dr. Dobson founded Focus on the Family with one employee—an assistant—and a once-a-week radio broadcast, aired on only 36 stations.

Now an international organization, Focus on the Family is dedicated to preserving Judeo-Christian values and strengthening the family through more than 70 different ministries, including eight separate daily radio broadcasts; television public service announcements; 11 publications; and a steady series of books and award-winning films and videos for people of all ages and interests.

Recognizing the needs of, as well as the sacrifices and important contributions made by, such diverse groups as educators, physicians, attorneys, crisis pregnancy center staff, and single parents, Focus on the Family offers specific outreaches to uphold and minister to these individuals, too. And it's all done for one purpose, and one purpose only: to encourage and strengthen individuals and families through the life-changing message of Jesus Christ.

For more information, or if we can be of help to your family, simply write to Focus on the Family, Colorado Springs, CO 80995 or call 1-800-A-FAMILY (1-800-232-6459). Friends in Canada may write Focus on the Family, P.O. Box 9800, Stn. Terminal, Vancouver, B.C. V6B 4G3 or call 1-800-661-9800. You may also visit our website: www.family.org, to learn more about the ministry or to find out if there is a Focus on the Family office in your country.

We are here for you!

THE 100 BIBLE MEMORY VERSES
EVERY CHRISTIAN TEENAGER NEEDS TO KNOW

(2 each week for 50 weeks)

Your word I have treasured in my heart, that I may not sin against You.

✍ Psalm 119:11

1.   Psalm 1:1
"How blessed is the man who does not walk in the counsel of the wicked, nor stand in the path of sinners, nor sit in the seat of scoffers!"

3.   Psalm 1:3
"He will be like a tree firmly planted by streams of water, which yields its fruit in its season and its leaf does not wither; and in whatever he does, he prospers."

5.   Psalm 1:6
"For the Lord knows the way of the righteous, but the way of the wicked will perish."

7.   Psalm 119:3-4
"They also do no unrighteousness; they walk in His ways. You have ordained Your precepts, that we should keep them diligently."

9.   Psalm 119:7-8
"I shall give thanks to You with uprightness of heart, when I learn Your righteous judgments. I shall keep Your statutes; do not forsake me utterly!"

11.   Psalm 119:10-11
"With all my heart I have sought You; do not let me wander from Your commandments. Your word I have treasured in my heart, that I may not sin against You."

13.   Proverbs 4:23
"Watch over your heart with all diligence, for from it flow the springs of life."

15.   Proverbs 6:17-19
" ...Haughty eyes, a lying tongue, and hands that shed innocent blood, a heart that devises wicked plans, feet that run rapidly to evil, a false witness who utters lies, and one who spreads strife among brothers."

17.   Proverbs 10:19
"When there are many words, transgression is unavoidable, but he who restrains his lips is wise."

19.   Proverbs 15:1
"A gentle answer turns away wrath, but a harsh word stirs up anger."

4.   Psalm 1:4-5

"The wicked are not so, but they are like chaff which the wind drives away. Therefore the wicked will not stand in the judgment, nor sinners in the assembly of the righteous."

2.   Psalm 1:2

"But his delight is in the law of the Lord, and in His law he meditates day and night."

8.   Psalm 119:5-6

"Oh that my ways may be established to keep Your statutes! Then I shall not be ashamed when I look upon all Your commandments."

6.   Psalm 119:1-2

"How blessed are those whose way is blameless, who walk in the law of the LORD. How blessed are those who observe His testimonies, who seek Him with all their heart."

12.   Proverbs 1:8-9

"Hear, my son, your father's instruction and do not forsake your mother's teaching; indeed, they are a graceful wreath to your head and ornaments about your neck."

10.   Psalm 119:9

"How can a young man keep his way pure? By keeping it according to Your word."

16.   Proverbs 10:1

"A wise son makes a father glad, but a foolish son is a grief to his mother."

14.   Proverbs 6:16

"There are six things which the LORD hates, yes, seven which are an abomination to Him...."

20.   Proverbs 22:1

"A good name is to be more desired than great wealth, favor is better than silver and gold."

18.   Proverbs 12:1

"Whoever loves discipline loves knowledge, but he who hates reproof is stupid."

21. Proverbs 22:6

"Train up a child in the way he should go, even when he is old he will not depart from it."

23. Proverbs 29:1

"A man who hardens his neck after much reproof will suddenly be broken beyond remedy."

25. Matthew 5:11-12

" 'Blessed are you when people insult you and persecute you, and falsely say all kinds of evil against you because of Me. Rejoice and be glad, for your reward in heaven is great; for in the same way they persecuted the prophets who were before you.' "

27. Matthew 5:27-28

" 'You have heard that it was said, "You shall not commit adultery"; but I say to you that everyone who looks at a woman with lust for her has already committed adultery with her in his heart.' "

29. Matthew 6:23

" 'But if your eye is bad, your whole body will be full of darkness. If then the light that is in you is darkness, how great is the darkness!' "

31. Matthew 6:33

" 'But seek first His kingdom and His righteousness, and all these things will be added to you.' "

33. Matthew 7:13

" 'Enter through the narrow gate; for the gate is wide and the way is broad that leads to destruction, and there are many who enter through it.' "

35. Matthew 18:3

" ... 'Truly I say to you, unless you are converted and become like children, you will not enter the kingdom of heaven.' "

37. Matthew 19:24

" 'Again I say to you, it is easier for a camel to go through the eye of a needle, than for a rich man to enter the kingdom of God.' "

39. Matthew 22:39-40

" 'The second is like it, "You shall love your neighbor as yourself." On these two commandments depend the whole Law and the Prophets.' "

41. Matthew 25:40

" 'The King will answer and say to them, "Truly I say to you, to the extent that you did it to one of these brothers of Mine, even the least of them, you did it to Me." ' "

43. Luke 2:52

"And Jesus kept increasing in wisdom and stature, and in favor with God and men."

45. Luke 6:38

" 'Give, and it will be given to you. They will pour into your lap a good measure—pressed down, shaken together, and running over. For by your standard of measure it will be measured to you in return.' "

47. Luke 11:9-10

" 'So I say to you, ask, and it will be given to you; seek, and you will find; knock, and it will be opened to you. For everyone who asks, receives; and he who seeks, finds; and to him who knocks, it will be opened.' "

24. Proverbs 31:30

"Charm is deceitful and beauty is vain, but a woman who fears the Lord, she shall be praised."

22. Proverbs 23:31-32

"Do not look on the wine when it is red, when it sparkles in the cup, when it goes down smoothly; at the last it bites like a serpent and stings like a viper."

28. Matthew 6:22

" 'The eye is the lamp of the body; so then if your eye is clear, your whole body will be full of light.' "

26. Matthew 5:16

" 'Let your light shine before men in such a way that they may see your good works, and glorify your Father who is in heaven.' "

32. Matthew 7:2-3

" 'For in the way you judge, you will be judged; and by your standard of measure, it will be measured to you. Why do you look at the speck that is in your brother's eye, but do not notice the log that is in your own eye?' "

30. Matthew 6:28-29

" 'And why are you worried about clothing? Observe how the lilies of the field grow; they do not toil nor do they spin, yet I say to you that not even Solomon in all his glory clothed himself like one of these.' "

36. Matthew 18:12

" 'What do you think? If any man has a hundred sheep, and one of them has gone astray, does he not leave the ninety-nine on the mountains and go and search for the one that is straying?' "

34. Matthew 16:24-25

"Then Jesus said to His disciples, 'If anyone wishes to come after Me, he must deny himself, and take up his cross and follow Me. For whoever wishes to save his life will lose it; but whoever loses his life for My sake will find it.' "

40. Matthew 24:44

" 'For this reason you also must be ready; for the Son of Man is coming at an hour when you do not think He will.' "

38. Matthew 22:36-38

" 'Teacher, which is the great commandment in the Law?' And He said to him, ' "You shall love the Lord your God with all your heart, and with all your soul, and with all your mind." This is the great and foremost commandment.' "

44. Luke 6:31

" 'Treat others the same way you want them to treat you.' "

42. Matthew 26:26-28

"Jesus took some bread . . . and said, 'Take, eat; this is My body.' And when He had taken a cup and given thanks, He gave it to them, saying, 'Drink from it, all of you; for this is My blood of the covenant, which is poured out for many for forgiveness of sins.' "

48. Luke 11:17

"But He knew their thoughts and said to them, 'Any kingdom divided against itself is laid waste; and a house divided against itself falls.' "

46. Luke 9:62

"But Jesus said to him, 'No one, after putting his hand to the plow and looking back, is fit for the kingdom of God.' "

49. Luke 14:27

"'Whoever does not carry his own cross and come after Me cannot be My disciple.'"

51. Luke 15:7

"'I tell you that in the same way, there will be more joy in heaven over one sinner who repents than over ninety-nine righteous persons who need no repentance.'"

53. John 1:3-4

"All things came into being through Him, and apart from Him nothing came into being that has come into being. In Him was life, and the life was the Light of men."

55. John 1:6-8

"There came a man sent from God, whose name was John. He came as a witness, to testify about the Light, so that all might believe through him. He was not the Light, but he came to testify about the Light."

57. John 1:11-12

"He came to His own, and those who were His own did not receive Him. But as many as received Him, to them He gave the right to become children of God, even to those who believe in His name."

59. John 3:16

"'For God so loved the world, that He gave His only begotten Son, that whoever believes in Him shall not perish, but have eternal life.'"

61. John 6:40

"'For this is the will of My Father, that everyone who beholds the Son and believes in Him will have eternal life, and I Myself will raise him up on the last day.'"

63. John 8:34,36

"Jesus answered them, 'Truly, truly, I say to you, everyone who commits sin is the slave of sin.... So if the Son makes you free, you will be free indeed.'"

65. John 11:25

"Jesus said to her, 'I am the resurrection and the life; he who believes in Me will live even if he dies.'"

67. John 14:2

"'In My Father's house are many dwelling places; if it were not so, I would have told you; for I go to prepare a place for you.'"

69. John 14:13

"'Whatever you ask in My name, that will I do, so that the Father may be glorified in the Son.'"

71. John 14:17

"'That is the Spirit of truth, whom the world cannot receive, because it does not see Him or know Him, but you know Him because He abides with you and will be in you.'"

73. John 14:20

"'In that day you will know that I am in My Father, and you in Me, and I in you.'"

75. John 15:4

"'Abide in Me, and I in you. As the branch cannot bear fruit of itself unless it abides in the vine, so neither can you unless you abide in Me.'"

52. John 1:1-2

"In the beginning was the Word, and the Word was with God, and the Word was God. He was in the beginning with God."

50. Luke 14:28

" 'For which one of you, when he wants to build a tower, does not first sit down and calculate the cost to see if he has enough to complete it?' "

56. John 1:9-10

"There was the true Light which, coming into the world, enlightens every man. He was in the world, and the world was made through Him, and the world did not know Him."

54. John 1:5

"The Light shines in the darkness, and the darkness did not comprehend it."

60. John 6:35

"Jesus said to them, 'I am the bread of life; he who comes to Me will not hunger, and he who believes in Me will never thirst.' "

58. John 3:3

"Jesus answered and said to him, 'Truly, truly, I say to you, unless one is born again he cannot see the kingdom of God.' "

64. John 10:10

" 'The thief comes only to steal and kill and destroy; I came that they may have life, and have it abundantly.' "

62. John 8:32

" 'And you will know the truth, and the truth will make you free.' "

68. John 14:6

"Jesus said to him, 'I am the way, and the truth, and the life; no one comes to the Father but through Me.' "

66. John 13:14

" 'If I then, the Lord and the Teacher, washed your feet, you also ought to wash one another's feet.' "

72. John 14:18-19

" 'I will not leave you as orphans; I will come to you. After a little while the world will no longer see Me, but you will see Me; because I live, you will live also.' "

70. John 14:16

" 'I will ask the Father, and He will give you another Helper, that He may be with you forever.' "

76. John 15:5

" 'I am the vine, you are the branches; he who abides in Me and I in him, he bears much fruit, for apart from Me you can do nothing.' "

74. John 14:21

" 'He who has My commandments and keeps them is the one who loves Me; and he who loves Me will be loved by My Father, and I will love him and will disclose Myself to him.' "

77. John 16:33

" 'These things I have spoken to you, so that in Me you may have peace. In the world you have tribulation, but take courage; I have overcome the world.' "

79. Acts 1:8

" 'But you will receive power when the Holy Spirit has come upon you; and you shall be My witnesses both in Jerusalem, and in all Judea and Samaria, and even to the remotest part of the earth.' "

81. James 1:4

"And let endurance have its perfect result, so that you may be perfect and complete, lacking in nothing."

83. James 1:6

"But he must ask in faith without any doubting, for the one who doubts is like the surf of the sea, driven and tossed by the wind."

85. James 1:13

"Let no one say when he is tempted, 'I am being tempted by God'; for God cannot be tempted by evil, and He Himself does not tempt anyone."

87. James 1:22

"But prove yourselves doers of the word, and not merely hearers who delude themselves."

89. James 2:17

"Even so faith, if it has no works, is dead, being by itself."

91. James 3:5

"So also the tongue is a small part of the body, and yet it boasts of great things."

93. James 4:7

"Submit therefore to God. Resist the devil and he will flee from you."

95. James 5:16

"Therefore, confess your sins to one another, and pray for one another so that you may be healed. The effective prayer of a righteous man can accomplish much."

97. Revelation 3:20

" ' "Behold, I stand at the door and knock; if anyone hears My voice and opens the door, I will come in to him and will dine with him, and he with Me." ' "

99. Revelation 21:3

"And I heard a loud voice from the throne, saying, 'Behold, the tabernacle of God is among men, and He will dwell among them, and they shall be His people, and God Himself will be among them.' "

80. James 1:2-3

"Consider it all joy, my brethren, when you encounter various trials, knowing that the testing of your faith produces endurance."

78. John 20:29

"Jesus said to him, 'Because you have seen Me, have you believed? Blessed are they who did not see, and yet believed.'"

84. James 1:7-8

"For that man ought not to expect that he will receive anything from the Lord, being a double-minded man, unstable in all his ways."

82. James 1:5

"But if any of you lacks wisdom, let him ask of God, who gives to all generously and without reproach, and it will be given to him."

88. James 1:25

"But one who looks intently at the perfect law, the law of liberty, and abides by it, not having become a forgetful hearer but an effectual doer, this man will be blessed in what he does."

86. James 1:14-15

"But each one is tempted when he is carried away and enticed by his own lust. Then when lust has conceived, it gives birth to sin; and when sin is accomplished, it brings forth death."

92. James 4:4

"You adulteresses, do you not know that friendship with the world is hostility toward God? Therefore whoever wishes to be a friend of the world makes himself an enemy of God."

90. James 3:2

"For we all stumble in many ways. If anyone does not stumble in what he says, he is a perfect man, able to bridle the whole body as well."

96. Revelation 3:15-16

"'"I know your deeds, that you are neither cold nor hot; I wish that you were cold or hot. So because you are lukewarm, and neither hot nor cold, I will spit you out of My mouth."'"

94. James 4:10

"Humble yourselves in the presence of the Lord, and He will exalt you."

100. Revelation 21:4

"'And He will wipe away every tear from their eyes; and there will no longer be any death; there will no longer be any mourning, or crying, or pain; the first things have passed away.'"

98. Revelation 21:1-2

"Then I saw a new heaven and a new earth; for the first heaven and the first earth passed away, and there is no longer any sea. And I saw the holy city, new Jerusalem, coming down out of heaven from God, made ready as a bride adorned for her husband."

LifE Training